Praise for *Take Their Breath Away*

"Are you bored? We're so spoiled that when something is merely good enough, we just walk away. Chip and John explain that the surefire method for growth and customer loyalty is simple: don't be boring."

—Seth Godin, author, *The Purple Cow* and *Tribes*

"*Take Their Breath Away* shows how legendary customer service delivery can win and keep devoted customers for life. I LUV this fantastic book."

—Colleen Barrett, president emeritus,
Southwest Airlines Company

"No one knows more about creating profit through service than Chip and John. If you want to know the best way to do it, read 'Take Their Breath Away.' The examples in this book will certainly start your creative juices flowing and help your organization take your customers' breath away."

—Howard Behar, president,
Starbucks Coffee International, retired

"*Take Their Breath Away* is a fun and inspiring book that provides a creative approach for achieving 'out of the box' customer devotion."

—Mike Vance, former director of Idea Development for
Walt Disney Productions and dean of Disney University

"Customer loyalty is at the heart of business success in the best of economic times and has even greater importance in the face of economic uncertainty. John and Chip have written the quintessential practical guide to securing profitability by serving your way to customer evangelism."

—Joseph Michelli, author, *The New Gold Standard*

Also by Chip R. Bell

Customer Loyalty Guaranteed: Create, Lead, and Sustain, Remarkable Customer Service (with John R. Patterson)

Magnetic Service: Secrets for Creating Passionately Devoted Customers (with Bilijack R. Bell)

Service Magic: The Art of Amazing Your Customers (with Ron Zemke)

Knock Your Socks Off Service Recovery (with Ron Zemke)

Customer Love: Attracting and Keeping Customers for Life

Beep Beep!: Competing in the Age of the Road Runner (with Oren Harari)

Dance Lessons: Six Steps to Great Partnerships in Business and Life (with Heather Shea)

Managers as Mentors: Building Partnerships for Learning

Customers as Partners: Building Relationships that Last

Managing Knock Your Socks off Service (with Ron Zemke)

Service Wisdom: Creating and Maintaining the Customer Service Edge (with Ron Zemke)

The Trainer's Professional Development Handbook (with Ray Bard, Leslie Stephen, and Linda Webster)

Understanding Training: Perspectives and Practices (with Fredric Margolis)

Instructing for Results: Managing the Learning Process (with Fredric Margolis)

Clients and Consultants (with Leonard Nadler)

Influencing: Marketing the Ideas That Matter

The Client-Consultant Handbook (with Leonard Nadler)

Also by John R. Patterson

Customer Loyalty Guaranteed: Create, Lead, and Sustain, Remarkable Customer Service (with Chip R. Bell)

Take Their Breath Away

Take Their Breath Away

How Imaginative Service Creates Devoted Customers

Chip R. Bell and John R. Patterson

WILEY

John Wiley & Sons, Inc.

Published by John Wiley & Sons, Inc., Hoboken, New Jersey.

Published simultaneously in Canada.

For general information on our other products and services or for technical support, please contact our Customer Care Department within the United States at (800) 762-2974, outside the United States at (317) 572-3993 or fax (317) 572-4002.

Wiley also publishes its books in a variety of electronic formats. Some content that appears in print may not be available in electronic books. For more information about Wiley products, visit our Web site at www.wiley.com.

Library of Congress Cataloging-in-Publication Data:

Bell, Chip R.
    Take their breath away : how imaginative service creates devoted customers/ by Chip R. Bell and John R. Patterson.
        p. cm.
    Includes bibliographical references and index.
    ISBN 978-0-470-44350-7 (cloth)
    1. Customer services—United States. 2. Consumer satisfaction—United States. 3. Customer loyalty—United States. 4. Service industries—Customer services–United States. I. Patterson, John R. II. Title.
    HF5415.5.B438 2009
    658.8'12—dc22

                                                                                    2008054902

Printed in the United States of America

10 9 8 7 6 5 4 3 2 1

To Lisa, Bilijack, Kaylee, Annabeth, and Cassie Bell
To Jay, Molly, Carrie, Chad, and Sarah Patterson
"You take our breath away!"

Contents

INTRODUCTION
A Call For Imaginative Service

Customers are bored! Service providers, chastised by the less-than-exciting results of their surveys, have put all their eggs in the improvement basket. Like the well-trodden story of attempts to free the 18-wheeler truck stuck in the overpass, too many units and organizations have sought the help of a jackhammer or a welding torch; too few have simply let the air out of the truck tires.

Getting better has meant improving efficiency—making the service experience faster, simpler, or more accurate. Service designers have typically asked, "How can we satisfy our customers?" rather than "How can we take their breath away?" "How can we make what we have better?" has taken precedence over "What if we made it completely different?" Enhancement has been about taking the next step rather than taking a completely new direction. We improve rather than invent.

The result? We hold up companies like Nordstrom, Starbucks, Ritz-Carlton Hotels, and the Container Store as exemplars. Not to say that they all don't deserve credit for elevating the standards from the mediocre levels of the '80s. But, take a closer look. These service greats focus on the customer (like remembering your preferences), design service processes around customer convenience, pay attention to service details, deliver consistency, and ensure you receive warm and friendly service. Most small-town merchants would probably say, "So what! Is that not what service means in the first place? When did such stock-in-trade start getting held up as something special?"

While we are sipping our pricey lattes, returning a shirt to the super gracious clerk, or getting turndown service with a personal note on the pillow, something else has been happening. We are getting way over-stimulated. Television has become both high definition and multimedia. The nightly news shows the weather report, ball scores, stock market numbers, and a crawling headline simultaneously on the TV screen. Internet servers have become a haven for colorful ads with video streaming at you while you try to concentrate on reading your e-mails. Even the Little League ballpark is cloistered among giant billboards. Hitting a home run makes a bragging sponsor as noteworthy as a budding sports star. That steady stream of sensory arousal has made a simple hotel check-in, taking Spot to the vet, or grocery shopping seem humdrum and plain vanilla.

One could argue for a slower pace and a simpler lifestyle. Instead why not enrich the clutter and harmonize the noise by offering ways to make customers laugh, reflect, swoon, or swell with pride? We have titled this book *Take Their Breath Away* because that is exactly the customer reaction to which customer service needs to aspire. Customers long to take from a service experience the emotional reaction they have to a golden sunset, perfect rainbow, magic trick, or poignant story. They want to be lifted beyond service that is pretty good to service that is remarkable.

This refreshingly novel brand of service leaves customers more than cheaply entertained—it leaves them richly stirred. Customers instinctively appreciate such an expression as coming from a solid intent to make a difference, not just a superficial desire to make an impression. Customers who experience such hybrid service want to return for more. They know it is rare and special; it is, in a word, imaginative.

This book does not attempt to "spamize" service but rather seeks to inspire and "nobilize" service. The path we have chosen is not the linear next step, but rather the quantum leap to a service expression that is fresh and novel. Get ready for a wild ride. The pages to follow will help you challenge conventional wisdom and upset the status quo. Want a quick taste?

As many chain hotels are struggling in the throes of "me too" competition and travel cutbacks, Hotel Monaco is thriving. Why? Because they deliver to the business traveler a funky, enchanting experience with goldfish in the room, leopard-skin bathrobes, foreign coins on the pillow instead of mints, and a psychic quietly reading palms in the lobby during the afternoon wine tasting. Not your cup of tea? Perhaps not. But for the market to whom the experience is targeted, it has been a winning recipe.

As Hotel Monaco and other imaginative service greats know so well, the desire to provide take-their-breath-away service spreads through memorable stories. Imagine the excitement that went through Walt Disney World theme park hotels when word spread that a housekeeper had cleverly moved Disney souvenir toys around in a guest's room to make the youngsters staying there convinced the toys had come alive while they were away at the park. This book is aimed at spreading that same type of thinking. The manicurist who not only opened the car door for her patrons, but also started their ignition no doubt left her customers with a story to tell. This is a story-building manual.

Stories have a viral effect. They unfold and spread very differently than the daily news. They broadcast more like rumors than reports. The value of such virus-like transmission is the way they swirl into the heart and thus lasso customers into their fold. The tale told by a friend is a far more powerful instrument for inviting customer devotion than the best ad or cleverest sales pitch.

The venue for take-their-breath-away service is not limited to those organizations whose names we can all drop. It is also the mailroom that dressed employees in costumes once a week, or the information technology department that built their service experience around the Road Runner cartoon character. It is the accounting firm that had partners wear Superman T-shirts under their business suits and to "think Superman" when meeting with clients. The tapestry of imaginative service spans the space from the wacky to the weird, from the silly to the sublime. The thread linking them all is an unmistakable quest for an experience that customers value, remember, and remark favorably about.

The need is clear—it is time for units and organizations to reignite the flame of customer experience. It is a conclusion heard from click-and-brick retailers, financial organizations, healthcare companies, restaurant companies, air carriers, and even non-profits coast to coast and, indeed, around the globe. Customer service is long overdue a wake-up call.

How Did We Get Here?

Customer service has been on a roller-coaster ride for the last 20 years. In the mid-1980s, the buzzword was "customer satisfaction." Winners worked hard to understand and meet customer needs. Satisfaction was the brass ring of choice, and the corporate drumbeat began its roll. Banners, bands, and banter told employees to start focusing on satisfying the customer. After all, the customer was always right.

In the 1990s, the customer service bar got raised. As quality initiatives began to impact product quality, simply satisfying the customer was viewed as nothing more than the price of admission in the game to win the customer. The real winners focused on customer loyalty and retention. The first wave of change, punctuated by Disney and Nordstrom stories along with words like "wowing," "outrageous," and "raving fans," characterized a new emphasis on loyalty and retention. It came replete with graphs and numbers that keyed off of the lifetime worth of a customer. The motto became "Keep the customer for life and your bottom line will be the envy of the industry." Names like Carl Sewell, Frederick Reichheld, Ron Zemke, Leonard Berry, and

Earl Sasser were the important prophets in the customer loyalty emphasis.

Toward the end of the 1990s, customer loyalty got a new wrinkle: customized service. The development of data-mining technology enabled organizations to gain and retain large amounts of information about the customer—not just demographics and financial information, but buying preferences and behavior. This enabled organizations to focus on customized (or as one popular business evangelist put it, "customerized") service. One became the key number, as in one-to-one (à la Don Peppers and Martha Rogers, Joe Pine and James Gilmore) and one size fits one (à la Gary Heil, et al.). Amazon.com and Ritz-Carlton became the exemplars. Organizations acquired the tools and software to capture more information about the customer than you'd find in a crackerjack salesperson's little black book. The thesis was this: Make customers perceive they are your only customer and you'll win their loyalty.

Many customers benefited greatly from all three initiatives— satisfaction, loyalty, and customization. Each has raised service quality. While customers still get lousy service more often than they would like, most would agree that service quality is not any better overall than it was 20 years ago. This is partly because customer expectations for service have gone up, often to the chagrin of service superstars that now have new customers walk in and think, "Okay, I've heard about you people—now blow my mind."

Take-their-breath-away service is about bringing a new spirit to the service world. It is intended as a practical blueprint and a courage builder for business pioneers who are unwilling to be lulled into complacence by the same old, same old. This book is designed to be your periscope for envisioning the future and a guidebook to ready you for the trip from here to there. It is a working book—one aimed at being more edgy than conventional, more vivacious than staid, more sensible than scholarly—and a book much more about practice than philosophy.

THE FINANCIAL PAYOFF OF IMAGINATIVE SERVICE IN A TIGHT ECONOMY

Delight your customer! Exceed your clients' expectations! Provide value-added service! These phrases have been the mantras of customer-service gurus for a long time. Such a focus on delivering more has no doubt raised the quality of service for many organizations. But, what's an organization to do when the budget-cutting ax is loosed and tight profit margins get even tighter? How does an organization avoid sending a very mixed message by telling the front line to wow their customers in the morning and announcing staff cutbacks and expense reductions in the afternoon? How do you add value when there are no more resources to fund the addition? In a phrase: imaginative service! The notion that exceptional customer service must cost more is pure myth.

Imaginative service is different from exceeding customer expectations. Ask customers what actions would be value added and they will focus on taking the expected experience to a higher level: "They gave me more than I anticipated." It's the upgrade, the extra helping, the complimentary dessert, the baker's dozen. But, imaginative service is not about addition, it's about creation. When service people are asked to give more, they think to themselves, "I am already doing the best I can." But, if they are asked to pleasantly surprise more customers, they feel less like worker bees and more like fireflies. If employees are asked to create a big customer smile instead of just working harder or faster, they suddenly feel a part of an adventure.

Ask employees to give better customer service and they will think of chores, tasks, and duty. But, make a request for imaginative service and you will find employees thinking about Ms. Jones or Mr. Smith—a shift from "all those customers" to "this customer." When employees get to create, not just perform, they feel prized and respected. When they are a part of an organization pursuing devoted customers, not just satisfied customers, employees extract enthusiasm and excellence from a growing reservoir of pride. Just ask a Southwest, Disney, Zappos.com, or Lexus dealership employee what they think about their job and you will get a smiling "it's awesome," not a shrugging "it's alright."

Imaginative service is sourced in joy and fun. It comes from the same part of the soul that plans a prank, organizes a party, or does a favor for a friend. When that part is used regularly, it raises self-esteem, increases resilience, and improves morale. Take a look at *Fortune* magazine's annual "100 Best Companies in America to Work For"—Nordstrom, Marriott, eBay, Zappos.com, Container Store, Wegman's Markets, FedEx, and the like—and you will find they serve their customers a large plateful of imaginative service. They also boast the lowest turnover (a cost saver), the best recruits (an investment), the highest productivity (another positive hit to the balance sheet), and the greatest profits. Companies in the top 20 percent of the highly revered American Customer Satisfaction Index outperformed the Dow Jones industrial average by 93 percent, the S&P 500 by 201 percent, and the NASDAQ by 355 percent. These companies yielded an average return of 40 percent.[1]

HOW TO GET THE MOST FROM THIS BOOK

This book is divided into two sections. Part One outlines 12 strategies for creating take-their-breath-away service. Each is fundamentally different, with its own unique set of principles and tactics. The explanation of each strategy will contain several tactics plus a host of examples aimed at making the strategy more understandable and implementation more practical.

Part Two focuses on how to select and implement one of the 12 strategies. Knowing about a strategy is not adequate; it must be put into practice to yield the rewards it embodies. This section is aimed at providing a blueprint for implementation. The sequence used in implementing this blueprint is important; a comprehensive approach to implementing the blueprint is vital. Pick and choose pieces of the blueprint at your own peril.

Half-baked in the world of imaginative service comes out raw, not rare.

We believe all service providers—those serving external customers and those serving internal colleagues—have the capacity to deliver take-their-breath-away service. And, we believe inventive service can be a consistent offering, rather than just an inadvertent or intermittent incident. This book is dedicated to that belief. Scan the book in a hurry or read it word for word. Read it in any direction; start anywhere. What matters most is that you do something with what you learn. Make a vow to start with your very next customer. Ignore the "we've always done it that way" past, elevate your intention to a higher plane, and simply make it happen.

"Take their breath away" is about a quest for being remarkable. "Remarkable takes originality, passion, guts, and daring," wrote Seth Godin in his best-selling book *The Purple Cow*. "Not just because going through life with passion and guts beats the alternative (which it does), but because it's the only way to be successful. Today, the one sure way to fail is to be boring. Your one chance for success is to be remarkable."[2]

Take-their-breath-away service requires an obvious display of passion—a focused zeal that touches as it contributes. We all know that passion is contagious. People smile at you and what do you do? You smile back. A stranger waves and you acknowledge their greeting. Passion is a way of retaliating against a challenging, difficult, and often indifferent world. The late comedian George Carlin wrote, "Life is not measured by the number of breaths we take but by the number of moments that take our breath away." So go take your customers' breath away.

Two requests before you do. First, please don't save this book. This is not a reference work. You are not going back to pull it off the shelf to check a formula, a quote, or a reference. So, give the thing away. Pick out the soul you think most needs it and pass the book on. No fanfare, no cute or caustic note, just simply say, "I liked this book and I thought you might as well."

Second, let us know what you think. You can find additional tools and support materials as well as our contact information on our Web site, www.taketheirbreathaway.com. It was our goal to create a quick read, a "single flight" tome that people could use immediately to start something with their customers. We hope that we have succeeded and that it will make a difference to you and your customer. The last page contains all the information you need to correspond with us. And we do need your feedback.

—Chip R. Bell, Lake Oconee, Georgia,
and John R. Patterson, Atlanta, Georgia

PART ONE

❀ ❀ ❀

Twelve Take-Their-Breath-Away Strategies

What is it that makes people pay four bucks for a cup of coffee at Starbucks, hundreds of dollars to watch the Green Bay Packers play in subzero weather, or $20,000 to be placed on a waiting list for a Harley-Davidson motorcycle? The answer lies way beyond customer loyalty. These brands generate a devotion in their customers. How? By giving them an experience that isn't limited to coffee, football, or motorcycles. To be sure, your unit or organization may not be selling a fragrant cup of steaming java, the legend of Vince Lombardi, or the freedom of the open road. But it is certainly possible to develop unique, customer-endearing practices that create a powerful experience and lead to a devoted customer base.

Customers who are devoted to your unit or organization act substantially different than the customers who are simply loyal. Devoted customers not only forgive you when you err, they help you correct what caused the mistake. They don't just recommend you; they assertively insist their friends do business with you. They vehemently defend you when others are critical. Even if

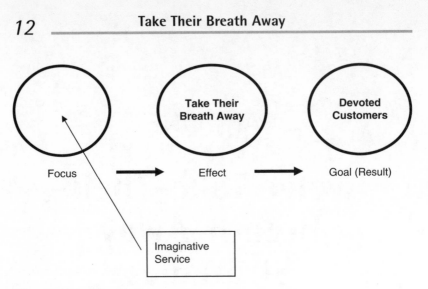

Figure I.1 The Link

the reason for the criticism is accurate, they quickly dismiss it as an aberration or an exception.

But there is even more to devotion. Some devoted customers of Harley-Davidson tattoo the company logo on their bodies. Devoted guests of Ritz-Carlton Hotels wear their logo-ed clothes and have Ritz-Carlton cobalt blue accessories in their home. Those connections become a part of the customer's identity and life expression.

The title of this book *Take Their Breath Away: How Imaginative Service Creates Devoted Customers* provides the structure for achieving the all-important goal of customer devotion (Figure I.1). In Part One, we will explore 12 strategies that help you deliver the kind of imaginative service that causes customers to be moved, motivated, and deputized as advocates. In each case, the idea is to create such an experience that it allures or draws the customer back time and time again.

Focusing on the delivery of imaginative service leads customers to having an experience that takes their breath away. The more frequently they get this effect, the more likely they will become devoted customers. And the unit or organization that took their breath away now reaps the rewards of customers who are more than simply loyal.

A HALF-DOZEN IMAGINATIVE SERVICE HORS d'OEUVRES

A preview of coming attractions can help whet your appetite for imaginative service. They are carved out of a menu of a dozen distinct strategies.

1. A family took a vacation on a Disney Cruise Line trip that began with a few days at Walt Disney World theme park. The morning they were to shift from their hotel to the cruise ship, they were instructed to leave all their luggage in their hotel room for pick-up and delivery. Imagine their delight when they arrived on board ship to discover that their luggage was already in their room with the same room number as the hotel—and the same hotel key opened the door!

2. A patient moved out of state and received a bill from Aurora Health Care in Milwaukee, Wisconsin, that exceeded the amount it should have been. When the woman called the billing department, they confirmed they had overcharged her. Remembering the woman complaining about having to call long distance to correct their mistake, the billing department included a complimentary phone card along with her refund check.

3. Several hospitals around the country are celebrating the arrival of newborns with a quiet lullaby. First Tune, a program developed by Mark Maxwell, a classical guitarist from Athens, Georgia, allows parents in the labor and delivery unit of a hospital to press a doorbell-like button that plays a 20-second lullaby over the hospital's public address system. The tune boosts the morale of patients, staff, and visitors as they share in the good news. Debra McKell, of Brandon Regional Medical Center in Brandon, Florida, says, "We are expecting to hear more than 3,000 lullabies at Brandon Regional Medical Center this year."

4. Clinique.com's tools help customers figure out their look and direct them to colors and product lines suited to their features. Once a Clinique.com customer fills out her color profile, it's permanently stored at the site. Whenever she clicks on a product category, the page automatically suggests shades and product lines that compliment her coloring and skin type.

5. At Grace Presbyterian Village in Dallas, a reinvented environment plays an important role in the treatment of Alzheimer's patients. Goodwin Dixon, Grace's CEO and president, took stock of the facility's physical look and feel: "We keep forcing residents to be in our reality, but they are more comfortable in their own, living in the past." Grace did a renovation that restyled the facility in a way that emphasized the comforting memories of Grace's residents. From posters of '49 Fords to baking classes held in a 1950s-style kitchen to an old-time front porch with rocking chairs to a sound system playing music of the era, everything about Grace now is purposely constructed to evoke memories of an earlier era when residents had a more positive self-image.[1]

6. Consider a common service experience: Taking a shuttle bus from the off-airport car rental lot to the terminal. A quintessentially unremarkable event? Not in Atlanta, at least not when Archie Bostick is driving the Hertz bus. After you turn in your car and go outside to catch the bus, the first thing you notice is Archie standing next to the doors with a big, welcoming grin on his face, and he's having a great time reinvigorating this service transaction. Instead of a tip jar (baited with a handful of bucks to encourage reluctant tippers), Archie paper-clips dollar bills across the front of his shirt. Nothing subtle about that ploy—it's an attention-getter that announces this is going to be a unique experience. Once on the bus, Archie

delivers a stand-up comedy routine instead of issuing the standard warning about the consequences of forgetting to turn in the keys to your rental car. He uses any excuse to break into song. ("The next time you're in Atlanta, maybe there'll be rain, and you'll be *'Singin' in the rain. I'm singin' in the rain....'"*) As Archie pulls up to the terminal, he announces, "Now that we're at your final destination, I may never see you again. I want us all to say together, 'I love Hertz!'" He invariably convinces a crowd of strangers to holler, "I love Hertz!" before they get off his bus. As customers exit applauding, they realize they have just witnessed a service innovator at work.

Archie Bostick

WALK ON THE INVENTIVE SIDE

The group of sales reps from a large after-market parts distributor gathered in a ballroom for the start of their annual sales rally. Excited to get their brand-new, four-inch-thick parts and price book, they largely ignored the CEO as he highlighted the company's previous year's wins and losses.

Then the meeting took an unexpected turn. The CEO introduced the opening keynote speaker, a business consultant who had entertained the audience the year before. But instead of opening with the expected clever joke, he walked into their midst and completely changed their view of their future with three questions.

If all your customers could at any time remotely look into your warehouse, find the solution or part they needed, and get it shipped overnight, what would they need you for?

If all your products were engineered to be "smart" and the part itself could alert the distribution center when it needed to be changed, replenished, or deleted, what would your customers need you for?

If all price shopping was driven by real-time, global comparisons via the Internet, and customers could request customized products and services, which in turn drove your production cycles, what would they need you for?

This is the type of mind-shifting perspective we have planned for you in the pages that follow. Our purpose is to completely challenge the manner in which you conceive of the service you provide. And the timing is crucial. "As globalization gives everyone the same information, resources, technology, and markets," wrote *The World Is Flat* best-selling author Tom Friedman, "a society's particular ability to put those pieces together in the fastest and most innovative manner increasingly separates winners from losers in the global economy."[2] Improvement will only take you so far; innovation is required to differentiate.

The skeptic might object: "I still have customers who expect quality products delivered on time. I still have shareholders who expect certain returns. I still have regulatory agencies that expect financial controls. I still have employees who expect to be paid." Of course you do! Everyone does! But meeting those challenging demands is simply the price of admission in today's business game. If that's all you do, you may survive but you certainly won't thrive.

Take-their-breath-away service can come from an array of random acts of service. However, sustainable reputations are best harnessed with a deliberately chosen strategy. A strategy is a spotlight or focal point that contains a set of tactics that fit together like pieces of a puzzle. An effective strategy reflects a keen understanding of the target audience for whom it is intended.

Consider the strategy used by a successful luxury hotel. Those that have stood the test of time did not do so by taking a page from the "How to run a good hotel" manual and simply ratchet up the service quality. Luxury has its own set of principles, fundamentally different from economy or moderate strategies. Luxury is a way of serving that consistently honors time-tested dos and don'ts. Understanding the luxury strategy enables its user to see actions, practices, and approaches that fit as well as those that do not.

The same holds true for all 12 take-their-breath-away strategies revealed in Part One: animation, reinvention, decoration, camouflage, concierge, partnership, cult-like, luxury, air, air defense, scout's honor, and firefighter. Each has its distinct philosophy and tactics and its unique principles and practices—all aimed at creating its characteristic connection with the customer. Yet all have the exact same goal in mind: devoted customers. And as the stories and examples prove, all are within the reach of the unit or organization that truly wants to take its customers' breath away.

CHAPTER 1
Animation

"My company created my role for one reason: to make you very happy, sir. And, the best part is that they picked me to do it!"

—*Charlie, a doorman at Marriott Quorum,*
Dallas, Texas

We knew we had a treat in the offing when the answer to our "Where's-the-best-lunch-in-town" question got escalated to "White's is the best in the state!" We were almost out of earshot when the local on the street corner added, "Ask for Katie."

The target of the local's affinity was White's Restaurant in Salem, Oregon. The restaurant had the look of a 1935 diner. The inside was neat and spotless; the atmosphere warm and upbeat. The hostess on the other side of the "Please wait to be seated" sign gave us a bright Steinway smile as we crossed the threshold.

"We heard Katie was the best in the house," we announced. "We'd like her table."

"Well, well, well . . . it's your lucky day!" the hostess teased. "There's is normally a two-hour wait to get Katie but we just had

White's Restaurant[1]

a cancellation," she said with a wink and a grin. "I think I can squeeze you in." The needle on our fun meter was already racing to the top.

"We are so glad to have you!" said our waitress. Her words came straight from the frying pan of a zealous spirit. "I'm Katie, and I'll check back with you in a minute. You know it's Thursday. Don's vegetable soup is already getting rave reviews." We were beginning to feel like locals.

When we noticed the breakfast menu listed "Don's Big Mess" as a headliner and the burger choices included a "Whoopee! Burger," we began to think we'd walked into a comedy club. Our spirits registered another uptick.

People throughout the restaurant were engaged in warm conversation, noisily greeting people they knew as they came through the front door. An hour later, we were back outside with satisfied stomachs and very happy hearts. The meal was awesome, but it was the animated service that told us we were witnessing the spirit of "take their breath away."

Animation is our moniker for the clear and present energy that reflects an unmistakable joy of serving. The label reminds us of what a great cartoonist does in turning stills into moving pictures—like the late Chuck Jones, who created such famous cartoon characters as Bugs Bunny, Daffy Duck, Wile E. Coyote, Road Runner, and Pepe Le Pew. When we interviewed him a few years back, the then-88-year-old genius sat in his studio in Irvine, California, and reflected on his 60-plus years as a world-renowned animator. "The secret to making a character come alive," he mused, "is not how you draw that particular character. Animation happens when everything in the frame moves with the character."

The power of an animated service person is how that person helps everything around them move with them. Katie was an animator. But, then, so was everything about the restaurant in which she worked.

THE SPIRIT OF ANIMATION

We all know customers are attracted to people with spirit. And, today's customers are frustrated with indifferent service; we're not talking bad service, just plain old boring, comatose service. Too often customers witness service people sleepwalking through the workday. They long to interact with—even relate to—employees who act like there is still a light on inside.

 The Bumblebee

Bumblebees are very useful pollinators, spreading the heart of the flower to other flowers, which enables them to reproduce. There is a popular urban myth that aeronautical engineers have claimed it was impossible for bumblebees to fly. This fueled the notion that it is the sheer determination of the bumblebee that enables it to fly anyway.

Think about organizations known for delivering over-the-top service: Apple, Ritz-Carlton, Southwest Airlines, Zappo.com, Chick-fil-A, Trader Joe's, USAA, JetBlue, Amazon.com, and Lexus, to name a few. What do they have in common? While their products and offerings may make their prospects' and customers' heads turn, it is the experience they create that makes their customers' hearts soar. They have cracked the code on managing the emotional connection with customers.

That connection has become even more critical in the digital age. Today, customer-generated media, especially via the use of the Internet, has dramatically increased customers' ability to tell stories about their experiences with those who serve them. This once-nerdy path has morphed into an information freeway, dramatically escalating your customers' power and capacity to influence other customers. Are customers always right in their blogs and "to whoever will listen" missives? Of course not. The customer is not always right. But the customer is always the customer. Pete Blackshaw, EVP of strategic services at Nielsen Online, has offered compelling research showing that customers will now tell up to 3,000 others (and rising) about their bad service experiences![2] While the dark side of that Internet gossip game can quickly demolish your reputation, the positive side can catapult your standing right into the stratosphere.

We begin our journey through the 12 take-their-breath-away strategies with animation for one reason: *Animation is a shade of engagement that every service encounter should be painted with*. Since the connection with the customer is an emotional one, the attitude you exhibit as a service provider is the most crucial key to success in attracting and retaining devoted customers.

The focus in this chapter will be on ways to take animation to such a level that customers become a part of the frame and eventually sign up for your cheerleading squad. We will examine five tactics—attitude, comfort, personal, respect, and sparkly—all important to pumping up the liveliness and the outlook needed to take your customers' breath away.

ATTITUDE

What's behind the sparkly Katie we witnessed at White's? What fuels her non-stop spirit of greatness? Katie selected the attitude she knew would likely unveil a customer smile and help boomerang that same spirit back. Her attitude is what philosopher/psychologist Rollo May had in mind when he wrote, "There is an energy field between all humans. When we reach out in passion it is met with an answering passion. . . ."[3]

Consider the characters kids the world over enjoy seeing at Disney theme parks. How can Mickey be Mickey, no matter what the circumstances? There is no "Mickey shot" to inoculate the character against crying babies, surly guests, or a costume without air conditioning. Mickey (like all the characters) selects the Mickey attitude to exhibit on stage, without regard to whether it is Monday morning or the day after late-night TV. It is the cast member in the Mickey costume who selects the Mickey attitude.

Spirit of Greatness Pledge

I promise to be in charge of my attitude each and every day, to let no one affect that attitude at any time, and to be a contagious spirit of greatness—24/7, 365 days a year!

Eighty-five percent of success in life, according to a well-known and often-cited Harvard study, is due solely to attitude. An attitude that shows the spirit of greatness provides the energy and magnetism needed to deliver an animated experience for customers and draw devotion from them. While customers like dealing with employees who are committed, they absolutely love being served by someone whose spirit to serve is unmistakable in its passion, pride, and commitment. Occasional animation is not sufficient. It is both the consistency and sincerity of attitude that brings customers back and causes them to tell all of their friends to "ask for Katie."

Leeches suck the blood from their target; *spirit leeches* suck the energy and passion from theirs. Some spirit leeches are negative—they remove optimism and hope. Mention an opportunity; they can tell you why it's a mistake. Some are transparent, preying on personal accountability. They play the blame game. Some are almost invisible, specializing in putting wet blankets on joy. Spirit leeches are removed the same way real leeches are—with fire. Not with a real match, of course, but with the warmth and energy of positive spirit. You do not inherit spirit, acquire spirit, or borrow spirit. You choose spirit much like you choose to introduce yourself to a stranger. Those who opt for an upbeat, positive spirit are happier, healthier, and more productive.

Take it from Vickie Henry, CEO of Feedback Plus, Inc., a Dallas-based mystery shopping firm with more than 30 years experience and more than a million anecdotes in their files from work with well-known retailers, restaurants, banks, and municipalities. Vickie was preparing for a keynote speech in London, England, and decided to do a few random mystery shops. As she walked into Sam's Club, Paul Hastings greeted her singing: *"Welcome to Sam's! We're so glad you're here!"* He pushed a cart her direction. She told Paul she was only there for a few items and really did not need a cart, at which Paul sang, *"You can't have fun without a cart!"* Vickie was blown away! "Paul made me feel very special," she told us. "And, Paul was having a great time! The one fact that is obvious from our years of mystery shopping: Customers love to be served by associates who love to serve them."

The most important thing to know about attitude is that it is something one *selects*. No normal person comes into the world with a particular attitude. It is chosen (or not). While we could blame our parents, our background, or our circumstances, the truth is we choose whether we want to soar through life as the passenger of our attitude or as its pilot. Eleanor Roosevelt said, "No one can make you feel inferior without your consent." Unless you are sick or hurt, your attitude is what you want it to be. Psychologist and concentration camp inmate Viktor Frankl observed that the major reason those who survived did was the fact that they never saw themselves as victims. "Every thing can be taken from a man but one thing: the last of the human freedoms—to choose one's attitude in any given set of circumstances," wrote Frankl in his classic book, *Man's Search for Meaning*.[4]

The second important thing to know is that an animated attitude can be contagious. When we are around happy, upbeat people, it is much easier for us to join in the spirit—especially if the invitation to join is coming from someone who clearly prefers we enroll. An unbridled spirit has a magnetic power on customers. It draws out their higher self. Being in the presence of a Katie causes customers to feel good about themselves. It's difficult to misbehave or stay cranky in their company. Few among us want to drag storm clouds into the perpetually sunny skies of such vivacious life forms.

University of Rhode Island students enjoy going to the nearby CVS/pharmacy in the Kingston Emporium to buy a snack and to see The Excellence Lady. The attraction is CVS head cashier Helen "Nonni" Plummer, who bids farewell to every customer with the phrase, "Have an excellent!" Should someone inquire, "Excellent what?" she quickly adds, "Whatever you want it to be." Her infectious spirit has spread to a Facebook.com group titled "You Have An Excellent" that has hundreds of members.

In his book *Authentic Management*, author Stan Herman captures the essence of this type of animated service. "No one grants you freedom," he writes. "You are free if you are free. I do not know how to tell you how to be free. But I do know some signs of freedom. One is in doing what you want to do even though someone tells you not to. Another is in doing what you want to do even *though* someone tells you to."[5]

It is the attitude of those who serve customers that provides customers with a peephole into the values and qualities most revered by the unit or organization. Remember what Chuck Jones said: "Animation happens when everything in the frame moves with the character"? One of the reasons we have such fond memories of White's is the way Katie was a character in the theatrical performance of "White's." Katie no doubt helped others get in the spirit of greatness; others like the wise-cracking hostess played their roles alongside her. And, owner Don Uselman—and inventor of the Whoopee! Burger and Don's Big Mess—was the cheerleader for them all.

Comfort

Think back about your very best friend as a child. It was the person who could tease you in a way no one else could get away with. It was the person who could make you laugh, keep a secret, and cheer you up when you were feeling downhearted. You had a relationship filled with a consistent enthusiasm. It was without pretense, free of anxiety, and laced with consideration and comfort.

As an animated service tactic, comfort comes from familiarity. It is all the ways a service-providing organization creates an "I know you" experience. Starbucks gets great marks from customers for turning the order-taking incident into a memory-making relationship. Step up to the counter to place your order and you'll hear "tall skinny cinnamon dolce for Chip" repeated several times—the information echoed from customer to clerk to the drink maker (barista) and back to the customer. The repetition not only creates the security of familiarity, it enables Starbucks personnel to quickly learn your specific drink preference so you do not have to start at the beginning each time you show up.

Comfort is the product of an emotional connection that feels familiar plus an experience that is anxiety-free. Don always makes Maynard's meatloaf on Wednesday at White's. The turkey club sandwich always tastes so fresh you expect to see feathers out back. Katie always teases her customers. The consistency makes customers feel empowered and secure. The reliability breeds a sense of contentment, the type that says to the customer's dissonance meter, "Calm down, we've been here before, and it's okay."

Katie was more than friendly. She was a pro working with a resourceful team in a well-oiled system. She had the White's menus in our hands before our bottoms touched the chairs. Our wait was not even noticeable. She refilled our iced tea glasses without prompting, brought more rolls, and left the check with the caveat: "Don't think I'm trying to rush you out. I just don't want you having to look for me when you're ready to leave."

Want to add comfort to your service experience? Take a close look at all the aspects of the experience that could make your customers feel apprehensive or nervous. Take an empathy walk with frequent customers willing to take the time to talk you through every step of their service journey with the goal of informing you of all the points where they experience the slightest unease. Call your own unit or organization, disguise your voice, and ask for something out of the ordinary, even something weird. Had we waited a long time for our menu at White's, we might have generalized that delay to the whole dining experience and concluded that lunch was going to take way too long. Had Katie been too hasty to take our order, we might have worried about her accuracy and wondered whether the apple pie we ordered was going to be Marionberry pie instead.

PERSONAL

Katie's version of animation works for Katie because she is authentically animated, delivering it in her own Katie fashion. Customers have a well-tuned sincerity sonar and will pick up even a hint of hypocrisy. Animation must come from the heart and be filtered through a conspicuous respect for the customer. Otherwise, it will feel as phony as a politician at a barbeque shaking hands and kissing babies. When you are Mickey Mouse, the costume can disguise your true self. But when you are serving out of costume, what you show to the customer must come from who you are, not who you pretend to be.

We arrived at the Marriott Hotel in Rocky Hill near Hartford, Connecticut, after a late-evening delayed flight. As we came through the lobby entrance the front desk clerk announced, "Where have you boys been? I waited up for you, but it is way past my bedtime." The affable sparring was coming from the front desk supervisor, Lillian Koster. We felt at home! Her animation was, as always, genuine and delivered with an approach that was signature Ms. Lillian. Not only did she make us feel like home, she showed unmistakably that she truly cared!

The personal tactic does not mean customized, it means *personal*. As one customer reported when describing her bank,

"They installed this new customer relationship management system so all my correspondence from them is now tailored—they even knew my son was heading off to college this year. Now, when I call and give them my account number, they do little chit chat about my neighborhood or comment on the fact that I have a new Buick, financed by their loan department. But all that is just mechanized. When I walk in any branch no one acts like they know me or even wants to get to know me! Give me back old fashioned personal service, not this customer-ized baloney. It's no more genuine than the ATM."

We reference this illustration because too many units and organizations confuse personal with customized. Most of us like tailor-made service. We enjoy a service provider that knows our preferences and caters to our unique needs and expectations. But, we still want the service provider to treat us like an important and valued person. We know that inside animated service is a human, not a program.

Look for ways to get to know your customers better. When now retired "Coach" Jim Miller was the CEO of Miller Business Systems in Arlington, Texas, he held a customer appreciation day each month. Miller Business (now Corporate Express) provides office supplies to businesses. On customer appreciation day, Miller employees constructed posters of the spotlighted customer company complete with displays of what the company did or made. All employees wore special "We love _____ " buttons. A special luncheon gave employees a chance to meet and talk with customer contact people they formerly only knew as a voice on the phone. The best part of the day was the opportunity for the customer's employees to observe Miller warehouse workers "picking" the customer's actual pending order!

RESPECT

Katie never commented on our way-too-obvious Southern accents. "You boys ain't from around here, are you?" would not have exactly made us feel like a neighbor. She was warm and a bit of a character, with a non-stop friendly tease. But even at the summit of her impishness, she never lost sight that we contributed to the currency that funded her wages. Katie's motivation was clearly not about tit for tat—her honor for our honorarium. She seemed genuinely thrilled and respectful we were there to eat Don's Fatso Burger.

Animation must always reflect respect. One important dimension of this is the degree to which the animation strategy fits your situation. The customer bond must make sense in its context. A complimentary bottle of champagne at a fast food drive-through would be as dissonant as a free serving of French fries at a five-star restaurant. But a congruent connection is more than matching connection with conditions or affirmation with ambiance. The connection must also be congruent with tone and style. As a former service quality instructor at the Disney Institute put it: "Disney makes magic with pixie dust. Whatever they do smells right, tastes right, sounds right as well as feels right. Bottom line, it is theatrically pure." Animation takes your customers' breath away when it is theatrically pure.

Zappos.com is fast becoming one of the country's leading online shoe retailers, with sales growing from $1.6 million in 2000 to more than $1 billion eight years later. It is not just their wide collection of goods or their renowned return policy that makes them great. It is the animated respect their phone reps deliver. One blogger wrote, "Awesome customer service. I didn't order the half size smaller and realized it before the shoes shipped. I was immediately helped and was so happy, then realized I went too small. I called back and again I was immediately helped and after a good laugh got the correct shoes shipped. I am sure Zappos people thought I had lost my mind but they were very supportive and had me laughing about my errors! It was the best customer support I have ever had! And I buy a lot online." Notice the reference to laughing. One of Zappos' core values is "Create fun and a little weirdness." Also, note the demonstration of respect. "Be humble" is another of Zappos' core values.

Respect is also about bigheartedness. There is nothing animated about greed. A miserly approach narrows relationships rather than expands them; it closes rather than opens doors. Customers value service providers who avoid the pound-of-flesh mentality. When the balance-the-books bean counters search for all the pennies to possibly squeeze from customer transactions, they risk losing the dollars of a devoted customer who desires a respectful relationship with a bit more give in it.

Several years ago, Chip purchased an industrial-strength sleeper-sofa and had it delivered to his lake house. This was his first experience with the furniture store. The salesperson neglected to tell him the standard mattress on the $900 sofa bed was a "pretend" mattress, one you might endure only for a short night after partying real late! After one night on it, Chip called the furniture store and was informed of the rules: An upgrade mattress would cost $60, but the pretend mattress could not be returned. There would be no free delivery on the upgrade mattress. Mattresses do not fold up to be neatly transported in the back seat of a car.

A friend with a truck and a half-day off came to his rescue. With prior agreement from the furniture store, Chip mailed in a check for $60 so his friend could pick up and transport the new mattress. No one called to learn if the new mattress worked better. Two weeks later, Chip received a bill for $1.80 with a note from Mr. Rules 'R Us: "You neglected to pay tax on the upgraded mattress. Remit immediately so we can balance our books!" This was Chip's last experience with the furniture store.

Customers remember what you give to them long after they have forgotten what you take from them. Customer devotion happens when the customer experiences service from providers willing to overlook imperfections in the math of the moment in exchange for the fairness of the future. Customers are particularly averse to service providers who wire their systems to their own strong advantage. Respect is not what you believe, it is what you show.

SPARKLY

Don's Big Mess, it turns out, is an everything-but-the-kitchen-sink breakfast amalgamation that is rather new to the White's menu. Owner Don Uselman likes to tease his customers now and then. "We don't tamper with the main menu, mind you," Don reported about his unusual entrée. "But a few little surprises once in a while help keep our customers coming back . . . sometimes, just out of curiosity."

Sparkly as an animated service tactic is designed to evoke a sense of adventure in customers. Service providers using the sparkly brand of animation serve as happiness scouts, convincing us to experiment and enticing us to expand our service horizons. Succumbing to their magic, we try that unique entrée we otherwise might have avoided, or embrace a color, style, or version of clothing we might have formerly thought outside the boundaries of our taste. Persuaded by their confidence and sheer joy in discovering the new, we are jolted out of our routines in ways that renew our spirits and help us see the value of taking calculated risks.

"A visit to the dentist" is hardly the phrase you would couple with "a wonderful experience." Yet that is exactly how Wayzata Dental, a 60-year-old, 20-plus person dental clinic in Wayzata, Minnesota, envisions their goal: to become the Nordstrom of dentistry. Dr. Jason McDowell, the clinic's owner since 2004, has pursued that goal with a passion, and he has succeeded. Warm smiles with a lively "Hello, John!" greet you as you walk in the door. Amenities are offered to each guest on arrival. They may choose to relax with a heated neck pillow, listen to an iPod, hook up to WiFi, or watch a movie during the visit. The reception area contains three flat-screen televisions (listened to via headsets so as not to disturb the other guests). There are Xbox 360 video games and a virtual aquarium. A refreshment bar completes the anti-dentist-office feel.

In a separate area of the clinic, designated the "Smile Spa," guests can have their teeth whitened using Zoom or Lasik's BriteSmile system. The procedures are offered with all the amenities to give the experience the feel of a mini-vacation with the result being beautiful, white teeth. No wonder the clinic is so enthusiastic about donating Smile Spa visits to silent auctions. Dr. McDowell states, "It's a great way to give to the community and reward an auction purchaser with something they will remember every time they look in the mirror." Creating a "Smile to Last Lifetime" is a very important theme at Wayzata Dental.

"We constantly work on making little things work right for our guests," says Brian Denn, clinic director. For instance, follow-up calls are made to guests who have had a particularly difficult procedure. Every guest has the doctor's business card, which includes the doctor's home phone number. There is a consultation area where the doctors can take guests and discuss their treatment in detail. "We don't think lying on your back with your mouth wide open is very good for communication or decision making," says Denn. "Time is really the most valuable service we can give our guests," says Dr. McDowell. "Each and every patient will be provided whatever time they need and never feel rushed. Even if they just need to talk about their day, our staff is happy to do this because we want every guest to feel like they are with friends." The experiment in patient-centered dentistry has paid off well. Growth has been remarkable, even in a down economy. The sparkle of the service they provide matches the sparkle of the smiles they help create.

Customer connections are about forging strong links, not about making superficial contacts. They create a bond when they stir our emotions, not just get our attention. This means they must be laced with spirit, energy, and attitude. And the most notable take-their-breath-away service providers are masters at balancing the familiar, the comfortable, and the respectful with the sparkly. In a word, animation is their forte.

Just like White's Restaurant, the culture that supports, encourages, and nurtures animation will be the one that attracts and retains devoted customers. And just as Wayzata Dental knows, animation is a service strategy that makes you, as well as your customer, smile. For the customer, animation stays in their memory banks for a long time afterward, or it quickly surfaces when someone mentions the service provider that created it. And it makes you, the service provider, look forward to delivering it with all the excitement of a nine-year-old waiting for Santa.

CHAPTER 2
Reinvention

"Breakthroughs come from an instinctive judgment of what customers might want if they knew to think about it."
    —Andrew Grove, former chairman and CEO, Intel

What do Bill Marriott, Debbi Fields, and Al Hopkins have in common? No, they are not all rich and famous! In fact, Al is a small-town accountant and part-time preacher in South Georgia. They all are (or were) innovators in ways to better serve customers. They saw the way a given service was being delivered and found a way to turn it completely on its ear. And in their heyday, they took their customers' breath away!

In 1937, J. Willard (Bill, Sr.) Marriott started the first catering service to airlines for meals on board after he noticed people at Hoover Field (now the site of the Pentagon) were going by his small Hot Shoppes restaurant and buying take-out food before boarding their flights. It was an intuitive leap that linked a customer need with an available resource via a novel path. He graduated from Hot Shoppes and in-flight catering to do hotels, and the rest is history.

Debbi Fields saw the growing popularity of shopping malls. She created a computer hookup with each mall-based cookie store that enabled the operator to make smart decisions by the hour on what cookies to offer and which to discount. The cookie maker linked together familiar pieces into a revolutionary combination that made her at one point the country's largest seller of cookies.

And Al Hopkins? When he was a young boy he watched the other 10-year-olds wait for customers to stop by their sidewalk lemonade stands in the hot summer sun. Al abandoned the stand concept and took his lemonade business door-to-door. He made enough money in one summer to buy a new Schwinn Flyer bicycle with a headlight *and* a siren!

The most common characteristic of take-their-breath-away service is that it is imaginative, distinctive, unique, unusual, atypical, unexpected, and all the other words you can think of that insinuate a super pleasant surprise. This brand of service yields in customers the exact same emotional reaction that might be created by witnessing a rainbow you did not expect, receiving a personal favor from an unlikely source, or getting a novel gift that communicates the giver knew you better than you realized.

Surprise can obviously happen unexpectedly. We have all experienced those serendipitous positive moments we knew were once-in-a-lifetime occurrences. The power in take-their-breath-away service is that it comes with a recognition on the part of the customer that it was planned, designed, or crafted that way on purpose—and therefore could be done again. Accidental greatness may delight us, but handmade greatness brings us back for a second look. And, the goal of such imaginative service is customer devotion, not simply customer pleasure.

🦋 The Butterfly

Caterpillars turn into butterflies. The process of starting out looking like one kind of creature and ending up like something else entirely is called *metamorphosis*. The word is derived from two Greek words that mean transformation and change.

Take-their-breath-away service is all about seeing what other people see but thinking about new applications. The losers are those who stick with "the way we have always done it." Television should have been started by the big movie studios, trucking should have been started by the firmly planted railroads, and the first motels should have come from the grand hotel giants like Hilton, not from upstarts like Holiday Inn and Marriott. Take-their-breath-away service starts with challenging assumptions about every aspect of the service experience.

Take a look at a short list of renowned service innovators. Despite a Yale professor's admonition that there was little practical about his theory, Fred Smith put his "C–" paper into operation and founded Federal Express (now FedEx). Michael Dell transformed a computer assembly business he operated out of his University of Texas dorm room into Dell Computer. Wall Street laughed at Jeff Bezos for thinking an online bookstore would work. Like the bumblebee ignoring the fact that, aerodynamically speaking, it cannot fly, Jeff created Amazon.com anyway.

THE REQUIREMENT FOR CREATIVITY

We have labeled our second take-their-breath-away strategy "Reinvention." It highlights a core requirement for imaginative service—creativity. Not creative? Whoa. Hold onto your seat! Our plan is to demonstrate that you *are* creative if you have the tools and techniques to unearth this important personal treasure, and we'll give you a starter tool kit in this chapter. Granted, some people are more creative than others; the demonstration of creativity comes more easily for some than for others. That said, you indeed have the capacity to design and deliver service that customers will view as inventive.

The short version of how to be creative is this: Your brain has a feature that helps you while it hinders you. Your brain is a pattern maker. From the time you arrived on the planet your survival depended on figuring out what made sense and what did not, what worked and what did not. Sense making happens in part by seeing regularities or patterns. You learned that a hot stove can be painful if touched, and a pattern was created in your brain that internally warned you each time you approached a hot stove. Without that pattern, you could continue to relearn a painful lesson.

Patterns can be very simple, like hot stoves; they can be very complex, like how to have a successful relationship or how to solve a complex puzzle. Patterns give us language. Patterns give us societal order. Patterns are the foundation of logic and the basis of all learning. Without patterns we would stay disoriented, confused, and anxious. Without patterns we would be unable to work with others in a group. English literary giant Aldous Huxley labeled the brain "a reducing mechanism" since people are confronted every day with far more data and inputs than their brains can possibly process.[1] Our brain patterns enable us to be selective about what we let in and what we ignore. The older we get, the more patterns we have in our brains and the more facile we become at recognizing and reacting to patterns.

Dung Mug[2]

Patterns also have a limiting side. Since we are always searching for patterns, we naturally gravitate toward the familiar, the tried and true, the tested. Imaginative service is effective because it is not typical. The essence of take-their-breath-away service is that it departs from the pattern. Patterned service can be ordinary, regular, and normal. There is nothing wrong with patterned service; it is just not a memory maker. What can you recall about the details of the last time you had your car washed, your shoes shined, or got a take-out order at a fast-food restaurant? If there was something out of the ordinary about it, you no doubt recall it. And, if it was a very positive out-of-the-ordinary experience, you probably told a few friends about it and made a secret promise to return for a second helping. The reinvention strategy is all about making the service experience an unexpected, positive memory maker that brings customers back.

Vujà Dé

The late George Carlin was credited with coining the phrase "vujà dé." It was his comedic flip of the familiar "déjà vu"—the feeling of "I've been here before." Carlin's made-up phrase meant seeing things through completely new eyes. That capacity enabled him to render such hilarious lines as "I put a dollar in a change machine. Nothing changed," or "What was the best thing before sliced bread?" or "So far this is the oldest I've been," or "Cloud nine gets all the publicity, but cloud eight is cheaper, less crowded, and has a better view," or . . . okay, we'll stop!

Vujà dé takes courage. Remember, our pattern-making brain is much more at home with the familiar. The quest for imaginative service requires being courageous enough to break from the familiar pattern to find a new service application. Traveling from comfortable to creative follows the path of ideation or reinvention. The route has calm on one end and gratification on the other. However, the course from start to finish includes a region of discomfort, even distress. The courage part comes with weathering the uneasiness long enough to get to the gratification end of the path.

Reinvention involves having a little contest with your brain, deliberately making it break the patterns it likes in order to explore new alternatives. Let's have fun with this by using an

Count every square you see.

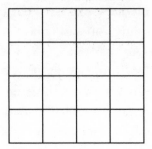

Figure 2.1   Pattern Breaking Puzzle

exercise to demonstrate how pattern breaking works in principle. Follow the instruction in Figure 2.1 before reading on.

Stop! Don't read the next paragraph until you have done the puzzle.

The first pattern your brain recognizes is the 16 squares in the figure. Then, your brain quickly reasons that there is one large square. With that discovery, you start counting 2-by-2 squares. If you looked closely, there are nine of these in all. Getting more advanced, your brain reasons that if two squares by two squares could produce nine, then three squares by three squares could yield even more. There are four. Adding up all of these, you proudly announce the correct answer is 30.

Now, here is the pattern breaker. Are there more than just the squares contained in the geometric figure? Look at the instruction again. The word "square" should also be included in your calculation. Your brain now reacts as if it has been tricked. This is the feeling of discomfort we mentioned earlier. The goal of reinvention is essentially to help your brain get past the geometric part of the analysis to discover a new, larger answer to the problem.

Nordstrom started in 1901 as a Seattle shoe store specializing in high-end merchandise. Nordstrom folklore has it that one of the three Nordstrom brothers (sons of cofounder John Nordstrom) vacationed at the classy Hotel del Coronado near San Diego in the early 1960s. While there, he was continually impressed with the hotel concierge who delivered over-the-top service to guests, no matter how unique their requests. He returned with a vision to create a chain of retail stores that had every employee functioning as a concierge . . . and you know the rest of the story.

Service reinventions seldom occur by examining best practices employed by others in the same industry. There are a lot of familiar patterns found in all the just-like-you organizations. Insights come through looking at a service offering or service process through the lens of great service exemplars outside your industry. A major hospital completely revamped patient admission after studying how a five-star hotel handled guest check-in. Cabela's and Bass Pro Shops did not get the idea of their sensory overload stores by studying Bubba's Bait and Tackle shop; they probably looked at Disney theme parks.

Make a list of great service providers. Now pick a service offering or service process of yours. Then, brainstorm ways that one or more of those service greats might reinvent that service offering or process. What if a great Lexus dealership service department could be in charge of your service department for a week? What improvements might come from Jiffy Lube's being in charge of your maintenance department for a few days? If the Geek Squad at Best Buy ran your IT department, what would customers likely notice changed? What would human resources be like if it embraced the "ladies and gentlemen serving ladies and gentlemen" philosophy of a Ritz-Carlton hotel? How about putting Disney in charge of the cafeteria or UPS in charge of the mail room?

JUICERS

Juicers are jump starters. They are a way of force-fitting a seemingly irrelevant attribute to unleash a new way to deliver service. They get their name from the way they help juice up the brain to break patterns—getting beyond "the way we have always done it." The technical term for juicers is *attribute listing* and was

Figure 2.2   What If Our Service Process Were . . .

Slower	Funnier	More entertaining	Divided into parts	Spiritual
Faster	Weirder	More instructional	Done with a helper	Wild
Longer	Cuter	More inspirational	Done anywhere	Empathic
Smaller	Uglier	More inclusive	Done remotely	Healthy
Cheaper	Sharper	More invisible	Done automatically	Green
Larger	Subtler	More responsive	Done backwards	Risky
Bolder	More	More attractive	Done with a manual	Expensive
Higher	Less	More challenging	Done randomly	Athletic
Quieter	None	More spiritual	Done anytime	Outdoors
Louder	Secret	More robotic	Done while you wait	Elegant
Flashier	Careful	More wholesome	Done in reverse	Effortless

made popular by Alex Osborne in his pioneering 1950's book *Applied Imagination.*

Here's how to put juicers to work: First, select a service application or process you would like to improve or alter. Then select a juicer from the list in Figure 2.2. If you thought of the juicer as a lens, what would your service process look like if you peered through it? Try a few and see what you get.

For instance, other organizations have asked questions like these:

What would a carwash be like if it was done greener?

What would boarding a plane be like if it was done funnier?

What would completing a requisition form be like if it was done with a helper?

What would contacting the call center be like if it was done more elegantly?

What would ordering a pizza be like if it was done automatically?

What would completing a tax return be like if was done more instructionally? Done with a mentor?

What would the checkout at a retail store be like if it was done completely invisibly? Or done automatically?

What would the reception area be like if it was flashier, more entertaining, or healthier?

Here are a few examples of how others have used the juicer tactic and forced it to apply to their service offering or process.

SERVICE DONE SLOWER

Starbucks made headlines for closing all their stores for four hours to do training. They smartly selected their slowest business hours—late afternoon. Employees told us that a part of their training was how to slow down. Some coffee baristas had been rushing the coffee ordering process to the point they were losing the relatively laid-back ambiance that had made them successful in the first place. Customers want to escape the frenetic and impersonal to get a latte delivered with calm and chitchat.

Catherine Davis, owner of the Davis Financial & Insurance Group in Louisville, Colorado, found that her Allstate agents and administrative staff had gotten so efficient at processing paperwork that they were not taking the time to build rapport with clients. To remind them to slow down, she placed turtle signs everywhere. "I chose the turtle because everyone remembers who won the race in the childhood story of the tortoise and hare," she reported. Her staff meetings included "turtle talk"—idea generation about ways to maintain efficiency while ramping up ways to demonstrate the staff had the patience and focus to make each client feel special.

SERVICE DONE REMOTELY

Blockbuster videos built an entertainment empire by buying up small video stores and transforming them into well-run franchises with the latest everything—the latest video titles, contemporary management methods, specialized software, and updated physical settings. Even as industry experts warned that technological breakthroughs would one day render it unnecessary to leave your living room to get the latest movie—it could be downloaded, stored, and watched at your leisure—Blockbuster continued to flourish.

Then an industry upstart unexpectedly came through a side door and upset the movie rental business. But instead of focusing on the Internet as the movie delivery system the experts had assumed in their forecasts, NetFlix relied on the old-fashioned U.S. Postal Service. Borrowing heavily from lessons learned from Amazon.com, the Netflix Web site included customer reviews and movie reviewer articles plus an easy-to-use search process. Customers could go online, order any DVD, and have it delivered to their home via snail mail complete with a simple return mailer. The company currently boasts more than four million customers and a market value of more than $1.5 billion. Even though the company is still quite young, it services 4 percent of all U.S. households.

SERVICE DONE WITH A HELPER

At Netflix, management is constantly on the prowl for new ways to improve the customer experience. That focus has led to a series of innovations, such as creation of the Friends network, which allows customers an online peek at movies their friends have rented and whether they've given them the thumbs up or down; allowing single customer accounts to create two or more profiles, so different members of a household can develop their own online queue of movies to be mailed out when current rentals are returned; and a feature that recommends new movies to users based on the customer's own reviews of movies they've rented before, not simply on types of movies rented in the past.[3] Some of these customer-friendly changes came as a result of input from the focus groups that Netflix holds every week.

SERVICE DONE BACKWARD

Rehabilitation and Health Center of Gastonia, North Carolina, had a problem. Residents enjoyed playing $1 and 50-cent bingo, a great activity for stimulating mental health, vital to their quality of life. But, too often, residents misplaced their money. Activities director Teresa Cochran solved the problem. They would pay residents "activity money" for every activity in which they participated. For an interactive game like bingo, residents might receive five dollars in activity money; for an activity in which an outside group came to entertain, residents might be given as much as 50 dollars of pretend money. So, how does the activity money get spent? At the end of every month, staff, family members, and friends donate items like sweaters, hats, socks, six-packs of soft drinks, snacks, and other goodies to be auctioned off to residents. A special item, an IOU, provides the winning bidder with a future trip to the store or a restaurant. If the winner of the IOU is unable to go out for dinner, the staff goes to the restaurant and buys the meal to go. According to Cochran, "Our auctions have been so successful we have had to limit residents to three items! We tell residents it pays to come to activities—and it does."

UNCONVENTIONAL PERSPECTIVE

In "vujà dé," we suggested looking at your unit or organization through the lens of service exemplars outside your industry. We are now going to give you another tool for seeing.

Stop and take five minutes to try and see everything around you. No really, go ahead and do it. We'll wait. Now, look around again, and this time notice all the things that are green. Bet you saw a few things you missed on the first look. Did green things come into your field of vision after your first look? Of course not. The difference was our third reinvention tactic: unconventional perspective. Changing perspective is one of the best ways to reinvent.

A friend of ours was staying at the elegant, antique Brown Palace Hotel in Denver while working there for a week. On the morning he was checking out he asked the desk clerk, "Can you give me really clear directions on how to get from the hotel to Denver International Airport? I have a rental car and don't know the city very well."

"I can do better than that," the desk clerk replied with a smile in her voice as grand as the one on her face. "I can give you this!" She presented the guest with a $3 \times 5''$ note card with detailed instructions for driving from the hotel to the airport.

"This is great!" our friend remarked. "I stay in a lot of hotels, and no one has ever given me a helpful tool like this."

"You want to know who came up with this idea?" she asked playfully. And before he could respond she blurted out: "The guys at the bell stand! Before we had these cards, we'd send you to the bell stand for driving directions since they're the ones who drive the hotel van. But sometimes they were tied up helping guests with luggage. They suggested we put answers to the most frequently asked guest questions on small cards. And it's worked terrific. It makes them more accessible, and it makes us look smarter."

"Oh, you mean you have others like this?" our friend continued, somewhat in awe. "Oh, yes!" she replied with great pleasure, as she pulled out a stack of different colored cards. "Where would you like to go?"

Getting people to help you change your perspective can land you lots of great ideas. What if you invited a guest to your next meeting to help you think differently? What could you learn from an artist, inventor, magician, musician, or clown? When our good friend John Longstreet (now with ClubCorp) was the general manager of the Harvey Hotel in Plano, Texas, he held weekly "What's Stupid" meetings with employees to learn ways to improve service to guests. But, he went one step further and frequently invited a hotel guest or a vendor to participate.

What if you involved a group of children in your reinvention strategy? A high-tech company was looking for a way to improve their proposal process. As an organization that got business by responding to requests for proposal (RFPs), they believed a more creative proposal could differentiate them from their competitors. They turned the challenge over to a group of elementary-school-aged children armed with host of art supplies—crayons, glitter, balloons, the works. They were amazed. The result was a totally reinvented process, and their "win rate" increased by more than 25 percent.

New people can be important gifts to the reinvention process since they are not yet stuck in "the way we have always done it." It takes about 90 days to go blind to the details customers see. As we get acclimated, oriented, and inculcated into a new culture, those illogical processes—the ones people are talking about when they say, "That's just the way we do things here"—fade away. We stop seeing what seemed obvious initially. This means new people are better able to see things like when the emperor is not wearing any clothes. Seek them out and tap their perception like an anthropologist in search of an explanation.

WACKY

Our look into reinvention as a take-their-breath-away service strategy would not be complete without considering its quirky and outrageous side. Before dismissing the wacky tactic as frivolous, know that many great inventions and discoveries have occurred in bizarre, screwball ways. Play-Doh was the accidental by-product of an effort to develop wallpaper cleaner. The Slinky came about when scientists were trying to design a spring to support sensitive equipment on ships. Silly Putty was a mistake in an attempt to create a synthetic rubber substitute. And the technology that made Cool Whip possible (that amazing whipped-cream–like stuff that stays fluffy after being frozen) was a sheer accident. A food chemist at General Foods was working on developing a new topping and accidentally left the blender on in the lab while he went to lunch. Incidentally, this same food chemist holds 70 patents, including ones for Tang, Pop Rocks, powdered egg whites, and quick-set Jell-O! Wacky works!

So, a detour through wacky can lead to a practical discovery. But it is important to know that wacky is not the destination; it's simply a detour on the route to practical results. Remember that little out-of-the-way diner your father insisted on stopping at for lunch when you were en route to your grandmother's? It may have made the trip a bit longer, but it made your travel a lot happier.

Another thing to know about wacky is it sometimes requires the highest level of courage. People in very rational, logical roles (engineers, accountants, attorneys, and physicians) may find this approach to reinvention particularly angst-ridden. Here are a few questions to use as a launch pad and ease the process.

What would your customer experience be like . . .

. . . if you had a magic wand and could change one important aspect of the customer experience.

. . . if you had unlimited resources.

. . . if you were a superhero with supernatural powers.

. . . if you wanted to invent a customer experience that was completely different from any other on the planet.

. . . if the new experience was going to carry the name of your child, your parents, or your best friend.

Now, let us take wacky up a few more notches. You could ask the following:

♦ What folk hero or character could represent the new customer experience you want to create?

♦ If that folk hero or character were to advise you on the new experience, what would he, she, or it recommend?

Here's another tack to take: Ask yourself, what's wrong with your current process? What if you could excise the wrong part and replace it with something that made your customers feel one of the emotions listed in Figure 2.3? Pick one and then brainstorm ways the replaced part could help capture the emotion you selected below.

Figure 2.3 How Could Our Customers Feel . . .

Pick One of the Top 40 Emotions			
Nostalgic	Entertaining	Ultramodern	Refreshing
Safe	Quirky/Funky	Traditional	Cultured
Efficient	Proud	Warm	Patriotic
Ritzy	Classy	Artistic	Confident
Cared for	Unique	Frugal	Smart
Elite/Rich	Special	Happy as a Kid	Wild
Secure	Pampered	Responsible	Macho
Feminine	Frisky	Tough	Sensitive
Neighborly	Relieved	Like Family	Healthy
Like a Partner	Romantic	Wise	Clever

Let's take wacky up yet another level. Earlier in this chapter you used a list of juicers constructed completely of attributes. Let's use a super-juicer designed to propel you into the realm of the truly wacky.

Here is an example of how it can work. When a group of human resource professionals were gathered to problem solve ways to reduce turnover, they chose a villain—Jack the Ripper— from the Famous People list in Figure 2.4 to apply to the issue.

When exploring what Jack the Ripper would do, someone in the group suggested that Jack would likely cut off all the employees' legs so they would be forced to stay on the job. Silly? You bet! But, it led to a rich discussion about hiring more people with handicaps, an employee group known to have a much lower

Figure 2.4 What If Our Service Process Were Like . . .

Arts	Lifestyle	Odd Views	Famous People
Character in movie	The other political party	You're the product	Military
Cartoon character	An occupation	You're the process	Comedian
Song title	A kitchen appliance	Kid's perspective	Politician
Subject of a painting	A room in the house	The other gender	Movie star
Colored differently	A vacation site	The customer's view	Inventor
A prop in a play	A make/type of car	Competitor's CEO	A villain
Musical instrument	A family	Worst nightmare	The other gender
Name of a band	A type of store	A dream come true	Your biggest hero
A type of dance	Mode of transportation	Wild inventor	News reporter
A well-known story	A computer program	Bird's eye view	Favorite author
Book title	Gossip column	It's alive!	Famous artist
A joke/cliché/ad	A recreation/sport	Guinness candidate	Superhero
	A type of food	Part of a circus	Favorite teacher

absentee and turnover rate than employees without handicaps. That is the power of the wacky tactic.

"Imagination is more important that intelligence," said Albert Einstein, arguably the 20th century's most intelligent person. "For knowledge is limited to all we now know and understand, while imagination embraces the entire world, and all there ever will be to know and understand." Imaginative service is much the same. Intelligent service makes us feel secure; imaginative service makes us swoon. Smart service builds customer confidence; imaginative service makes your heart skip a beat. Clever service gets customers talking; imaginative service takes their breath away.

As it brightens their world, it leaves them more patient and likely taking some of the irritation out of their next service grievance. As it brightens your world, that joy is passed to the next person you encounter who passes it on to another, elevating the geniality quotient for everyone. At the end of the day, repeat business and repeated stories are sourced from taking customers to a new, enchanting place with an implied promise that a return can be cheerfully arranged.

CHAPTER 3
Decoration

"There are two ways of spreading light: to be the candle or the mirror that reflects it."

—*Edith Wharton*

Guess where this is! You walk through the entrance and a big, fuzzy-costumed character greets you. Everywhere you look there are smiling employees and happy guests. As you wind through the colorfully adorned passageway, a mechanical rooster pops up and sings to the mechanical hens in the nearby cage. A peppy soundtrack is periodically punctuated by an announcement that the show in one section is about to begin. Think you are in a theme park? Nope! You are in a grocery store!

Clarence Saunders is credited with revolutionizing grocery shopping. Prior to his inventions in 1916, patrons handed their shopping lists to the grocer who went back into the stock room to fill the order. Saunders launched the self-service grocery store that incorporated such patented ideas as shopping baskets, checkout counters, and a store arrangement that enabled customers to view all the merchandise. Piggly Wiggly became the grocery shopping rage, and by the 1930s there were more than 2,500 stores.

The next revolution in grocery shopping came from the answer to our "where are you?" quiz: Stew Leonard's Dairy Store, headquartered in Norwalk, Connecticut, and currently operating eight giant stores in Connecticut and New York. Instead of focusing on overhauling the shopping process like Saunders, Stew Leonard decorated the shopping experience. He transformed a traditionally functional experience into one that was entertaining and fun. The concept was so successful that Stew Leonard's Dairy Store was listed in *Guinness Book of World Records* as having the highest retail sales per square foot of any establishment in the world. The company has been rated in *Fortune* magazine's "100 Best Companies to Work For" for eight years straight.

Stew Leonard's[1]

DECORATION BASICS

As Stew Leonard knows, the intent of the decoration strategy is to take a traditional service approach and embellish it in ways that make not only the outcome but the experience itself memorable. It works when it has an unforgettable positive impact on customers. It also works when it is kept perpetually fresh and original. That means keeping an unremitting flow of ideas in the pipeline from and to customers. At every Stew Leonard's store, there is a giant suggestion box at the entrance that announces "We get over 500 suggestions every day." Customers fill out the "Tell us what you like and don't like" forms because they see concrete evidence in stores that their two cents matters.

The decoration strategy first and foremost engages customers. If it is based on a theme or a story (as with Stew Leonard's), the customer is drawn into the story rather than simply being a witness. One way they do it at Stew Leonard's is to ask customers to play the Wow Game, whereby they target affirming feedback to frontline employees for over-the-top service. Customers are so engaged in the story they send in photos of themselves taken in exotic places holding a Stew Leonard's shopping bag. Over 40,000 photos have been posted.

🦚 The Peacock

Peacocks are large, colorful pheasants known for their iridescent tails. The showy train is used in courtship displays. Females are believed to choose their mates according to the size, color, and quality of this decorative plumage.

The decoration strategy comes in many forms. In this chapter we will examine four tactics: theme, sense, function, and comfort. Stew Leonard's uses theme as their tactic, harking back to their roots as a dairy store started in the 1920s by Stew Leonard Jr.'s grandfather. The sense tactic relies on the power of the five senses as a tool to ramp up the service experience. The tactic of function involves reframing the service experience to emphasize the emotional benefit rather than the obvious service outcome for the customer. Finally, the comfort tactic places a spotlight on everything needed to create a completely anxiety-free, zero-dissonance experience.

All four decoration tactics rely on a keen understanding of the customer as well as a realistic assessment of the service provider's capacity to keep it fresh. All assume delivery is done through animated, engaged employees. All are grounded in the recognition that, in today's economy, getting the product or outcome the customer desires at the price or investment they assume is fair is simply the price of admission; it provides zero competitive advantage.

THEME

"Eat it and get out!" That's the mantra for Ed Debevic's Diner in Chicago. At Ed Debevic's, guests step into a '50s–style diner to experience the ambiance of a misty yore, complete with bobby sox, saddle shoes, and jukebox. The surprise twist on this nostalgic experience is that the front-of-the-house employees are professional entertainers, trained to create a rollicking, in-your-face service experience—as well as to perform the odd musical entertainment, like dancing and singing on the countertop.

What is the origin of this unique dining experience? It was created in 1984 with its blueprint and script drawn from an important story: the story of Lill's Homesick Diner. But, let's give Ed a chance to tell it.

Those of you fortunate enough to have passed through
Talooca, Illinois, during the '50s and '60s probably

remember Lill's Homesick Diner on Highway 50. The Homesick knew how to feed you: fresh-baked bread and pies, homemade chili, real beef burgers (no soybeans), and plenty of good, hot coffee. And Lill knew how to treat people right—eat and get out, that was her motto. Unfortunately, when a fast food franchise moved in down the road, Lill closed the Homesick and moved to Florida to sell fruit at her sister Estelle's roadside stand.

The Homesick is where I learned the short-order business. And while I'm no Lill, I think I've made this place something she'd be proud of. So as Lill always said, "If you like what you're eatin', order more. If you don't, there's the door."[2]

Adhering to the motto "Eat and get out," Ed Debevic's service is anything but service with a sweet and dimpled smile. Dressed in mismatched orange and green floral prints that should have been lost in someone's attic, the comedic cast does more than take orders. They'll give them—to guests.

One of the stock cast characters at Ed Debevic's is LouLou Lewis, who tells guests to finish all the food on their plates, otherwise they'll get no dessert. LouLou will also demand that guests stop dawdling and talking and order a meal—"NOW!" Wait staff are frequently heard reciting Lill's famous refrain to diners: "If you like what you're eatin' order more. If you don't, there's the door." But their attitude—complete with foot-tapping, gum-smacking, watch-checking, eyeball-rolling hesitation—provides a quirky, magical charm that keeps customers coming back for more of their insults and meat loaf.

Ed knows how to run an effective restaurant. Ed also knows how to run a decorated restaurant. And the tactic he has selected is the one used by many of the service greats, including Disneyland, Walt Disney World, Universal Studios Hollywood, Universal Orlando, Hard Rock Café, and many of the top hotels in Las Vegas. They all start with a front story, a backstory, and a storyboard for the customer experience. To this they add set, costume, and, if need be, script to convey the story.

THE SCOOP ON THEME

Theme is all about having a compelling story. We label this tactic *theme* because its foundation is an alluring narrative, complete with a backstory. The front or main story is what you see—a fantasy land commanded by a mouse (Disney theme parks), a trip to Treasure Island (Treasure Island Hotel in Vegas), or a stroll through the streets of Paris (Paris Hotel), Venice (The Venetian), or New York (New York New York Hotel). Or take the Fantasyland Hotel at West Edmonton Mall in Edmonton, Alberta. It has rooms decorated around a dozen different themes, including Igloo, African, Truck, and Victorian Coach.

A *backstory*, on the other hand, is sort of the amplified, embellished, exaggerated story behind the story. It can be equally important in enriching the story and giving service people a more profound understanding of its nuances or mythology. Actors use backstories to help them get more deeply into character. When you witness an actor sob, scream, or deliver a sinister laugh, you are likely seeing a reaction to a backstory, not just the front story in the script. Audiences never hear the backstory; they just experience its impact.

Storyboarding is the process of experience choreography. It involves crafting the look and feel of the experience, complete with set design, parking, customer traffic flow, signage, and props. It considers every angle of the theme, from curb appeal to first impressions to the management of all the elements (tone and style, sight and sound) that impact the customer's experience of the story. The intent is to alter the customer's sense of reality. It enables all elements—space, time, and physical objects—be a cohesive, integrated whole.

The concepts of front story, backstory, and storyboard are three important organizing principles of the theme tactic. A good illustration is Walt Disney World's Hollywood Studios "Twilight Zone Tower of Terror" attraction—a 130-foot forced drop from the top of the tower to the basement below ground. The ride itself is housed in a building designed to look like an abandoned 1930s art deco high-rise hotel called the Hollywood Tower Hotel. The backstory or mythology of the ride that enriches the attraction and takes the guest's breath away is designed to both evoke the spirit of Rod Serling and *The Twilight Zone* television series and to shift the guest's amusement park thrill ride mindset.

Here is how the backstory comes in: Something strange happened in this one-time hangout of Hollywood's social elite. On a dark and stormy night in 1939, two glamorous movie stars, a bell-hop, and a budding young child star and her governess entered the hotel elevator. At the exact moment the doors closed, a bolt of lightning struck the hotel's tower with such force that the five passengers disappeared. As word of the horrible event spread, the hotel lost its clientele and was forced to close.

The storyboard of the customer's experience is a detailed plan of the structure of the experience—frame by frame so to speak. Tower of Terror guests are invited to enter the long-abandoned hotel and visit the site of the mysterious tragedy. The lobby is blanketed in dust. Suitcases and steamer trunks stand unchecked beside the front desk. An "out of order" sign hangs askew on the elevator doors. The queue for the ride winds through the lobby and down into the basement of the deserted old hotel. At one point guests stop in the hotel library where a black-and-white TV jumps to life—with the familiar "Welcome to *The Twilight Zone*" narration by Rod Serling. Following the welcome, bellhops lead groups of guests to the hotel's dark, creepy boiler room to see the haunted elevator. They step into the rusted and, until now, inoperable freight elevator. The doors suddenly close, and the guests re-experience the 1939 ride—rising slowly to the 13th floor, then plummeting back down to the basement. Riders may drop two or three times, depending on how the ride has been programmed—another mysterious element.

PUTTING THEME INTO ACTION

How to begin using theme as part of your service experience? Organizations that have mastered theme as their way to decorate their customer's service experience would say there are four main things you need to focus on.

1. *Find or develop a strong front story and backstory.* Most organizations have a proud history or founding vision to use as a backstory. For instance, Science Diet, a product of Hill's Pet Nutrition, traces its ancestry to Dr. Mark Morris, a veterinarian who in 1943 saved Buddy, the world's first seeing-eye dog, from death by kidney failure by feeding him a carefully crafted diabetic diet. Morris' dietetic approach to disease management became a hit with other vets and a company was born. Everyone at Hill's knows the Buddy story and takes great pride in being part of the tradition. Customers are carefully folded into the tradition of companion animal care through salespeople and company literature. What is your unit or organization's backstory? Is there a compelling person, event, or vision in your history? There's the start of your theme.

   No relevant story in your organization's legacy? Create one from another source. Walt Disney did not fashion his signature theme parks from looking at similar forms of entertainment. There were none. But he knew the carnival and circus could be morphed into something rare, something no one had ever seen. And, when the Walt Disney World engineers tried to encourage him to build the Magic Kingdom's centerpiece Cinderella Castle last, he insisted on a more costly route: build it first since he viewed it as the dramatic symbol of the front story.

2. *Develop and use a storyboard of the customer experience.* Porsche automobiles have a long history—their

backstory—that begins on the racing circuits of Europe. The typical Porsche showroom tells the tale of that racing tradition through photos, décor, and written materials. The front story—Porsche as worthy of the fast car aficionado's attention—is further supported by both an emphasis on performance data and a long list of available racecar-driver—like accessories. Many salespeople enfold the customer even further into the magic of the high-performance sports car fraternity by pointing out a unique Porsche engineering feature: The car's ignition switch is on the left side of the steering column. The reason? So drivers in cold-start races, like the 24 hours of LeMans, can turn the ignition with their left hand while simultaneously shifting into gear with the right—an advantage when tenths of a second count.[3] That tidbit of Porsche lore brings the would-be purchaser into the Porsche story in a personal, vicarious way.

3. *Dress your "set" in sync with your theme.* The story of a quick service restaurant is usually some version of decent food served up in a hurry. Speed. The set—and accoutrements—should reflect and reinforce that. So a McDonald's with sit-down dining accoutrements—silverware, plates, table service—would make no sense, and indeed would have a not right feel to it. On the other hand, a fast food restaurant on the shoreline of a popular vacation lake that is dressed with antique fishing gear, fun-in-the-sun sepia-tone photos, and posted info on current fishing conditions is clearly taking clever advantage of the enchantment of the locality. A particularly nice extra is equipping counter staff with a little information on what the big ones are biting.

4. *Dress employees to fit the theme.* Dressing employees to fit the front story is an obvious ploy in a theme park or

entertainment venue. Yet, even in professional settings there are customs that dictate dress—doctors in white coats, nurses in scrubs. Are there natural costuming options for your "cast"? Is there a way of dressing that will create a sense of commonality or comfort for your customers? Would an actual or approximate uniform make service employees in your organization more easily identifiable to your customers? Might there be a way to share parts of your dress with customers, like Mouse ears, pilot's wings, or a stage performer's scarf?

5. *Eliminate all the cues that distract from the experience.* Every detail and every nuance of a setting should not only support and further the theme but also the larger organizational identity and service vision. Evaluate your setting from the customer's perspective by experiencing it as a customer. Never get complacent, and always maintain your setting, whatever it is, in tip-top condition. The horse's head hitching posts outside City Hall of the Magic Kingdom's Main Street are rubbed and patted by hundreds of guests every day. So a maintenance crew repaints them every night.

SENSE

Walk into the lobby of a Westin Hotel and your nose knows the scent suddenly shifts from the smell of the street to a signature fragrance called White Tea.[4] Reach the checkout counter of Dallas garden center Nicholson-Hardie and you can pet one of the two big calico cats, named Frank Cat and Sammy Cat, who lie sprawled across the counter; their business cards in a holder nearby proclaim them Rat Pack. Walk around a Bass Pro Shop and take in the sporting goods displays amplified by such eye candy as a giant fish tank and museum quality wildlife dioramas. An antique and memorabilia shop in Memphis plays oldies; a shop specializing in silk flowers put a small waterfall in the center of the shop;

an upscale jewelry shop has all employees wear formal evening attire.

Cats' Business Card[5]

What's happening in these pictures? You are experiencing enterprises magnifying the power of the five senses to augment the customer's service experience. Some are performed with the bravado of Disney's Rain Forest Restaurant, a cacophony of sensory overload. Some are so subtle that only the customer's subconscious picks up the signal. When realtors suggest baking an apple pie before holding an open house, when cookie shops pipe their kitchen aroma onto the sidewalk, and when upscale retail stores put a pianist at a baby grand on the sales floor, all are declaring the common sense of uncommon senses.

However, the use of sense as a tactic for decoration requires a lot more than turning on a smell machine, putting in colored lights, or piping in nice music. Like all the decoration tactics, sense must rest on practices congruent with the core principles of design—focus, harmony, balance, proportion, and rhythm.

Atlanta-based Savor Specialty Foods and Tabletop is to food what Starbucks is to coffee. Walk into the store at the edge of the city's upscale Buckhead district and you immediately smell a blend of sweet balsamic drizzle with arugula and mango chutney. Strains of Italian baroque music or perhaps the 1940s sounds of a big band play softly in the background. Hundreds of rare cooking utensils and scads of gourmet paraphernalia adorn their walls, beckoning patrons to window shop while waiting for their gourmet sandwich—perhaps an applewood-smoked turkey with creamy Gouda, apple nut chutney, and sun-dried tomatoes on pumpernickel. Your sensory antennae are in state of sheer ecstasy.

Even the stunning wood floor is a part of this mélange of sensory delights. "These wood boards came from an old tobacco curing barn," says co-owner Ren Hodgson. "Some people wanted us to sand and stain them. But, we opted to leave them as they were to help communicate a fresh, genuine feel. Even the yellow paint markers we could have removed, we opted to leave in place."

"We are passionate about fine foods, a unique and interesting product mix, and customer education," says co-owner January Hodgson. "At Savor, we don't sell anything unless we taste it first. This allows us to explain product application as well as flavor profiles to our customers. We encourage our guests to ask questions and sample before they purchase."

The rich combination of sensory pleasures at Savor is the epitome of sense. Sight, sound, smell, taste, and touch come together to communicate a distinctive and unmistakable focus on the world and worth of a food connoisseur. There are cookbooks venturing onto the unbeaten paths of palates—*A Scavenger's Guide to Haute Cuisine* or *The Southern Belly*. There are cooking tools you would not likely find in Williams-Sonoma or Crate & Barrel—a salt cellar or whisk crafted from tigerwood or rarer-than-rare accessories like a chinoise (just Google it!). Yet there is no clutter, no conflict, no confusion. The store knows its role and does not allow anything inside that fails to harmonize with the sights and sounds of a cookery menagerie.

SIMPLE SENSE

The lessons to be gleaned from the Savor store are simple and exacting. Know your customer well. Select the response you believe your customers will value. Consider the emotion and sensations (real or imagined) you want to call to mind. But also pay close attention to those sense triggers that clash with your desired response and chase them away. Does that picture on the wall really add value? Are the restrooms compatible and congruent with the rest of your strategy? When was the last time you examined your parking lot, waiting area, or front entrance with a focus on sensory signals being conveyed? What should customers see first, second . . . last? How are key service transitions managed?

Does your place of business smell like Carpet Fresh or cleaning bleach? What does your customer hear in the background when phoning you that might clash with the desired response? "The first law of flavor and fragrance making," says Michael Heinz of manufacturer Bell Flavors and Fragrances, "is how they blend with the product they are added to." The same is true of service experiences. "When you create an extraordinarily beautiful mall like Galleria Dallas, Perimeter Mall Atlanta, or Water Tower in Chicago," says Jean Schlemmer, EVP of regional mall owner and manager General Growth Properties, "it is important there be soft seating and spotless bathrooms. Otherwise it is completely dissonant to our tenant's consumers."

The effective use of sense cries not just for congruence but for creativity. Take it from Billy Rivera of Karaoke Cab in Charlotte, who was the subject of a story by Simone Orendain on the NPR news program *All Things Considered* for his novel approach to a mundane service. With a laptop in the front seat next to him and a screen scrolling the words on the back of the seat that the passengers can view, he offers customers a choice of over 39,000 songs. Some passengers so enjoy the wild sing-a-long, they ask Billy to keep driving around the block until the song ends, not minding that the meter continues to run.

Learn from the best at sensory enhancement. Take a walk through Bellagio, the Venetian, or the MGM Grand on your next trip to Vegas. How do they blend music, mural, mystery, and magic? Log on the Web sites of Omiru, Popsugar, Picnik, Howcast, or Iliketotallyloveit; you'll find a treasure trove of sensory delights to adapt to your own situation.

Examine what associations might be caused by each sense attraction you consider. Sights, sounds, smells, and so on are all cues for customers that can surface pleasant or not-so-pleasant memories. A sign with red lettering might send a different message than the same sign in green. If it's ten degrees below zero outside, a silk kimono in the hotel guest's closet isn't nearly as sensuous as a thick terrycloth bathrobe.

Once you have decided on the senses to appeal to, find ways to introduce them in a way that customers discover and delight in. Also remember that sensory enhancement must reflect proportion and balance. Christmas trees are not the same visual experience if a few flashy ornaments grab all the attention. If your customers are singing along with the music, it might be playing too loud. Here's a final reminder: Sense is a tactic to implement the decoration strategy, which itself is intended to augment, enrich, and improve the service experience, not replace it.

COMFORT

Miller Brothers Ltd. is a men's clothing store in Atlanta that takes comfort to a whole new level. According to the store architect, Bill Edwards, "Owners Robby and Greg really listened to comments from their customers, and we incorporated those ideas into the design of the space. The outcome is a well-heeled clubby feel, with built-in clothing displays to blend with the architecture of the building."

Imagine a men's clothing store with a large fireplace, hardwood floors, comfortable leather couches, a seating and eating area with TV viewing for sports plus a full-scale and upscale bar. "We wanted our store to be a great place to hang out and have a beer with the boys but also be the best store in Atlanta. The goal was a place that was sophisticated but fun," Robby Miller remarked. "We care about customer comfort just as much as we care about the cut of a jacket or the superior quality of a dress shirt," adds Greg Miller.

The focus on comfort does not stop with design and décor. Miller Brothers combines a seasonal trunk sale with low-country barbeque and brew. They not only invited legendary University of Georgia football coach Vince Dooley to stage a book signing in the store, they held the special event in the late afternoon and early evening on the Wednesday before Father's Day.

We earlier examined comfort as a tactic in the animation strategy. There, the focus was on emotional comfort; for decoration, the tactic is more about physical comfort. It requires thinking through the lens of the customer with an eye to removing any hint of anxiety or apprehension from the service experience. Once the experience is essentially anxiety free, comfort involves elevating ease to a noticeable level. Miller Brothers did not simply provide comfortable seating; they provided cushy, melt-into-the-pillows comfortable seating. Their restrooms are not simply clean, they engulf you in calm. The beer is not just cold; it is super ice cold, like it was pulled right out of a barrel of ice cubes. The bar is not stocked with cheap whiskey, but features premium brands. And, the attention to comfort even extends to the potential little customer one might have in tow. On a table near the store entrance is a large, colorful gumball machine. Beside it is a child's dream come true: a glass bowl filled with pennies, there for the taking.

Gumball Machine[6]

Comfort works best when it fits the milieu. Low-country bar-beque might not work well in a men's clothing store in midtown Manhattan. But in the state of Georgia, barbeque is the caviar of comfort food. Also, comfort is most powerful when it is compre-hensive, when it permeates the customer's experience. Cushy chairs are soon deemed irrelevant if the customer has to wait too long at the cash register. The beauty of hardwood floors is forgotten if it's tough getting out of the parking lot. Comfort must envelope every aspect of the service experience. Especially important for would-be comfort purveyors: The tactic is most successful if your brand of comfort holds special appeal for your target customers. Miller Brothers created a "well-heeled clubby feel" because that is what they predicted their customers desired. The same brand of comfort might bomb in another part of town.

FUNCTION

Charles Revson said of Revlon, the cosmetics business he founded and managed for a half century, "We manufacture cosmetics, what we sell is hope." The notion communicated a strong concept: When an organization shifts their means–end focus, all manner of renewal can occur. What if you reconceived the real function of your unit or organization to focus on the benefit it offers, not just the outcome?

Let's try a simple example. What if a bait shop viewed their role as a fish-finding specialist, not just a fishing accessory supplier? If you walked into such a shop there would be a fishing location update on the wall, and a police band radio would be in constant contact with the local fishing greats who were pulling them in. The photos of the one that didn't get away would have been taken yesterday, not last season. "What are they biting today?" would replace "What's on sale today?" banter. Fishing superstars would stop by for guest appearances. The local newspaper would regularly send a reporter to get the latest scoop. And on and on and on.

Or take a real-life example. The Hotel Monaco is a hotel in the Kimpton Hotels chain. They target the same customers as Marriott, Hyatt, Sheraton, Doubletree, and Hilton—largely frequent business travelers. However, the Hotel Monaco has changed their function from business hotel operation to enchantment purveyor. Mind you, the basics are done superbly—check-in is efficient, the rooms are immaculate, the staff is friendly and helpful. But, that is what all hotels provide. The true function of the Hotel Monaco is to enchant its guests by indulging them in the sights, sounds, textures, and tastes of its special environment.

If you were to go to the Hotel Monaco in Chicago, this is what you'd experience: The lobby is inviting and intimate, very welcoming in appearance, color, and texture. Soft music plays in the background, never too intrusive. There is a zebra-print chaise that invites you to relax next to the roaring fireplace. The décor is somewhat Arabian, Moroccan, and Persian—eclectic, classy, original, almost bohemian. The concierge sits at a large circular desk supported by an antique leather trunk, like one you might see on the Orient Express around the turn of the last century.

You might see a woman walk through the lobby with her chocolate lab on a leash. At check-in, you would typically be asked if you would like a goldfish to stay with you in your room. All they require is that you give it a name. This is clearly a pet-friendly hotel. The Monaco provides beds for your pets, nature videos for them to watch in the guest room, a welcome treat plus a turndown bone/treat at night. The hotel can even arrange for pet-walking or -sitting service.

The Hotel Monaco's guest rooms are spacious and colorful. No sooner do you unpack than a bellman brings a basketball-sized glass bowl holding your goldfish swimming above a bed of colorful pebbles. The large bay window at the end of the room functions as a meditation station. Its plush satin pillows on the sill beckon you to take a seat and just reflect. Fully stretched out in the meditation station, wearing the leopard-print or zebra-striped bathrobe from your closet, you can see the city's towering buildings almost as though you were floating on a magic carpet above the calming flow of the Chicago River.

Back in the lobby for the complimentary wine party, you are likely to find a crackling fire burning in the fireplace. There are several guests in quiet conversation while a psychic in the lobby is unobtrusively reading palms for a small fee. Return to your guest room to turn in for the evening and the housekeeper has already made the rounds. On your pillow there will be a thoughtful note and perhaps a unique foreign coin, a flower, a small bag of popcorn, even a lottery ticket for a souvenir. The Monaco is more than a traveler's place for lodging; its real function is as a place for enchantment.

Debbi Fields, founder of Mrs. Fields Cookies, always told people, "I am not a businesswoman. I'm a cookie person." Southwest Airlines President Colleen Barrett states it this way: "We are not an airline with great customer service. We are a great customer service organization that happens to be in the airline business." Changing the way your business sees its function can dictate a complete overhaul of its form.

What is your core business? Too many enterprises respond with, "I'm just the print shop," or "I'm only a dry cleaner," or "I'm the accounting department." What if you completely rethought your function and then let form follow? The Hotel Monaco knew that being just another hotel would ensure neither a high occupancy rate nor revpar (revenue per available room). To quote Hotel Monaco Chicago general manager Nabil Moubayed: "We work to be a place of enchantment that just happens to be in the hotel business.

The word *decoration* has its origin in a French word meaning "to adorn." The word *adorn* has its roots in fourteenth-century Latin and it meant "to enliven." The important connotation here is the purpose of decoration—to make something come alive. Customers recall, return, and refer others to those experiences that help them come alive. Unlike a product, which by nature is inanimate, service is by definition alive. And, the more the service experience captures and reinforces the quality of aliveness, the more it adds value and takes your customer's breath away.

CHAPTER 4
Camouflage

> Customers who consider our waitresses uncivil should
> see the manager.
>
> —*Sign in a restaurant*

Watching a skilled magician at work is an exercise in awe. Try as
we might to see through the sleight of hand and illusions taking
place before our very eyes, we come away amused, amazed, and
astonished. Where did those cards fly off to? Where did those
doves come from? How did the magician do all those amazing
things? We know in our minds that there is a rational explanation.
But in our hearts we aren't so sure. It makes us smile. It makes
us shake our heads. It makes us wonder. And it leaves us with a
feeling of enchantment that stays with us for a long time.

Everyone knows, or at least suspects, that there are mechanical devices and subtle betrayals of the senses at work in the
magician's craft. But as important as clever physical aids are to
the magician's performance, they are the lesser of what meets and
eludes the eye. The successful stage magician is versed in the art
of practical psychology, human communication, and experience
management. The magician's ability to relate to the audience,
involve them in the magic, and make them feel good about the
surprises he or she brings to pass is as important as the mechanics
of the trick itself.

The creation of imaginative customer service—service so unique, so different, that it takes customers completely by surprise and leaves them with a smile and a story to tell—is often strikingly parallel in structure and outcome to fine stage magic. Just as the skilled stage magician is a master of audience enchantment, the service magician brings a touch of charm and delight to the customer's day, life, and world—even if just for a moment.

We have examined animation, the energy strategy, and decoration, the attraction strategy. Camouflage is the magical strategy of take-their-breath-away service. The camouflage strategy is what separates the food carrier from the professional waiter or waitress who has a devoted clientele. It separates the hair cutter from the personal stylist with an avid following. And, it distinguishes the trusted personal advisor from the forgettable, plain vanilla service rep. Making the difficult seem easy is what draws applause for the magician and gratitude for the service provider. Doing the seemingly impossible and unlikely creates wonder and respect in both audiences.

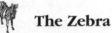 **The Zebra**

Even with their camouflage pattern, it's unlikely a gathering of zebras could escape a lion's notice. But when all the zebras keep together as a big group, the pattern of each zebra's stripes blends in with the stripes of the zebras around it. This is confusing to the lion who sees a large, moving, striped mass instead of many individual zebras. The lion has trouble picking out any single zebra, and so it doesn't have a very good plan of attack.

BEHIND THE MAGIC

There are many dimensions to the camouflage strategy of take-their-breath-away service. This chapter will outline four magical tactics: invisibility, transference, clairvoyance, and mystery. Each can stand alone, or they can be used as a collection. Before we unwrap each tactic, there are two perspectives vital to their execution.

The first perspective to embrace is that camouflage is about enchantment, not trickery. The goal is not to fool customers; the goal is to invite customers to join in a special adventure crafted specifically for their pleasure. A great magician has deep respect for the audience. And the service provider employing the camouflage strategy should have the same level of respect for their customers. Dupe your customers and they will dump you. Your con will be their exodus. One luxury hotel with a surprisingly detailed customer profile system had its front desk clerks say, "It says here in your guest profile, Ms. Smith, that you prefer a corner room on a high floor." Later, when the guest is enchanted with the fact that the oranges she is allergic to are absent from the fruit plate she ordered, she smiles in amazement without feeling concerned her privacy has been invaded.

The second perspective is the importance of careful planning and practice. No competent magician would set foot on the stage without preparation and rehearsal. What makes magic *magic* is not the cleverness of the maneuver but rather the smoothness of its execution. When a group of waiters at the exact same time lift the covers from the entrées for an assembly of diners, it is practice that makes it perfect. When the service manager alerts you that your car is ready at the precise time the mechanic brings it around to the front, that's practice at work.

There's one more thing about the customers' experience that is helpful to think about in planning the camouflage strategy: the outcome after the outcome. The outcome in grocery shopping, for example, is to get the groceries desired as conveniently as possible. But that is not the final memory the customer has of the grocery store experience. Ever gotten home and discovered two eggs were cracked? Ever purchased a large carton of a product that would not fit on any of the pantry shelves? Or have a bloody cut of meat soil the birthday card you bought to send to Aunt Molly? Too often the grocery store is in the mix of negative thoughts associated with the outcome after the outcome.

Considering the outcome beyond the outcome means thinking about what the customer will be doing with the service or outcome after you have done what the customer expected. For example, if you were a car salesperson, your customer's expected outcome might be purchasing a car. You might consider your selling role pretty much over when you see the taillights leaving the dealership lot. You might think, "Well, I've done my part, it's up to the folks in the service department when the customer returns for maintenance or repair." But, what if you thought about the customer's next outcome (arriving home with a brand new car) and staged a welcome celebration with balloons and banners? That's producing a ripple effect—creating an outcome beyond the expected outcome.

Nordstrom is famous for pursuing the outcome after the outcome effect. "We try to guess what is beyond our customers' purchase," says John McClesky of the men's suits department at their Dallas store. "If a customer buys a sports jacket, the obvious extension might be slacks or a tie. But if you learn the customer is buying the jacket for a cruise, you might explore dressy shorts, an ascot, or a Panama hat." John continues: "But, slipping a complimentary set of collar stays in the newly purchased jacket pocket (a frequently forgotten item on a trip) can leave a customer absolutely awed."

Play out in your mind the possibilities of what customers will be doing, thinking, and feeling after you have met their presented need. What small gesture would make this customer swoon? Sometimes a bit of subtle conversation about life after the met need can surface opportunities. Instead of asking, "How do you plan to use your new camera?" ask, "How will you use it in the next week or so?" Instead of asking, "Would there be anything else?" ask, "What have we not thought of that would make your hotel stay really special?" Make your queries reach into the future and the customer will provide you clues ripe for imaginative service.

Now, armed with those perspectives, consider which of the four basic tactics—alone or in combination—are most suitable for you in using camouflage to take your customers' breath away.

INVISIBILITY

Invisibility is the art of making invisible something traditionally visible (and perhaps less than exciting). This tactic is particularly suitable for service processes that have historically been done in plain sight but if hidden would enhance the customer's experience. Think of invisible service processes as operating outside the customer's line of sight, leaving only the effect or result visible. Some luxury hotels, for example, have put motion detectors in guest rooms. A computer program monitors movement and when it senses a long period of no movement during daylight hours it signals to housekeeping to clean the room. It seems awe inspiring to guests because they return to their room to find it clean without ever having experienced the intrusive knock on the door.

In some ways, the flashing-alarm system restaurants now use to alert guests their table is ready is a form of invisible process. Before, customers had been captive in the waiting area or had to keep checking with the hostess to find out when their table would be ready. Today, smart hospitals use the same type of flashing gadget to let patients know the nurse or physician is ready to see them. USAA uses invisibility in its system for capturing all customer correspondence and making it available to any call rep. It eliminates the need for customers to be passed around to find someone who knows how to help them. A large hospital experimented with a system whereby patients were given a plastic card to insert in a card reader in the parking lot before an appointment. It signaled the computer to find the family member on the card that had the appointment and automatically generate the admission paperwork.

The primary payoff of invisibility is that it makes service feel totally seamless. It frees up servers to deal with customers directly instead of being tied to administrative processes that frustrate both the customer and the server. And, it makes the experience seem enchanting.

How can one apply this tactic of camouflage? Let's take a common example: a grocery store. First, read the process and think of ways to invisibly accomplish the goal of that process. Then read our ideas.

PROCESS # 1: SHOPPING CARTS SHOULD APPEAR TO ALWAYS BE AVAILABLE.

Replenishing shopping carts should be invisible. They should just seem to always be there. If the customer arrives at a store and notices there are only a very few shopping carts, they subconsciously entertain the belief that they could show up and have them not be there at all.

How can you make this process invisible? Have someone round up the shopping carts from the parking lot and bring them in through a side door totally out of sight of the customer. The carts could be pushed into a tunnel that appears at the front door of the grocery store. Someone could constantly monitor the availability of carts at the entrance. Also have places in the parking lot where customers can get and return carts.

PROCESS # 2: PRODUCE IS ALWAYS IN STOCK.

For the most part, stock replenishment should be invisible; that is, the customer should never worry that an item was on the verge of running out. However, it is possible a retailer might want to make scarcity a virtue to communicate "buy yours early; they are rare or in very short supply."

Create shopping aisles with a tunnel in the middle traversed by employees constantly restocking (like some houses with alleys behind for the garbage truck to drive down so residents do not have to put the garbage on the street). Have restocking moments—times during prime shopping periods when an event in the store briefly attracts customers away from shopping so that shelves can be restocked. Design produce shelves to function like giant vending machines, stocked from above in the ceiling.

PROCESS #3: IMPERFECTIONS ARE NEVER NOTICED.

Who enjoys seeing imperfections or unpleasantries? One grocery store placed a large graffiti board in front of a part of the store being renovated. Instead of customers noticing the dirty clutter of construction, they enjoyed adding their two cents worth to the board. Another grocery store had a water pipe burst, leaving a giant hole in the side of the building. Quickly, the florist department moved its largest potted plants in front of the hole. Since it was Christmas time, they put out a large container of inexpensive ornaments and asked customers to help decorate the "trees." The pipe was repaired after the store closed for the night.

PROCESS #4: PARKING IS A BREEZE.

No one likes to spend time hunting for a parking spot. What are some ways to make the process invisible? Put in a sensor in the pavement and a large bulletin board that lights the spots available. Staff the lot with free valet parkers. Staff the lot with people who continually search the lot for parking places and alert arriving customers as to their location. Give frequent customers a GPS–type homing device for their car that beeps as it gets to available spots.

PROCESS #5: WAIT TIME IN CHECKOUT LINE.

Customers rarely like to wait. They value their time. Use the Disney approach of managing the perception of wait. Give the customer a new role, something to do other than waiting. Install something customers can watch, like bank lobbies do with their flat-screen TVs running stock market updates and financial head-line news. Create a special waiting area that removes customers from the checkout line while their groceries are scanned, tallied, and bagged. Let the customer go get their car while grocery store staff unload, scan, and sack items. When the customer arrives with their car, someone puts the groceries in their car while the customer pays via credit card, much like returning a rental car. Let customers buy groceries online and have them delivered.

TRANSFERENCE

Transference is the magician's tactic called *misdirection*. It involves establishing a frame of reference or stating a premise that occupies the customer's attention while something completely different is happening. The magician who gestures and looks off to the left or right of the audience is almost always moving the audience's attention to where the trick is not happening—or to be precise, away from where the effect is subtly being set up or staged.

Transference in everyday life is a frequent phenomenon, although—of course—we usually don't notice it. The nurse asks about the patient's weekend while giving a flu shot; the bellman calls the guest's attention to a beautiful plant or painting oppo-site the site of new construction; the dentist chitchats about his latest ski trip or the weather while the patient has a mouth full of stainless steel and goo—all are instances of transference. We even practice transference on ourselves. Listening to the radio while mowing the lawn or turning on the television while paying bills are, in fact, ways of distracting ourselves or redirecting our own attention.

Francie Johnson is a part-time pharmacist in a CVS/pharmacy in Dallas. She is also a master of redirection. When a frequent cus-tomer chooses to wait for a prescription, Francie has, for instance, been known to put the customer to work: "Nancy," she asks, "can you do me a really big favor? My eight-year old nephew's birthday is coming up in a couple of days, and I haven't had time to find him a card. Would you mind picking me out a cute card for him? I'll pay for it before I leave the store tonight." It's a simple, but flattering and effective use of transference.

Examine the negatives in the customer's experience that you might be able to remove from their consciousness by channeling the customer's attention elsewhere. What are ways to substitute a small gesture, token, or action that can replace the customer's adverse emotion with a positive one? Parents distract the children's focus on inappropriate or dangerous activities by providing a replacement. Inappropriate eats are replaced with tasty but healthy snacks; idle time is replaced with Scouts or soccer. What would be the customer version of this approach?

CLAIRVOYANCE

Another useful camouflage tactic is clairvoyance. It involves surprising the customer with what you know that they did not expect you to know. It requires a never-ending pursuit of customer intelligence and a knack for paying attention to the details. Consider the following example of a guest arriving at a hotel. The guest has only stayed at this particular hotel once, three years prior.

1. The bellman helps the arriving guest get his luggage out of the back of the taxi and asks, "How was your flight, Mr. Greenjeans?"

Clairvoyance: The bellman knows how much the fare is from the airport to the hotel and that the taxi service frequents the airport. The guest name was read off of the luggage tag.

2. As the guest approaches the check-in counter, the front desk clerk says, "Welcome back."

Clairvoyance: As the bellman brought the guest's bags into the hotel, he asked, "Is this your first time at this hotel?" When the guest said "no," the bellman pulled on his right ear as he wheeled the luggage cart up to the front desk, signaling this information to the check-in clerk.

3. The clerk asks the guest: "Would you like a corner non-smoking room again like you had the last time you were here, or would you like to try a different type of room?"

Clairvoyance: The clerk quickly checked the hotel records for the details of the guest's prior stay.

4. Taking the guest's luggage to his room, the second bellman says, "Nice to have you back again, sir."

Clairvoyance: The front desk clerk sends the same ear-tug signal to the next bellman transporting the guest's luggage.

5. When the guest awakes in the morning, his favorite news-paper is delivered to his door.

Clairvoyance: When the bellman took the guest's bags to his room, he asked the guest for information, such as the name of a favorite newspaper, that would help the hotel personalize the experience. Or, the bellman noticed the newspaper the guest was carrying when he arrived at the hotel.

6. On the guest's second night at the hotel, his favorite night-cap drink arrives with the room service dinner request.

Clairvoyance: Noting the nightcap the guest had drunk the previous night in the hotel bar, the lobby bar staff commu-nicated the guest's drink order to room service personnel so they could suggest it as a nightcap when the guest requested in-room dining.

A key consideration in using the clairvoyance tactic is the risk of invading the customer's privacy. We all enjoy a bit of personalization—some more than others. However, give us too much personalization and we get that uneasy feeling that we are being watched or someone is rummaging through our garbage cans at night. Another important step is to periodically ask customers how much personalization they prefer.

The centerpiece of our hotel example of clairvoyance is the keen observation and attentiveness of the staff during the customer service experience. For the team at Edwin Stipe, Inc., customer service does not end when the service call is over; it is just the beginning. Customer service reps from the Easton, Pennsylvania, plumbing company call each and every customer a couple of days after the work has been done with a list of questions about the service providers. While chatting with customers they make notes about items of a personal nature. "When a customer opens up to one of our employees and tells them about a birthday, an operation they just had, an anniversary, we make note of it," says owner Henry Scherer. "We send out a get well, birthday, or congratulations card. Everything is handwritten, the note, the signature, and the address on the envelope; it's even got a regular postage stamp."

Kauffman Tire in Woodstock, Georgia, enjoys taking their customers' breath away with their own special form of clairvoyance. When Steve Holloran walked in the store to purchase a tire, he was greeted with, "Welcome back, Mr. Steve." He was blown away since he not visited the store in long time. Pressing the clerk a bit closer on the secret of his incredible memory, the clerk reluctantly admitted how the magic was performed. "When you pulled in the parking lot, we plugged in your license plate number into the computer and then cross referenced the name with our records. We knew you were a prior customer by the time you got to our front door!" Advocate Steve has repeated his special story over and over.

Paying attention to the details can typically give you more than enough information to effectively surprise the customer with what you know. Once learned, the secret is to display the intelligence gained with the calm and confidence of a great magician. Never boast or show off what you know about the customer. Understated aptitude is more powerful than acumen under a spotlight.

MYSTERY

Mystery is a powerful tactic of the camouflage strategy. It makes maximum use of stealth and subtle use of surprise. Its best application is in the behind-the-scenes venue. There has always been a host of service providers whose only service signature was the quality of the work they left for the customer—the hotel housekeeper, the auto repair person on the other side of the "customers not allowed beyond this point" sign, and the night nurse who checks your medical stats after major surgery when you are too drugged to communicate. But what about service providers who depend on a strong interpersonal relationship with the customer for repeat business?

The route to creating a positive service relationship with customers requiring service without direct contact is to simulate a relationship. As with service in general, effective management of service details can turn an at-arm's-length encounter into a responsive, kinship experience. It means first making the relationship matter and then seeking subtle, but powerful actions designed to communicate care, trust, and authenticity.

Look at signage. Do your signs sound like warm instructions to valuable partners or like tough laws for crafty criminals? Just as the library that changed "overdue fines" to "extended-use fees" learned, the tone of your message can speak volumes to your customers. A coin operated laundry mat changed "Don't leave trash on the floor" signs to read "Thank you for helping us keep your Laundromat as clean as you want your clothes to be." "Our washers are allergic to liquid Clorox" communicated a completely different feel than the conventional "Thou shalt not . . ."

What about coming up with ways to personalize communication with frequent customers? Chip uses a service for refurbishing his laser-printer cartridges. When the "toner low" sign flashes on his laser printer, he pulls the cartridge, ships it to Toner Service, Inc. in St. Louis and within 48 hours gets a refurbished cartridge for about half the cost of a brand new toner cartridge. A "personalized" form letter accompanies the returned laser cartridge. But one letter contained a handwritten P.S.: "I'll bet you're real proud of those Cowboys!" The clerk or packer or someone noticed Chip's Texas business address and scrawled a little value-added to the letter.

Another application of the mystery tactic is to reduce the number of contacts the customer has to have with the organization. "The standard across most service operations is to report and track how quickly things were done . . . not how well they were done and how often, or why they needed to be done at all," wrote Bill Price and David Jaffe in *The Best Service Is No Service*. "At one company where managers imposed a target 'average handle time' (call time) of 12 minutes, phone calls miraculously shortened to just under 12 minutes. As the 12-minute mark approached, agents simply said whatever it took to get the caller off the phone. The call center at another company hit on the idea of reducing the number of phone lines so that the excess callers simply got a busy signal—and went unanswered."[1]

When Michael Dell, CEO of Dell Computer, watched Dell's customer satisfaction scores drop as hold time for customers dropped, he thought it was an unusual correlation. Closer examination found that shortening the telephone hold time created situations in which the call center rep simply ended the call prematurely before all of the customer's issues had been resolved. This necessitated a second call, leaving the customer feeling hassled and dissatisfied. When the primary metric was changed from "hold time" to "first call resolution," the overall efficiency of the call center increased right along with the customer satisfaction scores.[2]

Mystery does not have to be silent service, stoically given without customer rapport. The superior service provider finds ways to build a relationship with distant customers even if that relationship must be more like a dedicated pen pal than a friendly neighbor. As customers require better service delivered more quickly and with greater convenience, serving in the dark can become, to paraphrase the familiar ad line, the next best substitute for actually being there.

The power of camouflage is well known in nature. While the motive is to hide or disguise, the technique is to blend or match. The earth tone color of a deer or the stripes of a tiger or zebra only work if they effectively match their surroundings. The same is true of camouflage as a service strategy. Its motive is to hide or disguise the operation of service, leaving the customer to experience its effect. Watching a magic trick done in slow motion might reveal its secret but destroys its charm.

Camouflage in service like camouflage in nature will only work if it blends with its environment. It must be grounded in what customers value and synchronized with what customers enjoy. If it is employed with a sense of pride and respect, it will be experienced by customers as a symbol of your commitment to their well-being.

CHAPTER 5
Concierge

"To give real service you must add something which cannot be measured or bought with money, and that is sincerity and integrity."

—*Donald A. Adams*

Nick Caballero is a concierge. No, he is not a securer of show tickets nor can he get you a great table at a popular restaurant, although if asked he probably would for his customers. He is a salesman at the Façonnable store on fashionable Fifth Avenue in New York City. And, he knows how to make his customers feel very important.

We are both fans of the Façonnable brand of men's clothes. In addition to being a brand typically available in the men's clothing section of most Nordstrom stores, the more than 50-year-old French high-end tailored clothing company opened a few (four to be exact) self-standing Façonnable stores in the United States. But this story is not about their product. It is about the man who delivers the experience that wraps around the product.

Nick Caballero In Action

If you could pay a visit to Nick's Rolodex, you would get a peephole into the man's obsession with taking his customers' breath away! You would not likely find entries with just contact information and clothing sizes. You're likely to find notations like "writes books on customer service, enjoys Mexican food, drinks Jack Daniel's, has three granddaughters, call only during the week, favorite color is plum," et cetera, ad nauseam. This is way more than your usual customer profile; Nick is like a super-sensitive electron microscope trained onto a particular customer's makeup that gets the DNA map needed for completely tailored service.

"John, I found a perfect shirt for that jacket you bought last April," the voice mail says with the excitement of a kid opening a birthday present. "I went ahead and shipped it to you along with a tie I thought would match. If it doesn't work for you, just put it in the mailer I sent along and return it as you get a chance." Not only is the perfect shirt perfect, it is obvious Nick has spent time thinking about John's preferences.

"We don't have the exact navy sweater you want, Chip, but let me do some research. I'll find it and get it to you the week after Christmas. That way you'll also get it at the after-Christmas sale price." Nick is passionate and driven as he works his laser lasso to match the man with the merchandise. It is glaringly obvious he loves his customers as much as he loves his role. And, he never takes for granted any aspect of the relationship, acting as if he is perpetually courting and forever grateful. No purchase is complete without a passionate and heartfelt thank you as well as handwritten note.

The concierge strategy is the essence of what we think of when we think about truly great service. The word *service* obviously has its roots in the role of one who serves. There was a time when the word conjured up the image of servant—as in "The customer is always right" or "We'll do whatever it takes to make the customer happy." But, the concierge brand of service connotes the comportment of a very competent butler or a highly skilled military general's aide. There is nothing deferent about Nick. He's too busy plumbing his vast reservoir of service talents, thinking about the next way he can make you smile.

 The Mockingbird

The mockingbird can mimic the songs of 40 different birds, as well as sounds made by other animals, including cats. A mockingbird continues to add new sounds to its song repertoire throughout its life. A male may have two distinct repertoires of songs: one for spring and another for fall.

We were in New York to appear on a national television show. En route to the hotel the evening before, we stopped at the

Façonnable store. An hour later, Nick had sufficiently ravaged our respective credit cards. "Need a recommendation for dinner, gentlemen?" he asked with the same confidence he might say, "Can I ship that to your home so you won't have to pack it?" Knowing we were Mexican food fans he indicated the best place in town was right next to where he parked and was owned by friends. "I've already worked past my shift, so why don't I walk you there?" Along the way he took his concierge orientation to the next level: "I would never ever want to butt into your evening plans, but I would be delighted to be your host." Needless to say we had a great dining experience, with Nick escorting us through the menu, the staff, and many of the diners who all knew Nick. Deferent? Not a chance! Passionate about service? You bet!

THE HEART OF CONCIERGE SERVICE

The concierge strategy is all about you, the customer. The strategic intent is for the customer to feel as though they have been bestowed a unique gift, specially selected just for them. When it works well, the target of the strategy feels valued, special, and appreciated. And, it works well because the care and handling of the experience clearly communicates a commitment both to the customer as well as a concern for the endurance of the relationship.

Think about the features of Nick's concierge approach. He pays very close attention to the details the customer cares about as well as the details that govern the service experience. He clearly cares more about the worth of the relationship than the return from the transaction. Out of that abundance mentality he is willing to deliver unexpected value. He puts as much effort into anticipating as he does into responding. He knows his customers and acts on that knowledge. Finally, he never lets customers think they are taken for granted. The architecture of his role yields five tactics—the net of which leave his customers devoted.

DETAILS

Steve Win, owner and operator of Win Signature Service, a limo service in the Chicago area, was a star in our last book, *Customer Loyalty Guaranteed*. Steve is still our driver when we work in his geography. Like Nick Caballero, Steve Win is an ace when it comes to delivering concierge service. He is always early for appointments. His car is immaculate. He handles his passengers' luggage as if he were handling a crate of eggs. He always greets customers with a large smile, a handshake, and a very warm greeting! We never have to ask him to adjust the heat or air conditioning; he just seems to know the correct temperature for us. If we call him from one of our cell phones, he sees the number and answers, "Hello, Dr. Bell, how are you, sir?" or "Greetings, Mr. Patterson. What can I do for you today?" If he is unavailable to pick up one or both of us, he makes arrangements with a fellow driver to fill in, and each, without fail, demonstrates the same friendly manner and fastidious attention to detail.

The masters of the concierge strategy are intensely loyal to a customer. Read that line again and pay attention to the singular object of the phrase "loyal to." They do not think of the target of their service efforts in the plural; they think only in the singular. When you are around Steve Win he seems completely absorbed in you and you alone. The truth is that he is processing a million details as he works to ensure that clients get from here to there on time and safely. But all of that is kept behind the scenes, and all that customers see and feel is a laser-like, in-the-moment focus on their unique needs and concerns.

Taking care of the little things sends a signal to the customer that you are watching out for their interests. The concierge strategy requires service providers to be service choreographers; a great customer experience requires managing an amalgamation of diverse elements. Fail on even one performance dimension and the concierge knows it can color the whole experience **negative** for customers. A waitress might be warm and friendly, but if she can't get orders right or remember the daily specials, her weaknesses overshadow her strengths. The call center phone representative might be knowledgeable and efficient, but if he has little patience for customer problems or is short with coworkers, his cognitive gifts are lost amid the interpersonal flaws.

Effective service choreography requires integration, organization, and alignment; it means mastering the little things and managing the customer's experience from end to end. Executing the concierge strategy well means combining a jack-of-all-trades capacity with exceptional resourcefulness. Like seasoned event planners, concierge service organizations manage the flow and pace of the experience—concentrating on the ease, agility, and effectiveness of the service they provide.

The concierge strategy takes a focus on backward serving. That means having a clear picture of what the outcome should be, then working backward from that goal to ensure the reality matches the vision. It means having a sixth sense for anticipating what can go wrong in service encounters. Only with this clear picture and early warning capacity can you set about ensuring the experience *product* matches the experience *plan*.

EXTRAS

Recall the last time you used the services of a great concierge. In that picture of the past is likely to be some "something extra." It could sound like "and I also got you upgraded," or "and also these seats were the best in the house," or "also, they will have a stroller ready for Kaylee." The concierge strategy is about the *also*, the addition of something unrequested and typically unexpected.

MedStar Health in Baltimore has a brand new cancer center. Realizing they were operating within the long shadow of a nearby renowned competitor, they saw a new building, world-class physicians, and state of the art technology as important ways to attract customers. But they went for occasional extravagance as a powerful differentiator. The hospital commissioned a new breed of hybrid rose called the "Rose of Hope." (The rose is the symbol of hope, life, and empathy.) When it came time for the center's grand opening, MedStar invited survivors treated at the old facility to attend, as you might expect. But what do you imagine was the most memorable feature of the event? The poignant stories of courage and survival each of the survivors related to the audience while holding a bouquet of yellow Hope roses. Today each patient of the new center receives a Hope rose as he or she begins treatment—a reminder, in the fight against cancer, that care and compassion are as important as the best physicians and technology.

Ron Skipski is a superintendent for EDiS, a construction company headquartered in Wilmington, Delaware. EDiS had just completed a project to renovate an old home and transform it into the headquarters for a company we'll call AB & C. Ron had been the superintendent on that job. In the middle of a second project EDiS had with AB & C, a heavy weekend snowstorm triggered an opportunity for Ron to perform an unexpected miracle. Even though Ron was not assigned to this new project, he remembered the company had no snow removal service contract and was likely facing a Monday morning challenge. And he still had the key to the fence surrounding the lot. Late Sunday afternoon he personally cleared the lot for a powerful Monday morning surprise.

Chanaka Demel was working the front desk at the Holiday Inn Select hotel at the Toronto Pearson International Airport when two men came in to register late one evening. As he was checking them in, the guests communicated their anger over the fact that the airline had lost their luggage. Both men were scheduled for important interviews beginning early the next morning and did not have the proper clothes. Realizing both guests were about his size, Chanaka signaled to another clerk to fill in for him and went home to secure two business suits, complete with shirts and all the appropriate accessories for the guests. They returned to the hotel late the next afternoon after completing a successful day of interviews in Chanaka's clothes. "He's a miracle worker," the men told the general manager. "We plan to tell everyone to stay at this hotel in the future."

Marlene Moran, a collections rep at Aurora's Forest Home Center in Milwaukee, contacted an elderly customer about his overdue medical bills. During the call, she learned the man was unable to pay anything; in fact his eyesight was so bad he could not even read his bill, plus he was an amputee. Marlene contacted an Aurora financial counselor who dispatched Kathy Paul for a home visit. "I was able to find and help him complete his application for senior care which had expired," said Paul. "We also contacted the county, which arranged for a social agency to visit him weekly to provide personal care. I left him my phone number to a call anytime he had a concern." Her actions were like the story of the boy returning starfish trapped on the beach back into the ocean, despite the fact there were thousands washed up on the shore. When a passerby chastised the boy for pursuing a task that was too massive to make a difference, he retorted, as he tossed another starfish into the surf, "It made a difference to that one!" The story is now a part of Aurora's book of patient-centered care stories entitled *This Side Up*.

Extra goes to the heart of the concierge strategy. It telegraphs affirmation. William James, the famed psychologist, wrote, "The deepest principle in human nature is the craving to be appreciated." Extra says you are worth it. Extra says, "I care enough to go the extra mile for you." It is Southern California Edison troubleman Vincent Coburn organizing a crew just getting off work to remove a cat from a power transformer. The cat's owner, a woman recently widowed and living alone, called the power company after getting no help from the fire department. It is Bryan Jones, an electrical services worker with show management company Freeman, after learning one of the exhibitors at the Aviation Expo had gotten food poisoning toward the end of the show, meticulously packing up the display machinery at the customer's booth for shipment back to his company. Remember: the strategic intent of the concierge strategy is "all about you, the customer." Proof comes through the alsos.

MENTOR

John Goodman, Stephen Newman, and Cynthia Grimm of TARP Worldwide in Arlington, Virginia, did a research study that appeared in *Customer Relationship Management Journal* in an article entitled "The ROI of Delight." The goal of the study was to dissect the components of a service encounter in order to determine which factors created the greatest increase (they called it "lift") in the likelihood that a customer would repurchase or return. The factor that yielded the greatest lift (32 percent) was "proactively provides me new and useful information."[1]

Today's customers can be confused by a gazillion options, overwhelmed by information excess, and oversaturated by media spam. Their lives have less certainty, more anxiety, and fewer resources to help with it all. When they find a service provider who can help create calm, they hand over their devotion and their dollars. Target gets great marks from customers for the store layout that seems simple. Best Buy gets great scores for having people who seem to know the products. Publix Super Markets get raving reviews for taking the hassle out the most hassling part of grocery buying: checkout. All these examples spotlight the power of a concierge who can be a tutor, not just a tour guide.

Today's customers value service providers who can act as mentors. We chose *mentor* as the label for this tactic rather than teacher, because mentors foster discovery; teachers convey knowledge. Mentors guide; teachers instruct. Now before we get in trouble with all the teachers on the planet, we know there are many teachers who care more about facilitating wisdom than simply ensuring students learn the facts. But the traditional connotation of a mentor is one who nurtures insight; the traditional connotation of a teacher is one who dispenses information. Concierges are mentors.

Early in the rise of the Starbucks-on-every-corner era, John became a devoted fan and Starbucks junkie, often visiting the store more than once a day to secure the "small town size" latte with extra shots of whoopee. Chip, on the other hand, steered clear of the new and fast-growing chain of coffee houses. But when he finally visited one, he was immediately overwhelmed with a totally new and confusing language (tall means small?). Even more intimidating was the large herd of devotees, all of whom seem to know the drill as if they had been lifetime members of this secret club.

An observant and sensitive Starbucks barista read Chip's reaction and immediately put on her mentor hat. "I know it can be daunting," she said with that I-was-once-just-like-you sound. "I'll be glad to translate for you. You just tell me what you like and don't like." Then she led Chip to the next step of coffee-ordering mastery. "Here is a little book to take with you. It explains all the strange words and the unique ways we do things at Starbucks. Next time you'll be a pro." There was no public comparing of neophyte Chip to expert John who was standing nearby. And, her approach was not just a "here's a flyer on the museum" instruction. It was guided insight targeted at leaving Chip more confident, not just more competent.

The mentor tactic requires being ever vigilant for opportunities to add learning to service—sometimes in the most unexpected places. Monsanto's training center in St. Louis added a unique accessory to the bathrooms often frequented by customers there for product training. Over the urinals and on the backs of the stall doors at eye level are large plastic picture frames that contain the *Stall Street Journal*. The comical giant newsletter contains an array of helpful information, from the weather forecast to a how-to product tip to the thought for the day. The message is clear. Monsanto is eager to increase customers' learning, not just their buying. That is a technique straight from the mind of a mentor.

KNOW ME

The *know me* tactic requires an in-depth knowledge of the customer, a continual effort to keep it up to date, and a capacity to demonstrate that knowledge to the customer. It means a perpetual attentiveness for ways to know the customer at a personal level. However, a great concierge knows there is a difference between personal and private. Familiarity can be a positive to most customers; intimacy is a benefit to only a few.

For several years, Chip was working three to four days every month in Miami on a long-term consulting project. He chose a comfortable chain hotel within walking distance of the client's headquarters office. He got to know everyone in this "home away from home" hotel. They would do small favors for him; he would sing their praises and encourage his clients and others to use the hotel for major meetings. After a year, however, the shiny wore off, and he began to be treated with too much intimacy. Employees told him their hard-luck stories like he was a fellow employee; one even gave Chip his resume to help him find another job and leave the hotel. Then they gave him a poor room when a key group of executives came in. Their explanation: "We knew *you* would understand and not mind!" They never bothered to ask Chip ahead of time! Here's the punch line: He plotted his escape and switched hotels for the final 36 months of his Miami work.

Dave Lockin of Hennessy Automobile Companies in Atlanta practices the know-me tactic with all his customers. When John's mother wanted to replace her 2000 Buick with 56,000 miles on it, John called Dave to find a suitable vehicle for an 86-year-old driver. Dave has two vital talents: He knows GM cars, and he knows how to quickly get on the other side of *know me* through his warm Columbo-like pursuit. After John's brief outline of his mother's interests and Dave's skillful probing for details, it took Dave a few hours to locate the perfect vehicle in his vast inventory. He scanned and e-mailed John the vehicle window sticker so John could describe the features to his mother.

The know me tactic is not just about great questions, dramatic listening, and a superb memory. It must be embellished with an "all about you" treasure-hunting approach to acting on what you know. When John informed Dave that his mother lived two hours away in Montgomery, Dave exhibited his concierge spirit with a solution: "That's not a problem. I'll deliver the new car to your mom and drive her trade-in back. I'll get the *Blue Book* appraised value and send her a bill. She can just write me a check and drop it in the mail." John's mother is very happy with a new car. She is also very happy with her son! That's car buying, concierge style.

THANKS

The *thanks* tactic may seem to be rather obvious and pedestrian, particularly in a book about imaginative service. However, it can set an organization apart in an era of take-you-for-granted service. The goal is not simply the expression of a statement but rather the conveyance of a feeling. We have all heard "thank you" directed at us, knowing full well there was little sincerity behind it. In concierge-style service, thanks means communicating gratitude in a fashion that makes customers feel your authenticity.

Twenty-Five Ways to Thank Customers

Here are 25 ways to show thanks. Use this list to jump-start your own list. Amplify the suggestions to suit your situation and customer. Remember, what turns on one customer may be a turn off to another. Recognition comes from the root word *cognoscere* meaning "to know"; tailor your affirmation.

1. Invite a customer to an important staff meeting.

2. Arrange for a special learning experience for customers.

3. Hand write a thank-you note to a key customer.

4. Send customers greeting cards on all key holidays.

5. Name a policy, building, or conference room for a key customer.

6. Provide a special parking space for a key customer.

7. Start a fund or scholarship in the name of a key customer.

8. Provide a donation in the name of your customer to his/her favorite charity.

9. Provide a special discount for loyal customers.

10. Create a forum that allows for public recognition of customers.

11. Remember a customer's birthday in a unique and personalized way.

12. Send customers a subscription to a magazine they value.

13. Buy helpful books for key customers (like this one! Just kidding).

14. Invite customers to your home for a cookout.

15. Provide tickets to an event valued by the customer.

16. Nominate your customer for a special award.

17. Find a way to compliment your customer to their customer.

18. Put up pictures of your customer in the cafeteria.

19. Invite customers to your facility to talk about their needs and goals to all employees.

(*continued*)

(continued)

20. Feature key customers in your organization's news-letter.

21. Give your customer a gift that you won, like a weekend at a local fishing camp or a nearby theme park.

22. Poll your customer for their input on important changes you plan to make.

23. Ask your customer for advice on how to better run your organization.

24. Purchase an ad in a key publication to thank your customers.

25. Have an executive write a thank-you letter to a key customer.

"People don't learn from conversation, they learn from observation," said cowboy humorist Will Rogers. And, while he was talking about politicians at the time, his remark is a powerful reminder that customers pay less attention to our mouths and more attention to our moves.

If you do business with Charlotte, North Carolina-based Wilson Fence Company, expect to receive a letter beginning, "All too often, we do business with nice people, such as yourself, and then go on as if nothing had ever happened or without giving the customer a second thought. We would like to take a few minutes out of a busy day to personally thank you for your business."

Most customer relationships don't end in dispute. Most wither away from disregard and absent-minded inattention. Neglect is more dangerous than strife, and indifference is more costly than error. Customer relationships are fueled by affirmation. Nurturing the bounty of customer devotion requires more than proper cultivation and seeding. It must be fertilized with attention and care. And bucketfuls of thanks.

The essence of the concierge strategy is customer courtship. Nick never lets us forget he is working hard on our behalf. We know it is on his behalf as well. A note in the mail or a message on the phone tells us he is on our case. But he has learned that too much attention can feel smothering and intrusive. No competent hotel concierge would call you every hour to report on the progress of your show tickets.

Remember that customers vary in their requirements for attention. When your insurance agent asks you periodically, "How would you like me to communicate with you and how often is about right?" you know there is an effort being devoted to calibrating attention. Concierge is about tailor-made service. And, what fits one customer might be too snug for another.

It is also important to know that courting the customer does not end with the sale or transaction. Take-their-breath-away service providers never take a valued relationship for granted and remain ever attentive for ways to celebrate the joy of the relationship and express gratitude for the return it provides.

CHAPTER 6
Partnership

"The meeting of two personalities is like the contact of chemical substances. If there is any reaction, both are transformed."

—Carl Jung

Picture this. You and your spouse own and operate a small restaurant in a low-income, inner-city neighborhood. As competition increases, your profit margin gets razor thin. A freakish accident strips away your savings. But your personal contribution to your neighborhood plus the great food and service you provide keep your customers raving. Then, your spouse (who's the restaurant's business manager) is paralyzed by a stroke. As you devote time to taking care of your spouse, the bills pile up. The bank is demanding their money, and your restaurant is on the edge of going completely under. Would your customers step in and save your business?

What if they did? What if they made flyers, held fund-raising benefits, went door to door seeking contributions, and raised the $50,000 you needed to get out of debt? What if they helped out in the restaurant, did needed repairs, offered free advice, and assisted with tons of chores as you struggled to get back on your feet? And, what if your restaurant survived? Sound like a fairy tale? Nope. It's a partnership!

Now for the facts. The restaurant in the story is Cole's Café in the Anacostia area of Washington, DC.[1] It is a neighborhood long on history and pride but short on income and investment. The owners of Cole's are Evangeline "Mama" Cole-Thompson and her husband. Mama is known for her community generosity. She buys gloves and scarves for neighborhood children. When they show her their good grades, she rewards them with free burgers. Seniors get reduced prices. Sometimes a needy senior might get a meal "on Mama."

When Mama's husband had a stroke, the restaurant seemed doomed. "But God blessed me with wonderful customers," Mama Cole said in an interview with us. "They took charge of our lives when we could not make it alone. Without their love and hard work for us, we surely would have gone under."

Now, for the big question we asked at the end of the first paragraph: Would your customers step in and save your restaurant?

PRINCIPLES OF PARTNERSHIP

The partnership strategy yields highly engaged customers. If you scanned the table of contents, you may recall one of the twelve strategies is "Cult-like." This strategy yields the most evangelistic customers. We will be examining this strategy next. A customer under the influence of a partnership strategy might use "extremely fond of" where one under the sway of a cult-like strategy might say, "I absolutely love them." They may not be as insanely devoted as the customers the cult-like strategy produces, but they are every bit as personally invested. They may not be completely irrational in their financial investment in you like the fans of Build-a-Bear Workshops are, but their emotional investment will be just as significant.

Service by nature is already a partnership of sorts. Lying between server and servee is a relationship, an experience, or both. The relationship or experience is co-created by both parties. Service cannot happen without this two-sided value-for-value exchange. Service probably should always happen as a partnership except that the infection of power sometimes devitalizes the potential of the union.

Power in a customer relationship can take two forms. The most prevalent is servers who treat customers with indifference or disdain. This superiority is often expressed with attitudes that say "We know what is best for our customers so we don't need to ask them," "What will these customers want from us next?" or "I can't help you . . . I guess you'll have to talk with a manager." The condescension leaves customers retorting with thoughts like "They have completely forgotten that without me they would be unemployed" or "Why do they make it so hard for someone trying to give them money?"

Power in a customer relationship can come in another form: the customer as king. It is born from the unfortunate and unduly deferential belief that the customer is always right. Since we are all customers, we know this is not true. While the customer is truly always the customer and should be valued for their role in our welfare, such a one-down subservient position can lead to decisions and practices that risk putting the unit or organization in economic harm's way. Giving away the store out of an interest to keep the customer happy is just as flawed a service strategy as only giving customers just enough to keep them satisfied.

Partnership as a take-their-breath-away strategy relies on several tactics found in all highly complementary, power-free relationships. Examine a strong business-to-business alliance, a successful marriage, or an effective professional firm and several elements will always be present. The partnership strategy works to create a relationship of equality—one with a strong sense of fairness plus mutual give and take.

The Egret and the Buffalo

The back of the African water buffalo is a natural draw for the bugs the cattle egret most enjoys eating. In exchange for this special dining spot, the cattle egret provides a service to the water buffalo. Armed with a keen sense of hearing and unmistakable chirp, the cattle egret provides the water buffalo early warning of an approaching pride of lions.

What if the relationship with your customer felt a lot like the one with your best friend? What if you had a relationship in which customers worked as hard to make the service encounter work as you did? What if customers went out of their way to ensure your success, not just their return? More than simply advocates, customers as partners worry about you, invest in you, celebrate with you in the good times, and come to your aid in the tough times. Mama Cole and her husband are beneficiaries of this strategy. But then, so are Cole's Café's customers.

How so? You don't have to be in a disastrous situation like Cole's to reap the huge benefits the partnership strategy offers. Smart service providers know that marketplace success today demands that units and organizations be incredibly agile. As organizations stretch and bend to meet both ever-increasing requirements for turn-time and turn-on-a-dime response, they can ill afford to waste precious time guarding their backside from unscrupulous relations eager to cash in on a moment of vulnerability. As the economics of service get more and more challenging, units and organizations benefit greatly from customers willing to help out, pitch in, and advocate.

On the customer end of the equation, a benefit of high-quality partnership is that it answers the customer's growing fatigue with superficiality. We are already seeing a renaissance of a focus on substance. Customer-centric and customer-focused organizations are finding ever-innovative ways of combining compassion with "countability." "Soft" is emerging as the glove of a results-driven hand, not the disguise of an oppressive fist. And, employees enjoy living in congruent worlds. Life contains far less stress when the principles that make their home life work are equally valued at the water cooler, on the shop floor, and in the board room.

What makes a partnership strategy work? What follows are five tactics that can turn a transaction into a relationship and a relationship into a partnership. They come from years of research on successful and unsuccessful partnerships with customers. Inserting these principles into your service experience mix will transform the customer's attitude from taker to collaborator; from "what have you done for me lately?" to "how can I help?" However, don't expect transformation overnight. It will take time for customers to let go of their skepticism or suspicion that a scheming motivation is at work.

INCLUSION

Bose is brilliant! Buy a pricey set of their QuietComfort headphones and they come with a stack of courtesy cards for the new owner to pass along to potential buyers. On the back of the courtesy card is every conceivable way to contact Bose. And, the strategy works—at least according to the many users who continually request replacement courtesy cards. Bose turns consumers into partners. Politicians would be wise to learn the ways of Bose.

The most striking ingredient of partnership is inclusion or participation. Inclusion begins by being comfortable enough to ask the customer for assistance. It also means being willing at times to sacrifice a bit on efficiency or effectiveness for the commitment gained by inclusion. However, seeking customer participation can backfire if mishandled or used inappropriately. We have included a sidebar with a half-dozen dos and don'ts to make customer inclusion work.

Six Principles of Customer Inclusion

1. Only ask for what is reasonable.

Make certain the request is one appropriate to make of a loyal customer. Avoid any customer request that makes the organization or customer in any way liable or puts either at risk if things went wrong. While the goal is to help the customer feel like a member of the family, it is important to remember the customer is always the guest of the organization.

2. Make the request the way your mother taught.

The "may I?" and "please" courtesies we learned growing up are always important. Preface your request with a simple statement ("I need your help") or a simple question ("May I ask of you a small favor?"). Simplicity and sincerity are important tunes and tones to help the customer get with the rhythm of partnership.

3. Provide customers with a brief background.

Avoid complaining or whining. Simply and positively describe the reason for your invitation for help. And, be clear and specific about how the customer can assist. It might be as simple as: "We are a bit swamped today, and I could really use your assistance. If you could complete your own paperwork on this order while I get the part, I can get you processed and on your way a whole lot quicker. What do you think?"

4. Be sure the request contains the element of choice.

The customer must clearly have an option to pass on involvement. Make a customer demand and you are asking for resistance. Avoid managing the encounter so the customer feels guilted into meeting your request. A customer made to feel guilty may comply and respond today, but he or she will quietly disappear tomorrow.

5. Give the customer plenty of breathing room.

This means being selective in how and when customers are invited to participate. Too little participation and the customer never gets to feel the glow of inclusion. But, too much can be worse; the customer will feel crowded and leave feeling "they knew me too well" or "they took me for granted."

6. Never forget to express your gratitude.

Asking a customer to assist should be as unique as it is special. The customer will remember it that way if you remember to always communicate appreciation for their efforts. Remember, customer requests should be seen as an option for the customer. Reward their caring enough to accept that option by letting them hear, and feel, your thanks.

On Southwest Flight 22 from El Paso to Phoenix, the flight attendant accepted assistance from two adoring passengers to help pass out peanuts to fellow travelers. The most important part of the occurrence was not the obvious fun the two guys in Bermuda shorts and ball caps had. It was the noticeable positive effect the incident had on everyone on board. Even super-serious passengers could not help but grin as they received the all-too-familiar snack from the flight attendant-wannabes!

Inclusion involves finding a way to invite customers to put skin in the game. The power lies more in the opportunity to participate than actual involvement. Most passengers on the Southwest flight knew that, had they volunteered, their services would have been equally welcomed. That means that they participated vicariously and had almost as much fun as the two guys doing the peanut passing.

The wise organization makes the path to customer contribution comfortable and obvious. As you find opportunities for customer inclusion, remember this: There are some customers who want to be pampered, not partnered. They would be insulted if you suggested they do more than give you their money and/or their time. Let them be as they are and put your extra effort into those customers who are willing to join in.

GENEROSITY

Great partners are generous. Partners are willing to give more than they receive. Mama Cole lived generosity every day of her life. And, she gave not because it was the other end of getting. She gave because that is who she is. In her darkest hour, with Cole's Café teetering on the brink of bankruptcy, one neighbor suggested she cut back on her propensity to make food "on Mama" if the customer was a little short of cash. She quickly set the neighbor straight. "I won't stop feeding the older customers, even if I have to cook for them at home. They're on a fixed income." When her banana pudding became so popular she couldn't make enough for everyone, she gave away copies of the recipe!

While the very essence of service is to give, a partnership strategy involves more *gifting* than giving. Giving can imply a tit-for-tat component: I gave you something of value, now you have an opportunity to return the favor. Gifting, on the other hand, suggests doing something for the sheer joy of giving and the pleasure of watching the response. With gifting, reciprocity is solely in the reaction of the receiver; there is no expectation of future payback.

"Where is the worth in giving when taking is so crucial to survival?" some may chide in challenging economic times. "Besides, before we can talk bounty, we need to get past survival. Our stakeholders cannot spend good customer feelings or deposit thank-you notes in their checking accounts." Ask Mama Cole about that perspective!

We are not suggesting that anyone give away the shop. However, trusting a generosity attitude is a far safer bet than putting your stakes on greed. Of course there are fickle customers on the prowl for a cheap one-night stand they can brag about as a financial conquest. However, smart service providers seek more mature customer relationships with patrons in whom they can invest for a long-term payback. The smart money is on fostering customer devotion, not simply customer acquisition; the wise enterprise counts on the depth and length of an ongoing relationship, not a single transaction.

A generosity attitude has a captivating impact on customers. It attracts them because it conveys to the customer the kind of unconditional positive regard that characterizes relationships at their best. Customers like the way they feel when dealing with service providers who have such an orientation. They feel valued, not used. They believe they are the recipient of a sincere desire to serve, not just a ploy for payback. They enjoy relationships laced with substance and value far more than encounters that are functional but hollow.

"A cash-and-carry customer brought a small rug in to clean," reports Ellen Amirkhan of Dallas-based Oriental Rug Cleaning. "All the parking spaces were taken so she parked on the sidewalk; when she came out she had gotten a parking ticket. She came in and told us, and we wrote her a check for the ticket. When the rug was ready we delivered it to her and did not charge her for the cleaning! We have a customer for life."

Bouquets is an award-winning flower shop located in the heart of downtown Denver near many parking meters as well as a bus stop. Many businesses refuse to give change for meters and buses, except to customers, because it depletes their cash till and takes employee time to go to the bank for more change. Bouquets replenishes a bag of quarters daily, specifically designed to make change for anyone who asks, says co-owner B.J. Dyer. "Coins are offered with a smile and a business card. Many people later become our customers when they need flowers." Dyer adds, "But, even if they didn't, we get a kick out of treating people different from the way others treat them."

We were staying at the Marriott in Rocky Hill, Connecticut, while working with a client nearby. We both had a very early meeting, but Chip was returning to the hotel afterwards to work in his room. Before getting in the rental car John planned to keep, Chip stopped by the front desk and asked the night auditor and early morning front desk clerk, Linda Zieller, if the hotel had a van that could pick him up at the meeting site 10 minutes away and bring him back to the hotel at 8 AM. Without hesitation Linda said, "We don't have a hotel van, but I will be getting off at 7:30 AM and will be glad to pick you up and bring you back to the hotel before I go home." We made other arrangements, but the generous offer increased our devotion to the hotel.

The worth of great customer service requires a focus not on the transaction costs, but on the relationship value. Transaction costs are not irrelevant, but they can, if we aren't careful, become destructively dominant. Focus on the transaction and you get a satisfied customer; focus on the relationship and you get a devoted customer.

TRUST

What is it about trust that makes customers feel so valued? In part, it communicates that one-half of a partnership is reaching out to the other half. And customers truly reward partnerships. The amazing power of trust is that it creates even more—show trust to customers, they'll trust you back.

The trusting service person, unit, or organization generously puts more focus on nurturing the relationship than miserly squeezing every dollar out of every transaction. Everyone in the organization should protect and grow the assets of the organization. However, customers remember organizations that refrain from nickel and diming them to death. Look for opportunities to say, "No charge" or "That one's on us." Find ways to do little extras for customers they didn't expect. The small, personalized, unexpected extras gain more devotion mileage than big, splashy ones. Remember, value-added may make them smile, but value-unique will take their breath away!

Think about what you would do in this situation: A customer calls your trophy and engraving company seeking imprinted wine glasses for a fund-raising event. You quote her a price of 144 glasses with two-sided imprint at $2.16. She misinterprets the quote as $216 for the whole order and excitingly informs her board of directors. She learns of her error when she stops by to place the order. After a lengthy tirade, her director offers to put an ad for your company in the event's program and would allow you to put your banner on the sponsor wall if you will honor the bargain basement price. Do you take the deal and save the relationship, or do you play hard ball and avoid taking an economic hit?

This was the dilemma faced by Richard Schaefer, CEO of Awards & More in Enfield, Connecticut. "We took the position that we knew the customer made a mistake," says Schaefer, "but it was our job to help her save face to her peers. But we also learned to avoid quoting final prices over the phone and always confirm our quotes in writing." The customer may not always be right, but the customer is always the customer. And, they are a lot different than they use to be.

Trusting actions can be as small as the cup of pennies next to the cash register with a sign that reads, "Got a penny, give a penny; need a penny, take a penny." Or the dry cleaner's poster on the wall that says, "We DO take personal checks." Examine the signs around your organization that say "Don't," "No," or other negatives. Can the same message be communicated in a more trusting way? And in the back room, out of sight from the customer, put reminders for employees to think through the customer's eyes.

Would you want yourself for a service provider if you were the customer? What signals do your actions send to your customers? Take a look at the sidebar of "we don't trust you" signs customers hate.

Signs Customers Hate

The line starts here
Next window please
Your call is important to us.
No loitering
Keep off the grass
No personal checks
Take a number and wait until your number is called

Arriving in Dallas for work, we went to the rental car location at DFW airport when we landed on time. The rental car company is one we use so much we are in their "Super Customer Club." Our reservation had been made for weeks. We went into the Super Customer Club booth and waited in line with all the other Super Customer Club members. When we reached the counter, the agent informed us that our car was not ready. "Why not?" we queried. His flatline response: "We were out of cars, but it's not your fault." That's like Kentucky Fried Chicken being out of fried chicken!

When we finally got a car, there were no keys in it. We looked everywhere. Stopping a nearby rental car employee with a radio, we explained the situation. Her response: "Get out, I'll look." Message?

When she came up keyless too, she sent us back to the Super Customer Club booth. All the other Super Customer Club members watched again as we informed the counter agent of our plight. His response: "Wait here. I'll go look!" Message?

We ultimately got a rental car. And, he upgraded us to a Dodge! And guess what? He threw in a free GPS! Message?

Trust is like a billboard. It can loudly proclaim how we feel about the customer through the subtle actions we take. Everyone in the rental car story was doing what they thought was right. The problem was, they were thinking about tasks to be performed and not about customer relationships to be nurtured into a partnership. The most important part to keep in mind is that customers read mistrust long before we become aware of it. As the Polish proverb goes, "The guest sees more in an hour than the host in a year."

WIDE AWAKE

We asked a partnership expert what she thought most characterized successful partnerships. "They glow in the dark," she said with a smile. Great partnerships are "on." They bring a perpetual energy and intensity to every encounter. When they are there, they are *all* there. "When the partnership with the customer is hot," says John King, founder and president of J. Kings Food Service Professionals, Inc. in Holtsville, New York, "we are good when we are together, and we are good when we are not."

Partnerships work best when they are wide awake. Partners bring all they are to the relationship. When it comes to the partnership, they are never lazy, disinterested, or indifferent. In conversations, they are attentive, curious when they listen, animated when they contribute. They show up in life with completed staff work. They care enough to bring their very best.

Part of being wide awake includes dramatic listening and over-communication. Tom Berger, world-class financial consultant with the CBC Group of Merrill Lynch in Charlotte, enjoys a rich, long-term relationship with all of his clients. Their allegiance to Tom is grounded in an intense curiosity that drives his pursuit of client understanding. He not only is accessible 24/7 to his clients, he finds an array of ways to keep his clients constantly plugged into the ever-changing financial world. His proactive style creates the unmistakable impression that he has one mission in life: to ride herd on each client's portfolio as if it were his only one, and to do it with the passion that says his entire career is hanging on that client's portfolio performance. His enthusiasm for his profession coupled with his fervor for his clients make him a valued partner with his devoted clients.

Partnership pros like Tom are primed to be enamored by the possible, treasuring the process as much as they do the outcome. And, while they enjoy harmony, they are more pleasured by the energy of encounter. As one senior manager stated of his relationship with a key customer, "Our partnership is sometimes easygoing and sometimes feisty, but it's always vigorous." "If we keep the relationship with our customers turned up wide open all the time," says Lillian Koster, front desk supervisor of the Marriott Hotel in Rocky Hill, Connecticut, "then we don't get complacent, we don't take customers for granted, and everybody benefits. They make our lives easier as we make their lives better."

At Kindred Health Care, following nonclinical staff training on how to respond to call lights of their patients and residents, graduates wear buttons that say "I stop at call lights" to heighten awareness and engage all team members. Great customer service is all about bringing forth obvious energy. And when that energy is focused on the customer like a spotlight on a stage performer, it communicates commitment and care. Does this mean great partners never rest? Of course not. But, while they do not take themselves too seriously, they take the partnership very seriously. When they cannot be all there, they serve notice. Their continuous energy is not fueled by a desire to never disappoint, but rather by a need to squeeze the most from every important moment.

I Stop For Call Lights

BONE HONESTY

"'Truth Rules' is the motto of our company," reports Ted Townsend, CEO of Townsend Engineering headquartered in Des Moines, Iowa. "You have to have the courage to speak the truth. When conflicts come up, you put the honest approach out there. You can tell very quickly if people are comfortable or not with that approach. If they are not, watch out. You will probably pay for it later."

Partnerships that work are bone honest. They are willing to go overboard sharing information. They are also willing to go out back sharing private intelligence. Sharing is premised less on an obligation to reciprocity ("you tell me your secret and I'll tell you mine") and more on a commitment to baggage-free interaction. Frankness might not always be comfy, but it is always clean. Constant pursuit of truth also fuels mutual learning, and winning partnerships never stop learning.

Take it from the City of Santa Clarita (California), selected by *Money Magazine* as one of the top-25 places to live in the United States. Santa Clarita Mayor Bob Kellar holds regular town hall meetings, which are promoted by his posing for a spoof "Got milk?" commercial. Four different communities are the settings for these events featuring his active listening to issues and then facilitating citizens' involvement in finding solutions. The meetings are extremely well received, especially the milk and cookies served at each gathering. The city also shows its willingness to be frank and make information a two-way street with its citywide Citizen Participation program. For example, when a new parks and recreation facility is planned, the neighborhood impacted is involved in every aspect, from initial design to grand opening.

Got Mayor Poster[2]

Wait. There's more. Imagine how many people a hairdresser talks with every day. Now, picture a whole room full of local hairdressers. In the spirit of bone honesty, Santa Clarita's municipal leadership holds "Hairdressers' Luncheons" to find out about the issues and concerns people express about their city government. And the hairdressers love it!

What wild animal is the most efficient hunter? Conventional wisdom would suggest a pride of lions, or at least some other animal in the wild cat family. Yet, a pride of lions only has a 20 percent success rate when pursuing their kill. There is another species with an 80 percent success rate: a pack of wild dogs!

Zoologists were curious about what made the difference in their hunting success. It was, in a word, partnership. Lions only come together for the hunt, like a project team (!), and typically fight among themselves over the spoils. Wild dogs partner before, during, and after the hunt. They make certain all the dogs in the pack get their share of the kill. If partnership is to be your chosen strategy, it will only work if it becomes a part of your organizational DNA. Organizations known for customer partnerships *think* partnership, therefore they live partnership—before, during, and after.

Partnership is a take-their-breath-away strategy that requires a significant emotional investment. It also provides a significant return. And, the benefits go beyond a devoted customer. The Ritz-Carlton Hotels has a reputation for extraordinary service and intensely loyal guests. Part of their success lies in creating a culture of partnership. "Ladies and gentlemen serving ladies and gentlemen" is practiced in the back of the house with the same fervor as at the front desk.

Staying at the Ritz-Carlton Hotel in Naples, Florida, during a business trip, we were enjoying attentive service at breakfast in the hotel restaurant. Wearing our consultant hat, we asked the cheerful waitress, "What do you like most about working at this Ritz-Carlton?" Without hesitation she responded, "Working here has made me a better wife and parent." Surprised by her answer, we probed further. "It's more than respect and trust," she explained. "Whether at home or at work, whether you are serving your family or the guest, it is all about love."

Mama Cole would concur.

CHAPTER 7
Cult-Like

"The relationship between the band and the Deadheads needs to be nurtured because they are us and we are them."

—Phil Lesh, bass guitarist, The Grateful Dead

He brought down the heel of his Lucchese boot hard on the kickstand and dismounted his Harley Fat Boy. Wiping the dust off his Levi's jeans, he entered his favorite bar. As he walked through the door the bartender began pouring the customer his favorite adult beverage—Jack Daniel's straight up. He was about to wet his whistle when he felt the buzz of his Apple iPhone attached to his large leather belt.

Stop! What's going on in this story? In a word, devotion. But, we're not talking just ordinary devotion; this is the kind we associate with a cult following. The essence of *cult-like* as a take-their-breath-away strategy is the way the product or service becomes a part of the customer's identity. You know you have achieved cult-like status when your customers wear your logo, name their children after your brand, or act possessive when you change some aspect of your service offering they do not particularly favor. You know you have a cult-like following when patrons fiercely protect and defend you. "I love the little restaurant around the corner from my house so much," says Lynn Goldberg of Goldberg, McDuffie Communications in New York, "that I find myself tidying up their bathroom when I am there just so their next customer does not see them in any way less than extraordinary."

This sort of exaggerated faithfulness appears insane to some, odd to most. However, units or organizations are wise to court such intense customer devotion. The research shows that loyal customers will pay a premium because of a provider's service distinction (think Nordstrom or a five-star restaurant).[1] However, when customers act like rock star groupies or those team fans who paint their faces and wear funny hats, all normal financial expectations go completely out the window. Those customers are willing to pay exorbitantly because of their adoration.

Think about the questions asked in the introduction of the book: What makes customers spend $4 for a cup of coffee at Starbucks, put up 20,000 bucks to wait several months for a Harley-Davidson, or stand in line for hours to get tickets to see the Green Bay Packers or Madonna? These exaggerated investments are not about a beverage, transportation, ballgame, or song and dance show. They are all about enjoying a special experience—an unforgettable service experience! Granted, the product or outcome must be good, but it doesn't have to be the greatest. Harley devotees reluctantly acknowledge that there really are technologically better bikes. Nine out of ten voice teachers would rate Charlotte Church's voice better than Madonna's. And the Green Bay Packers? Being fans of the Atlanta Braves and Dallas Cowboys, now that's an attraction we can appreciate but not really understand!

But most would say that Charlotte Church can't electrify an audience like Madonna, any more than Suzuki can match the gratification a Harley owner feels on a Sunday afternoon ride. Devotion springs from all the texture and nuance of an experience—a totally unforgettable positive experience. People who pay $4 for a cup of coffee at a Starbucks might not put 16 quarters in a vending machine to get the exact same beverage.

THE PRINCIPLES OF CULT-LIKE

Dissecting the cult-like service experience that gives rise to extreme devotion is not a simple process. There is clearly a psychò logic to extreme brand appeal. Color, shape, sound, and touch form an intricate pattern in the brain that links with learned preferences and spell magnetism. There is also a social component at work. Somehow, watching Green Bay in the privacy of your living room is not the same as elbowing your way through the noisy, frozen bleachers with two hot dogs and a cold beer.

But organizations can't turn on a tape of a cheering mob or flood the showroom with the smell of motorcycle exhaust every time customers enter. What are the service actions that elicit serious affection? Is there a formula that, if consistently honored, would dramatically increase the chances customers would become zealots for a service provider?

Your Dog

The devotion that dogs demonstrate as part of their natural instincts as pack animals closely mimics the human idea of love and friendship, leading many dog owners to view their pets as full-fledged family members. Dogs seem to view their human companions as members of their pack and make few, if any, distinctions between their owners and fellow canines.

Cult-like customers are the crown jewels of any unit or organization. All organizations want more; few know how to position their enterprise to dramatically increase their share of these customer groupies. Granted some customers don't want to be this sort of devoted customer (nor should they be). However, just as a rising tide raises all boats, elevating the unit or organization to attract a bigger share of cult-like customers can increase the quality of service to everyone served.

Dissecting cult-like is a bit like unraveling motivation. We don't have to study long before we learn motivation is the response to certain conditions. Leaders do not motivate employees; they create conditions that result in motivation (employees chose to motivate themselves or not). The cult-like strategy is an invitation for customers to join. It is an effect or result that is fostered and then nurtured or kept alive. And, as sinister and evil as some real cults are (the ones that parents hope their teenagers never join), some of the principles that make the bad ones work can make the good ones possible. It is for this reason we have labeled this strategy "cult-like" rather than "cult."

Bottom line, it is always important to recognize that customers have free will. Intense devotion to a service provider needs to be something customers joyfully join in and can freely abandon should their needs or opinions change. Devotion should also be achieved with integrity and never manipulation. If customers ever feel duped or conned to become an advocate, then they will loudly proclaim their disgruntlement to anyone who will listen. Stated differently, if whatever strategy or tactic you select to create take-their-breath-away service is not one that would make your mother proud, leave it on the shelf!

Creating the conditions that heighten the probability a customer will manifest their devotion at the highest level involves five tactics: network, identity, daring, secret, and character. Consider making these tactics part of your invitation for customers to be inducted into your special club where membership has its privileges.

NETWORK

Network creates ways of socializing the service experience, thus ramping up affirmation that the customer made a wise choice. It is also a way to encourage customer storytelling—the best network glue there is. Smart organizations using cult-like as a take-their-breath-away strategy often seed their networks with stories. Walk into any large Starbucks and you will see evidence there are stories ready to spread. Watch how Apple uses a major trade show as a story-starting venue. Look at the posters on the walls of a Mazda Miata showroom. Newsletters, blogs, and special takeaways can similarly be rich outlets for stories.

Another approach to network is to create happenings—events and alliances that attract loyalists. MacWorld is one example of this network approach; Mary Kay cosmetics is another. Then, there are the Tupperware parties and Herbalife's regional gatherings, aimed not only at selling product but also creating a sense of belonging to those who feel the same adoration for the company and its products and services.

Buckhead Boutique provides a unique buying experience for customers. All the upscale women's apparel is purchased in the privacy of Lynn Dinkins' gorgeous Atlanta home. Her clients are women who are senior executives, attorneys, or entrepreneurs with little time to shop at the mall or women from wealthy homes who have major social schedules, or both. These women want a private shopping experience, they want quality, and they do not want to encounter someone wearing the same outfit at a business meeting or charity fundraising event. Lynn becomes their super fashion consultant.

Lynn's Front Door

Four times a year, Lynn holds a private show. Decorative invitations are e-mailed to her clients; appointments are made with ample time for browsing in her no-pressure buying environment. On the day before the show, all the furniture in her spacious family room is removed and the room is transformed into a stunning and shoppable boutique. Clients select and order their wardrobe in comfort and privacy; the clothes are delivered to the clients' homes immediately after the shipment is received at Lynn's house. A Neiman-Marcus trained alteration specialist is a part of her network of professionals and available to work with clients on any required tailoring. And, clients are given a 10 percent discount as a referral fee for friends who become Lynn's clients. She has clients who fly in to work with her several times a year; others who drive hours to her Atlanta home.

Network obviously links customers to service providers like Lynn; as a cult-like tactic, it can also forge a connection from customer to customer to customer. The Harley Owners Group is a well-known organization that creates opportunities for Harley employees (including senior leaders) and customers (including famous celebrities) to get together for Sunday afternoon rides. "It becomes a barrier to exit," said Michael Keefe, a former HOG director. The Harley corporate Web site has a whole section accessible only to members of HOG.

Network can also mean facilitating participation in a collective cause. The Rehabilitation and Nursing Center in Monroe, North Carolina, has a program called Magic Moments. "We ask our residents to tell us something they would really like to have or do, and then we involve everyone in making it happen," says Program Manager Brian Rife. Sometimes the Magic Moment is funded through contributions; sometimes it happens through the connections of a resident's family member or friend. One example was a resident who wanted to move to the state of Ohio where her family lived. Rife persuaded a company to donate a $7,000 medical flight to transport the woman home to her loved ones. The overarching benefit is that new bonds among residents, families, friends, and the community are formed from participating in the program.

Network means creating events that can function as a watering hole for your customers. Facilitate their interaction with other customers. Provide giveaways or drawings to promote a spirit of warmth and camaraderie. Ensure there are value-added takeaways that tie your organization to the network experience. Invite a special person your customers will want to meet. Wilmington, Delaware-based construction giant EDiS sponsors an annual EDiS Institute. Invited are clients, members of the trades, local officials, and others with ties to the construction industry. Top speakers on topics relevant to the audience and interactive workshops are a part of the day-long crucible for the less-than-devoted to become ardent company loyalists. "It is one way we give back to our community and our industry," says Brian DiSabatino, president of EDiS Building Systems. "It also is a great opportunity for our clients to network and reaffirm their loyalty to EDiS."

Do something super special for your best customers. American Airlines turned their frequent business travelers from mild supporters to passionate devotees through their Executive Platinum desk. Executive Platinum status requires a person fly 100,000 air miles a year on American. The airline turned an affinity group into aficionados by asking these ultimate road warriors the one travel perk they valued the most. The Executive Platinum desk was their overwhelming choice. The desk can only be accessed through a secret phone number given to Executive Platinum members who must requalify each year. On the other end of the phone is a team of American's very best agents. World-class problem solvers, these helpers delight in surprising their patrons with their capacity to work miracles. Their confident, warm style is often a great relief to the tired traveler caught with an unexpected layover in Peoria and no apparent way out until morning.

IDENTITY

Identity involves finding ways the experience can be integrated into the customer's individuality. It is the principle behind all the logoed paraphernalia that many customers collect. Identity might employ physical objects. It could be a coded greeting, a special expression, a mannerism, or a style. The key to making it effective is how easily it becomes a part of who the customer is and their style of living.

Lynn Dinkins taps into identity through a function that very few clothes boutiques provide: She goes to her clients' homes to assess their clothes closet. She works a closet like an interior decorator might work your living room. It is not just about looking for holes to fill; Lynn looks to create and accessorize new combinations of clothing in the client's wardrobe. She catalogs the information in her vast database. Should a client call to request a new navy blue skirt, she might ask, "Do you want another like the one you purchased last year?" Sometimes her clients forget what they have hanging in the closet. The end result makes her boutique an extension of her client's closet and vice versa.

Figure out what makes your customers different from others and then capitalize on it. Try to get inside your customers' minds to figure out what unique need or desire your service can address. Lynn knows privacy is a vital desire to her clients. "The average woman in America is a size 14. The last thing she wants is a size 4 sales clerk at Neiman's trying to tell her what looks good on her," she told us. "Besides," she continued, "the public display nature of the fitting room can make her avoid shopping all together. But she can shop without inhibition or anxiety in the privacy of a home under the watchful protection of her own fashion consultant who respects her uniqueness and cares about her happiness."

Helping your customers feel they are a part of a special group holds the same allure that the "The Few, the Proud, the Marines" has for a Marine recruit. When Jeff Bezos started Amazon.com he wanted to create an online experience of the neighborhood bookstore. Since there was no bookstore clerk to tell patrons about an obscure new mystery or the best book on crocheting, he turned the job over to customers, encouraging them to write book reviews. The result was a cult-like community of book lovers, or to quote Bezos, "neighbors helping neighbors make purchase decisions." Linus Torvalds' open source PC operating system allowed users to customize it and share their insights with other users. Soon Linux became the David to giant Microsoft. Devoted users made the open architecture better and better, investing countless hours almost like a second job.

Turn the familiar and routine into something quirky, adventuresome, and just plain fun. Jack Daniels not only sells whiskey, like most of their competitors, they sell a host of logoed paraphernalia: belt buckles, hats, shirts, drink glasses. But, Jack Daniels went one step further. They created a semisecret club called the Tennessee Squire Association for devotees. Only members can nominate new members. Not only does a new member get an impressive certificate, they get a deed to part of the Jack Daniel Distillery in Lynchburg, Tennessee. That's when the fun begins.

Members begin periodically to get letters from their supposed neighbors in Lynchburg. You could get one from Herb at the Lynchburg Hardware wanting to take horseweed worms from your property to use as fish bait. "Porky" Roper might write you to be on the lookout for his lost hog since his farm is near you. Or the County Executive of Moore County, Tennessee, might write to request an easement across your property so locals can take a shortcut past the distillery to reach Spencer Hole, a popular recreation area. Some letters might want your ideas on how to make the distillery tour better. You could even get a postcard photo of your property taken from three miles up. Along with the folksy, tongue-firmly-in-cheek letters will come calendars, coasters, and catalogs for ordering more JD paraphernalia. The upshot is that through a Tennessee Squire experience, customers become so emotionally tied to the Jack Daniel's brand, they would never consider accepting a substitute at a social gathering serving adult beverages.[2]

DARING

Daring is our label for actions that help customers feel special because of choosing you as their service provider. Daring can range from providing a thoughtful solution to an uncomfortable situation to making a generous gesture to customers who are in the club to taking a controversial stand.

One of Buckhead Boutique Lynn Dinkins' clients had a challenging figure and panicky situation: She was obligated to go for a few days to a dude ranch. With great calm and confidence Lynn coached her through the apparel she would need for her visit to this unique upscale but rustic setting. The pinch came when the topic of jeans surfaced: "Oh, I don't wear jeans! I never wear jeans," reported her client with the defiance of a child asked to take a bitter pill. The challenge was heightened by the fact that the jeans were a low-rise style, designed to be worn at the hips, not at the waist. With continued calm, Lynn invited her client to be daring in a safe environment: "Take these jeans home and just wear them around the house for a couple of weeks. If you don't like them, we'll find something else." The client fell in love with the jeans. She invited Lynn to her house to help her pack for the trip so she would choose clothing that worked well together. She was the hit of the trip as her friends raved about her clothes, especially her jeans!

Cult-like service greatness comes from knowing that necessity is the mother of invention. It also relies on an unwavering service greatness philosophy, which can come from any number of persuasive rationales. It might come from a value system that says, "This is the right way to *be* in the marketplace." It might originate in a David–Goliath imbalance between you and your resource-rich competitor. It could rest on the recognition that the beaten path is too crowded with copycats and that a fresh approach will be a productive wake-up call to the customer. Whatever the reason, the attraction to cult-like service greatness is strongest for people with daring in their nature and restlessness in their practice.

Daring is the realm of the maverick, the nonconformist, the eccentric, even the weirdo. The truth is that great organizations and great units are spawned by the daring. Breakthroughs and record bustings are generally done by those wild ducks who fly to the beat of their own drum. The late Peter Drucker noted that after 30 years of studying organizations, he had concluded that the only time something truly worthwhile got done in organizations was when it got done by "a monomaniac with a mission."[3]

Daring people focus on improving, creating, shaping—not on enhancing their self-image at someone else's expense. Daring breeds focus and honesty. Political gamesmanship, deception, and weasel tactics are simply clutter. There's no need or time for that. There's cool stuff to be done. Accordingly, people engaged in daring can sometimes threaten people with their strength, foresight, and commitment. They're also the ones who get things done and build new value for customers. When he was an executive producer with *NBC Nightly News*, Steve Friedman gave his troops this advice: "I believe the people who work below you should love and admire you, and the people who work above you should think you're somewhat insane. They should have a bit of a pause, a bit of nervousness, before they pick up the phone to call you."

SECRET

Secret is not about covert actions; it's about practices that help customers feel like an insider. The tactic can range from inventing a special language or process to making certain folklore known only to customers to having customers be the first to find out about some new development.

Walt Disney World fans know the gold paint on the carousel is really 23-karat gold leaf, and they enjoy playing the insider's game of how many hidden Mickeys they can spot in a shadow made by a lamp post on the pavement in Tomorrowland or formed by the lights in the loading area of the Pirates of the Caribbean attraction. Harley-Davidson devotees know the role Willie G. Davidson (grandson of one of the founders) played in rescuing the company from AMF as it was teetering on bankruptcy. Apple fans look at

Steve Jobs as their "man in black" savior; Mary Kay cosmetics disciples know Ms. Ash came from Hot Wells, Texas.

Buckhead Boutique's Lynn Dinkins invented a creative financing system for her clients. With the average purchase running several thousands of dollars a trip, Lynn thought that her clients would welcome a way to have the business end of the shopping experience feel as comfortable and effortless as the rest. "I tell my clients that I take payment in any form—check, cash, and credit card," Lynn says. "Then, I wink and tell them, 'or any combination that works for you.'" For Lynn's clients, learning that they can spread a major purchase across several forms of payment is like getting the secret password to a VIP club.

Secrets is a broad label for insider information. "Grande, quad, ristretto dry cappuccino" makes complete sense to a true Starbucks fan. The Varsity in Atlanta is the world's largest drive-in restaurant, accommodating more than 600 cars at one time. Its fans know the meaning of "walk a dog," "Mary Brown steak," and "N.I.P.C.," or that "Joe-ree" means coffee with cream.

Secrets can be rituals. Starbucks fans know there is a set ritual for properly ordering a beverage. Die-hard University of Texas football fans know they haven't properly attended a Longhorns home game without a ritual beer at Scholz Garten, which has been serving devoted locals since 1866. In the hills above Hollywood stands a spookily elegant Victorian mansion, complete with intricate gingerbread trim and towering turrets. Tour guides point it out with great reverence, but it's not a movie star's home or elegant hotel. It's the Magic Castle, home of The Academy of Magical Arts Inc., a private club for magicians and lovers of magic. Open only to members or guests of members, the Magic Castle sets the tone from the moment you step into the foyer, which has the look of the bookcase-lined library from the board game Clue.

You utter a secret phrase given to you by an Academy member, and—voilà!—the bookcases separate, and you enter into a bar and dining room that gleams with fine old woods and crystal lamps.

From the dining room, you pass through a corridor covered with photographs and playbills of some of the world's greatest magicians. And, finally, the main attraction: three performance stages. On a typical evening, magicians and their guests dine and watch the best of the best of their colleagues on one of the three stages. The connection between magician and audience creates a bond that has everyone in attendance eagerly awaiting a return.

CHARACTER

Cult-like service greatness has a quality that in some way touches the customer's soul. Customers find such service ennobling and a compelling model of merit. It leaves the customer moved and eager for a repeat experience. It is a kind of awakening that causes life's colors to be richer and the day's emotions to be rounder. Watch a person who has just had such an experience and they act more considerate, more confident, and more carefree. It can be so profound that it is added to the customer's storehouse of significant life recollections—a wedding, birth of a first child, or the celebration of a major accomplishment.

We call this feature *character*. It means finding a way to support the customer's view of self at a superlative level. It is captured in comments like "When I ride my Harley it takes my head to another place where I am free, strong, and bold," and "Staying at the Ritz-Carlton Hotel reminds me of life lived with elegance and style. At home I have diapers to change and beds to make. At the Ritz, I can be a queen."

Lynn Dinkins is committed to leaving her clients confident in their wardrobe and knowledgeable about fashion. "Some of our clients could be buyers for a fashionable women's wear company. But most are not. My job is to teach them to make wise choices that fit their body, their personality, and their unique taste," Lynn told us. She continued, "Some of our clients view clothes buying as a necessary step, akin to acquiring an important professional accoutrement like a well-appointed office; some view clothes buying as a sport, like golf or tennis. My role is to start where they are and make their buying experience seamless as well as ennobling, efficient, and respectful."

Character can mean standing up for your customers. The Tattered Cover in Denver continues to enjoy a reputation as the largest independent bookstore in the United States. It also has a major cult-like following. The bookstore came under attack when owner Joyce Meskis refused to release information about customers as a part of a criminal investigation. Losing her case in lower court, she funded an expensive appeal on the grounds of her customers' right to privacy. Not only did she win the appeal, she won the admiration of customers around the globe. Even those who disagreed with her stand praised her courage to honor her convictions, even at the risk of significant financial loss. Look around at how many independent bookstores have survived with the advent of giant chains. The Tattered Cover thrives as it basks in the admiration of its fans who feel privileged to be associated with a national treasure.

Character means being true to your beliefs and values, never waffling even at the risk of losing market share. Truett Cathy, the 88-year-old founder of Chick-fil-A, the fifth largest fast-food chain in the United States, is deeply religious. Like Eric Little, the 1927 Olympic gold medal runner whose refusal to compete on the Sabbath formed the plot of the Academy Award winning movie *Chariots of Fire*, Truett has honored his religious convictions and elected to remain closed on Sunday. While competitors KFC, McDonald's, Burger King, and the like serve customers seven days a week, Truett has gained favor in the marketplace for his courage in remaining faithful to his values. And, devotees rave about Chick-fil-A's respectful style with customers. "Next guest please" is heard at the counter rather than "Take your order?" "My pleasure" is the preferred response to a guest's "thank you" rather than the "no problem" heard in most fast-food restaurants. Managers work side by side with frontline employees to ensure guests consistently and continually get over-the-top service.

"I like dealing with an organization whose leaders 'stand for something!'" was a frequent answer when a major research firm asked customers, "What do you like most about the organizations to whom you are most loyal?"[4] Chick-fil-A, USAA, Southwest Airlines, The Container Store, Charles Schwab, and Enterprise Rent-A-Car were some of the companies that received high marks.

Character is also about authenticity and naturalness. Cult-like organizations remain true to themselves. Popularity with the masses is not their quest; connection with their niche is. And they view marketing and sales more as an invitation than an enticement. "There is absolutely no pressure on our clients to buy anything," says Lynn Dinkins of Buckhead Boutique. "If they buy, great; if they don't, that's fine too. We are just happy to see them. Some come to one show and decide it is not for them. We don't chase them. We are not for every woman."

Cult-like service greatness leaves you stunned. It is not simply imaginative, it is also provocative. Delivering such unique service causes the customer to be a bit amazed and left with a compelling memory that quickly turns into a story that starts with "You're not gonna believe this." It is also the kind of experience customers subconsciously hold up to competing organizations in a kind of "Can you top this?" dare.

But cult-like is different from fad-like. Fads rise suddenly, gaining a lot of buzz only to sink in popularity about as fast as they soared. When was the last time you played with your Pet Rock or Hula Hoop? Cult-like works when it is sustainable. And, sustainability relies on perpetual and renewed value. Lynn Dinkins is in her eighth year of business; many of her clients are in their eighth year with her. Their devotion springs from the worth Buckhead Boutique contributes to their lives. Customers accelerate their ardor from the transience of "I shall return" to the permanence of "I do" when their union with a service provider touches their essence and not just their assets.

CHAPTER 8
Luxury

"Luxury customers seek stimulation not standardization.
They are drawn to the potential of inventive encounters
and unexpected episodes."
                    —*James Brown, president and CEO, Brownstone*
                                        Hotels & Resorts

It had been six months of hard negotiation. Todd Singley and
Sheldon McAllister, with the aid of a wise investment banker,
finally inked the billion-dollar deal. Now it was time to celebrate.

A call to the concierge from Todd triggered their shift from
his hotel suite to the hotel restaurant; the maitre d' ushered the
banker and the two CEOs to Todd's favorite table. The simple
candle on the table cast a soft glow on the nearby teak paneling.
The setting sun cast a soft glow on a lush patio garden just outside
the restaurant window.

Slow forward four hours. The waiter is telling the backstory
behind the wine the trio just enjoyed. Purchased by the restaurant manager at a Christie's auction, it had been bottled at a tiny
vineyard near Josephine's home the month Napoleon went into
Waterloo; there were only 10 bottles left in the world. Cigars
were presented in a mahogany box autographed by Castro, also
purchased by the restaurant manager himself on a recent trip to

Cuba. Some two thousand dollars later, the threesome departed with the memory of a special evening permanently etched in their brains.

Luxury. The concept stirs mixed feelings. The dark side spells opulence, conceit, and gluttony. But luxury also is associated with excellence, majesty, worth, and reward. When we use the handle to revere an automobile, abode, or aperitif, it implies a sense of class, refinement, and elegance. It is the choice of the rich and famous, and the aspiration of wannabes. Dreams of luxury have fueled lottery ticket sales, TV game show participation, and sweepstakes entries.

Luxury products are expected to come equipped with the best of everything, and they even have a special language to communicate their prestige. There are no "selections," only "appointments;" objects are "hand-crafted," not "built." In the playpen of upscale advertisers, luxury talk is the secret code. Peruse ads in *The Robb Report*, *Worth*, *Architectural Digest*, or *Town and Country* and you will find over-the-top attempts to create mind-pictures the color of rich. Branding luxury has ensnared the attention and budget of countless enterprises striving to increase their share of this lucrative market segment.

Yet ads do not a luxury brand make. Todd, Sheldon, and the banker were not seeking a brand-name beverage nor were they concerned about who witnessed them drinking pricey wine. They were driven by a hunger for a luxury experience, and all the trappings that evening simply decorated the memory. Bottom line, luxury brand-making requires crafting an unforgettable experience that matches the price tab.

"Luxury is fundamentally a state of mind," says David Williams, VP of sales and marketing for Orient-Express Hotels. It is foremost an expression of excellence—particularly one that exhibits fine craftsmanship, obvious pride, superior training, and a perpetual attention to detail. Luxury service is that which is performed in a relaxed, but refined ambiance.

UNDERSTANDING THE LUXURY-SEEKING CUSTOMER

The high-end customer segment is one of the fastest-growing components of today's marketplace, even in a challenging economy. While there are a limited number of organizations in the world that exclusively serve the luxury customer—Rolls-Royce, the Hotel Bel Air, Learjet—more and more organizations have a portion of their customer base at the upper stratum of wealth. From financial services to consumer products to law firms, these organizations now grapple with how to give distinctive treatment to their more discriminating customers and clients. Additionally, many wannabe high-end customers are emulating the buying behaviors and service requirements of the true luxury customer, extending the reach of potential attraction.

The House Cat

Dogs have owners; cats have servants. Dogs eat; cats dine. In ancient times cats were worshipped as gods; they have not forgotten this. A cat is a puzzle for which there is no solution.

While much has been written about the design and creation of luxury products, there's been little guidance for people tasked with delivering and managing luxury service. Those that exist are often the expertise of butlers, concierges, and valets passed to protégés as lessons from experience rather than instructions from a manual. What are the principles that guide the creation of the service experience of someone buying a very expensive wine, vacationing at a posh hotel, or indulging in that once-in-a-lifetime cruise? What are the components of the customer service a wealthy client might expect from his or her attorney or financial advisor? How is the true luxury customer who is chauffeured in a Rolls-Royce different from the upscale customer who drives a Lexus or Porsche?

Luxury-service-seeking customers are unique, and luxury-service-seeking customers are very similar. The challenge of the service provider is to honor their uniqueness while pursuing ways to respond to their similarities. While all market features change over time and all generalizations are precarious, today's high-end customers share certain characteristics.

Luxury-seeking customers know they are different and search for service that acknowledges that difference. This does not necessarily imply arrogance or superiority.

Luxury-seeking customers count on quality throughout, and most know it when they see it. Cutting corners in perceivable service dimensions will net an overall mediocre experience.

Luxury-seeking customers rely on obvious quality and carefully monitored safety as an entrée to the experimentation and risk that can yield a new, exciting adventure.

Luxury-seeking customers value classy over flashy and authentic over pretentious; they expect close and personalized, but not invasive, attention. Err on the side of being real and respectful.

Luxury-seeking customers have an aversion to opulence and excess. Granted there are wealthy wannabes who think helicopters and champagne baths signal they have arrived. The true luxury-seeking customer prefers experiences unmarked by puffery and waste. Err on the side of being understated.

Luxury-seeking customers are enamored by extremes; they are as stirred by the simple silk mat on the floor by the bed as by the magnificent painting in the hotel lobby. The more their senses are stirred, the more the experience is memorable.

Luxury-seeking customers value privacy, yet enjoy an inclusive connection and a special bond with those who serve them on a repeated basis. Connections yielding adventure and relationships founded on confidence are more apt to encourage their emotional participation in a luxurious experience.

Despite the continuing quest to "make mine unique," there are protocols that, if honored, help assure the experience is perceived as special by the discerning patron. These givens must be implemented against the characteristics of today's luxury-seeking customer.

THE PROTOCOLS OF LUXURY SERVICE

What are the features that customers label "a luxurious experience"? Luxury service is not just the purview of an affluent customer, although that is most typically the target market. Granted the affluent customer is often able to recognize the subtle features of luxurious quality—the gilding on a chair, the thread count of the sheets, the effortless style of the club pro. But even the blue-collar worker with an affinity for expensive cigars or enjoying that long-saved-for special occasion evening at a swanky hotel senses luxury when he feels it, even if he can't detail exactly why.

The ability to recognize the take-their-breath-away service strategy we call luxury is not just an accident of good breeding, prep school training, or globe trotting. Walk into the lobby of the Raffles Hotel in Singapore or board the Eastern & Oriental Express train in Kuala Lumpur bound for Bangkok, and you instantly know the milieu has been carefully crafted and managed from the playbook of a palace butler.

This does not mean you will experience the familiar banter or predictable script governing most service experiences in the disciplined, branded world of commerce. In fact, what makes luxury luxury is that it is unique, not uniform. Affluent customers do not want the Windsor Court Hotel in New Orleans to be like the Hotel Cipriani in Venice, even though both are owned by the same company.

"Luxury customers," says James Brown, president and CEO of Brownstone Hotels & Resorts, "seek stimulation, not standardization. And, because they have likely 'been there, done that,' they are drawn to the potential of inventive encounters and unexpected episodes." "My hotel" in the most possessive sense of the phrase is preferred by luxury customers to a brand flag, corporate colors, or a recognizable trade name that marks predictability. Luxury customers avoid cookie-cutter experiences and will not be shoehorned into a situation like an economy tour group.

LUXURY SERVICE IS AUTHENTIC AND SYMMETRICAL

There is nothing artificial about luxury service. It must be seen and experienced as authentic and natural. In fact, luxury service or surroundings almost always have some clear link to nature: water, light, plants. This alignment with nature creates a grounded feeling that luxury-seeking customers find wholesome and comfortable.

One product of this alignment is the natural symmetry of luxury service. The chairs in a Bentley automobile dealership are fashioned from the same leather as the seats in the vehicle on display; the table on which papers are signed at purchase is constructed of the same burr walnut found in the automobile. "Our clients value a harmonious experience," says Kirk Frederick, general manager of Bentley Dallas. "We are constantly looking for subtle ways to give our clients congruence between the appointments on our motorcars with the aspects of their showroom experience."

LUXURY SERVICE IS MAGICAL AND SUBTLE

The brass railing at the Desert Falls Country Club in Palm Desert, California, is polished in the middle of the night so guests never see it being cleaned. The five-star Las Brisas Hotel at the edge of Acapulco, Mexico, has the grass cut after hours with non-motorized push mowers and manual clippers so guests never hear the unpleasant sounds of maintenance underway. As we mentioned in the chapter on Reinvention, some very upscale hotels even have a motion detector inside the guest rooms and a watchful staff so guest rooms can be unobtrusively cleaned when guests are out. A version of this concept was practiced over a century ago when housekeepers leaned a straw from their broom against the bottom of the outside of the guest's room door.

Straw Against the Guest's Door[5]

A part of the magic of luxury service is that it always strives to happen at the right time. It is never late or early. And, it is in sync with other time-bound events that surround the experience. Wait time is carefully managed to ensure customers do not experience it as a delay. Nikolai's Roof, a five-star restaurant in Atlanta, presents guests with the chef's special appetizer and later a taste of the chef's preferred vodka, both complimentary diversions to help patrons remain enchanted as their meal is prepared.

LUXURY SERVICE EDUCATES TO INVITE EXPERIMENTATION

Luxury service-seeking customers are not daredevils. While they are passionate pursuers of novel thrills, their propensity for risk taking is born of education. They are willing to trust the service provider to guide them through a new experience if they know there has been close attention to crafting a quality outcome and a constant focus on safety. Special knowledge opens up previously unknown vistas and opportunities.

"Our guests like to be in the know," says Michael Tompkins, associate managing director of the world-famous Canyon Ranch Health Resort in the Berkshire Mountains of Massachusetts. "That 'being in the know' encourages them to try an experience they would not try without tutoring. For example, when we educate guests on the use and power of acupuncture while reassuring them with our focus on quality and safety, they try it and love it. It's not about attaining 'first on the block' bragging rights; it is about a new experience that exalts their life."

LUXURY SERVICE ELEVATES AND ENRICHES

Luxury service awakens the spirit in the customer and elevates ideal virtues. It typically causes customers to feel they had an experience that was better than the context required—sometimes even better than they thought they deserved. When GM Rick Jelinski of Cruisers Yachts tells his dealers, "Our customers are the best in the world," he is appealing to this "pursuit of elevation." As we write this, Cruisers Yachts has won the National Marine Manufacturers' Association's CSI award several years in a row. Why? In the words of Customer Relations Manager Joy Todd, "Because we live class, we don't just manufacture class."

Luxury-service providers enrich by adorning the mundane. An example is the hotel that installed brass fire sprinklers when plain-vanilla metal ones would have sufficed. Or the financial consultant who sends papers by courier when regular mail would be adequate. Or Sewell Village Cadillac, whose service bay floors are invariably clean enough for a healthy picnic.

LUXURY SERVICE IS A UNIQUE SENSORY EXPERIENCE

Luxury service often involves the rare, unusual, forbidden, or difficult-to-get. However, the use of those elements is in sync with the overall experience. Take the five-star Rosewood Mansion on Turtle Creek in Dallas. The flowers throughout the hotel don't all look like they came from the local nursery; some look like they came from the jungle. A fruit plate at the Hotel Bel-Air in Los Angeles might contain passion fruit, heirloom figs, or slices of kumquat. The Hyatt at Gainey Ranch in Scottsdale blends the aroma of mesquite wood burning in the giant fireplace with romantic candle lighting and the sounds of a guitar-piano-steel drum ensemble quietly playing near the lobby sitting area to craft an atmosphere as mystical as the Native American artifacts that adorn the walls.

The Spa at Cap Juluca Resort in Anguilla, BWI not only puts fragrant plant material (like bougainvillea petals) in the bath before a massage, they blend the same scent into the oil used by the masseuse and put a sprig in the bottom of the guest's locker so the special fragrance is "worn" by the guest after they leave the spa. Carl Sewell of Sewell Village Cadillac spent more than $250 a roll for bathroom wallpaper at his automobile dealerships. Customers in his service waiting area enjoy freshly brewed designer coffee, delicious pastries, and classical music.

LUXURY SERVICE IS THE PINNACLE OF COMFORT

Luxury service provides psychological comfort by being reliable and trustworthy. Luxury service also provides physical comfort. Few organizations weave comfort into the service tapestry like Steinway & Sons. Their piano showrooms match their history—floors of marble, chandeliers of crystal, chairs of teak. Salespeople are impeccably dressed and chosen for their musical knowledge and understated manner. On the showroom walls are photos of the great pianists who made a living at the keys of a Steinway. In Steinway Hall in Dallas, visitors report encountering the likes of Van Cliburn practicing pieces on different Steinway models.

"Purchasing a piano over $50,000 can seem daunting to even our wealthy customers," says Steinway Hall Retail Sales Manager

Steve Tunnell. "We help our customers discover they are purchasing not only a piece of beautiful furniture, but also they are investing in an important musical heirloom. We try to make their experience with us comfortable by anticipating their needs and responding to their unspoken wishes. It means you have to be part musician and part psychologist."

ELEGANCE WITH ALL THE ARROGANCE REMOVED

A new member of the Pyramid Club in Philadelphia and her guest were stuck in traffic for two hours trying to get to the club's Friends of the Vine wine-tasting event. By the time they arrived, the wine event was just about over. However, Rashida Ali-Campbell, evening bartender, suggested they stay around for a bit. She reenacted the entire wine tasting/presentation just for them!

Luxury service begins and ends with the guardian of the experience, the server or service provider who demonstrates enormous pride in their workmanship. Their personal gratification comes from delivering an excellent performance or crafting a superior product. However, the server also must exhibit great respect for the customer (the recipient of the experience, performance, or product). That respect is manifested as a kind of invitation to the experience. It is as if the server were saying, "Come witness and experience my excellent work, crafted just for you."

Luxury service is born of ingenuity. Think of ingenuity as the blue-collar cousin of creativity. Ingenuity is inventive problem solving, not just blue-sky dreaming. It is more than breakthrough innovation; it is made-it-work resourcefulness. It happens when leaders and employees communicate goals as problems to be solved, not just hills to climb. Ingenuity is cultivated when everyone is invited to think like owners. It is nurtured in a context of partnership, where communication is candid and information is shared. It thrives in a world where original is valued more than orthodox and unique more than uniform.

Luxury service is fundamentally the product of employees with a passion for customers multiplied by a willingness to be inventive. Where there is the zeal and courage to serve, luxury service will emerge; where there is supportive leadership, luxury service will endure.

CHAPTER 9
Air

"Change is good, but you don't want to lose what you really are."

—Jim Koch, founder, Boston Beer

Customer satisfaction has been the hallmark of customer evaluations. However, if you look up the definition of "satisfactory," it says "good enough to fulfill a need or requirement." The verb "to satisfy" comes from the Latin word *satisfacere*, which means "to do enough." It also means adequate or sufficient. Because we live in an era of too many choices, data overload, and sensory excess, our taste for sufficient is, well, insufficient.

Customers want sparkly and glittery, a cherry on top of everything. We want all our senses stimulated, not just those linked to the buyer-seller exchange. Features have become far more titillating than function; the extras are more valued than the core offering. The way-too-simple secret seems to be this: Provide a consistently superior product (or outcome) with a consistently excellent service experience and customers will reward you with their loyalty. Yet this elementary solution to the customer loyalty puzzle is much more difficult for some than others.

A few years ago the *New Yorker* ran a cartoon showing a discussion between a salesman and his sales manager. The despondent salesman asks, "I know you're always telling us to sell the sizzle and not the steak, Mr. Bollinger, but just what *is* the sizzle of a 90° elbow flexible-copper fitting?"[1] The question touches the core of the issue. What are the options if creating a unique devotion-producing experience is way too far a reach?

Starbucks, Ritz-Carlton Hotels, Lexus, and Walt Disney World have infatuated the marketplace as great exemplars of customer service. Clearly there are principles such organizations have mastered that are relevant for all enterprises. But, just like our plumbing supply salesman, not every industry is as glamorous as a gourmet coffeehouse, luxury hotel, expensive car, or theme park. Even leaders armed with a zeal for the remarkable can find it a daunting challenge to change the product or experience into one that engenders customer devotion.

Consider this. If you were in charge of the Department of Motor Vehicles, how would you make the DMV more like a Starbucks and still stay within the state-mandated cost controls? And, what about your insurance company? Aside from the relationship with your agent, how would you suggest they reinvent the insurance process to be more like Walt Disney World? What would you do to make your local bank more like a Ritz-Carlton hotel and still stay within the razor-thin profit margins that now characterize the financial services industry? As one senior executive told us, "No matter how customer-friendly our employees are, our processes are still customer-hostile, and many are decreed by our regulators." Another exec put it this way: "The way we deliver service to customers might be possible to fix, but it is impossible to fund."

THE MANAGEMENT OF SERVICE AIR

Frederick Herzberg's legendary research into worker motivation found that the opposite end of those factors that produced worker dissatisfaction did not result in worker motivation.[2] Take away worker pay or provide poor working conditions, for example, and workers will become dissatisfied. But, increasing worker pay or improving working conditions only leads to worker satisfaction, not worker motivation. Factors that created motivation were completely different from those that yielded satisfaction. Workers were motivated by factors like recognition, advancement, and the work itself. The Herzberg concept is similarly true for customer motivation. Those factors that lead to customer dissatisfaction are not the other end of the continuum of factors that lead to customer devotion. They are on a different continuum.

🐜 The Ant

Ants live and work with other ants in a colony. In this living arrangement they have developed a clear division of labor, where different ants are tasked with doing different jobs. There are home builder ants, food collector ants, home maintenance ants, reproducer ants, even leaf cutter ants. By sticking to the basics they are able to thrive almost anywhere in the world and have for over 100 million years.

Think about it this way: A value proposition is the complete package of offerings a seller proposes to a customer in exchange for the buyer's investment of funds, time, or effort. It includes the product (or outcome for non-object-selling companies), the price, and the process (or experience) involved in getting the product or outcome. There are certain qualities or features all buyers assume will typify that value proposition. For instance, buyers assume the products or outcomes they buy will be as the seller promised, the price fair, and the process relatively comfortable.

These givens are a lot like the air we breathe. We tend to take air for granted unless it is removed from our surroundings, leaving us dissatisfied. But adding more air to our environment does not necessarily make us happy campers. If the commercial plane we board lands in the right city, we do not cheer, but, if it lands in the wrong city, we are very upset. We assume banks will be safe, hotels comfortable, hospitals clean. These taken-for-granted attributes are what we call service *air*; they are noticed only when they are absent (or perceived to be at risk of being absent). Capitalizing on service air might provide a competitive strategy for units or organizations that seek customer devotion but are severely challenged by the stretch. Ensuring that service air attributes are in place is a prerequisite for any organization wishing to successfully pursue a service strategy that goes beyond the basics.

AIR-PLAIN

Majoring in the minors is rarely a compelling competitive strategy. Most leaders long to make their units or organizations distinctive. Marketing experts would scold us if we opted for a me-too approach. However, providing a unique, valuable benefit only has traction if all the givens the customer expects are done correctly. The afterglow of an incredibly friendly flight attendant will be completely erased from the customer's adoration memory bank should the flight land three hours late. The recollection of an exquisite gourmet meal will be totally overwritten by the nightmare of food poisoning because the restaurant failed to pay attention to routine health standards. Service air may be boring stuff, but it is called *air* for a reason!

Let's assume your bank is not a particularly central part of your personal life. You have an auto loan, a checking account, a safe deposit box, a small savings account you keep for overdraft protection, and an ATM card. You do your banking largely online, visiting the local branch only for an uncommon need like getting a cashier's check or having a document notarized. Now, what if bank employees were accessible, friendly, and consistently seemed to know what they were doing? And, what if your statements were always accurate and there was rarely a wait in the teller line? Nothing remarkable, nothing unique—just all the basics done very well. What would it take for another bank to get you to pull up stakes and abandon First Vanilla Bank?

Consistently doing the fundamentals exceedingly well can be a potent competitive take-their-breath-away strategy. This is usually true when the unit or organization is a part of an industry fraught with hiccups, broken promises, and a less-than-glowing reputation. Granted a plain-Jane strategy would flop in some market niches or industries. Imagine paying nosebleed prices for a room at a hotel that always provided soap and shampoo, a well-lighted parking lot, a quiet setting, and beds that were made daily with fresh sheets. However, that unadorned but distinctive strategy at the appropriate price point has worked well for Motel 6, AirTran Airways, and Krystal restaurants.

What makes the *air-plain* approach work? It works if your unit or organization takes care of the basics perfectly *and* ensures customers remain keenly aware of that fact. It works as long as the organization is in a sub-par niche with no other enterprise that's getting its air perfect, *and* it really works when the organization adds a little something unique. Unique trumps air, but only if air is done exactly as customers expect. An air-plain strategy requires crystal-clear standards and easy-to-understand metrics. It must include a means to monitor key incidents linked to the perfect execution of core requirements. It means having an early-warning process to signal when any aspect of service air is endangered. And it takes a culture that values continuous improvement and rewards honest assessment of how well the basics are being performed. Finally, it requires the kind of customer intelligence that alerts the unit or organization should the customer's definition of what is service air ever change.

Air Apparent

"At Third National Savings Bank you can always count on hassle-free banking." At first blush, this advertising tagline seems completely absurd. How could *not* beating you up have any competitive advantage? It would be as zany as saying, "Our dry cleaners promises to get your clothes clean," or "Buster's Butcher Shop: Where you can always find meat." Yet there may be a bright side to this seemingly counterintuitive tactic.

The competitive logic of making a core component of the value proposition more apparent is a strategy that's only relevant in a broken market segment. If, for instance, banks in general fill the banking experience with aggravations, then promising to *not* do that could be perceived as an asset. Southwest Airlines effectively reminds customers of their on-time record because most major airlines frequently arrive late. Do consumers believe airlines should always be on time? Of course. And, airlines in general are on time enough for customers to not ditch that service attribute as a part of their core requirements; therefore, it's still in the realm of service air.

Air apparent means singling out a service air feature at which the organization believes it can excel and then reminding the customer of that fact. It is the dry cleaners that brags, "Your shirt buttons are always safe with us," or the movie theater that boasts, "We get a lot of complaints about the smell of our fresh popcorn—from the store next door!" It is the residential real estate firm that proclaims, "We want ugly houses!" or the auto repair shop that promises, "Your engine knocks stop at our front door." T-Mobile made their billing process (with a focus on accuracy, clarity, and timely resolution of problems) the very finest in their industry. Publix Super Markets did the same thing with the speed of their checkout process.

Underscoring the merit of a particular service feature is effective only when it is consistently true. Accentuating service quality in word and not matching it in deed is as risky as the voice mail that tells customers, "Your call is very important to us" and is followed by a 30-minute hold. The air apparent tactic succeeds as long as employees have faith in it. Hollow promises are quickly spotted by employees who then alert customers of the falsehood.

It can sound like this: "This car rental company wants you to believe that buying a full tank of gas up front is a good deal, but trust me, most customers lose money on it."

Like air-plain, air apparent can be a short-lived route to customer devotion. It is vital to remain vigilant for copycats. If a me-too competitor can one-up your air apparent, you will soon be scrambling to find a new way to differentiate your offering. A well-known retail discount chain banked heavily on a lowest-price strategy as one way to dominate their target market. Service workers were simply stationed at the cash registers and their interactions with shoppers were too often robotic ("Thank you for shopping at Kmart...next"); products were not known for their great quality. Their Blue Light Specials worked for a while. But then along came Wal-Mart, offering the similar products and prices but with folksy service delivered with a smile. Soon Kmart was in bankruptcy and Wal-Mart was spreading like wildfire. There is obviously more to the Kmart versus Wal-Mart competition than a myopic strategy. Kmart emerged from bankruptcy in 2003, and in 2005 merged with Sears. But, it is hard to deny that Kmart's shortfall came when they put too many of their strategy eggs in the low-price basket.

AIR SHOW

Once in a while an organization can take a service air factor to a high or unexpected level, turning a customer core requirement into a delight factor. The Columbia Tower Club in downtown Seattle is an illustration of what our friend Doug Johnson at General Growth Properties calls "air show." Five of the stalls in the ladies restroom were designed so the commodes face toward the outside of the building, and the exterior wall they look out on is wall-to-wall, floor-to-ceiling window. Since the Club is the top floor of a high-rise building, a visitor sitting on one of these toilets can enjoy a panoramic view of downtown Seattle! Patrons of the club would naturally assume the women's restroom would be spotless, comfortable, and well-appointed. They would not expect the club to sport johns with a view!

Columbia Club Bathroom[3]

Taking a core service component and showing it off can be a powerful strategy that can make competitors seem out of touch by comparison. When Domino's Pizza hit the marketplace with their promise of pizza delivery in 30 minutes or the pizza was free, they quickly owned the pizza delivery market. The truth was that before there was Domino's, the average time to deliver a pizza was about 30 minutes. So the guarantee was a fairly safe bet. If you asked pizza delivery customers if they expected their pizza to be delivered in 30 minutes or less, they would say "yes." Attaching a guarantee not only made the feature apparent, it showed off the feature to the point other pizza delivery companies were soon scrambling to match the Domino's offering.

Federal Express (now FedEx) promised overnight package delivery to be "absolutely, positively there by 10:30 AM." Again, they took a service air attribute and put such a spotlight on it that competitors soon had to match it. Today, which major airline does *not* have a frequent flyer program? Which coffee house does *not* provide a sleeve for handling hot to-go cups? Which auto repair shop does *not* provide a loaner to frequent customers? Which rental car establishment does *not* have a plan that allows frequent users to bypass the counter and go straight to the vehicle? All these features were at one point someone's air show.

The power of the air show strategy is its capacity to enable an organization to leapfrog competitors and gain competitive advantage very quickly. What makes it work? It must be bold enough to create a marketplace buzz. It must be complex enough to preclude competitors from being able to quickly copy it. It must be a feature that either meets a pent-up customer need ("Well, it's about time!") or one that customers never knew they needed but once offered could not do without. Customers were not pining for fax machines. However, once introduced, customers quickly embraced the new technology.

However, as a strategy, air show can be short lived as competitors ultimately catch on and catch up. Blockbuster has added movies-by-mail, a space NetFlix formerly owned. Consider the intense fight for market share between FedEx and UPS or between Walt Disney World and Universal Orlando. And, who would have ever thought Best Buy would be compared with Nordstrom for making customer care a special feature of their value proposition?

"Stick to the knitting" was one of eight tenets of success that Tom Peters and Bob Waterman discovered in the best-run companies in America and detailed in their runaway bestseller *In Search of Excellence*.[4] It continues to be solid advice. At its nucleus is a view that unwavering attention to an organization's core offering will pay rich dividends from customers perpetually disappointed by "they can't even get the basics right."

Air-plain, air apparent, and air show are solid tactics of an air strategy. The compelling case for an air strategy done properly is the paucity of strategies available to keep an organization successful for a long time. The likes of Sears, Holiday Inn, and Ace Hardware have long weathered onslaughts from competitors offering flashier features and more exciting experiences. Still, it goes without saying that any strategy is effective only as long as it differentiates, elevates, and distinguishes.

CHAPTER 10
Air Defense

"Responsibilities are given to him on whom trust rests.
Responsibility is always a sign of trust."
   —*James Cash Penney, American businessman*

It was her first flight. Her parents had finally settled a bitter divorce
resulting in her dad moving three states away. The 10-year-old was
nervous about pretty much everything. As soon as she was settled in her seat after being handed off to a flight attendant, the
pilot announced there would be a brief delay due to a mechanical problem. She heard a dog whimpering from the storage bay
in the belly of the plane below her. There was an empty water
bottle under the seat in front of her, obviously missed by the
maintenance clean-up following the previous flight.

After a 30-minute delay, the plane was finally in the air. Her
view of the ground disappeared as the plane moved into the thick
clouds. The plane began to bounce and fall as it encountered
predictable air turbulence. She began to cry and pray.

"God is in the details," said renowned architect Mies van der
Rohe. The essence of his adage has always been a fundamental
of great customer service. Customers use detail management as
an indicator of a service provider's commitment to delivering a
positive service experience. But there is a more profound element of detail management that service providers often miss or
misunderstand.

Service is an implied covenant between a service provider and a customer. The covenant is simply this: A service provider promises to deliver an outcome at a fair price with a satisfactory experience in exchange for some investment of time, effort, and money paid by the customer. Satisfaction to both provider and receiver hangs on whether each party keeps their promise in the manner expected by the other.

Customers judge whether the promise has been kept through concrete, irrefutable *outcomes*. The fact that a hotel guest with a guaranteed reservation is being walked to another property because the hotel overbooked is undeniable by both the guest and the front desk clerk. Passengers and pilots alike know if the flight they share landed two hours late.

Customers also judge whether the promise has been kept through their *perception* of the experience. Perceptions regarding promises kept are almost always the source of hurt feelings in relationships, including the one between service provider and customer. While server and customer might agree that a certain outcome occurred, assessment of the experience is in the eye of the beholder. Effective service recovery from a broken promise is typically less about correcting an obvious breach in the outcome promised and more about soothing the bad feelings of the customer triggered by perceived shortcomings in the experience.

There is more to the perceptual side of the covenant than might be initially apparent. It is easy to think of outcome and experience as two halves of a whole. But they are often linked together in much deeper fashion. The customer's perceptions about a bus driver with obvious alcohol breath are not just about the driver's personal habits. A nurse with dirty hands shows more to a patient than simply shoddy hygiene. As customers, our perceptions can take us way past what we observe to what we conclude. And, when those conclusions leave us anxious about the outcome, then the message to a service provider is irrefutable: be a constant guardian of the details that feed a customer's perceptions.

PROTECTING SERVICE AIR

Air is necessary to survival; it is also a feature in our lives we take for granted until it is either removed or threatened. In much the same way, the outcome side of the service covenant is the taken-for-granted part of the equation—as you learned in the last chapter, we call it *service air*.

Service air is important to protect because it is the very core of the covenant made by the service provider. Too many organizations, enwrapped in the euphoria of creating customer delight through sparkly experiences, sometimes forget to take care of the basics—in other words, service air. Service air may be plain vanilla, but it is as vital to service as the gas that fills our lungs.

Look back at the opening story. There was nothing unique or abnormal about the flight taken by the 10-year old. Delays due to mechanical problems are quiet common. Clean-up crews sometimes miss trash as they hurriedly clean the plane between flights. Pets in the storage area often register their displeasure loud enough for passengers to hear. Air turbulence is typical at the point the plane enters the clouds. But all these details, examined through the eyes of an already anxious passenger, stand out like a beacon and have a completely different meaning than routine and normal.

The Turtle

Turtles seem to have a character of dedication with a reliable gait that convinces they will always get where they are going. The most striking feature of a turtle is its shell (carapace), which is made up of 50 different bones all connected together. The bony portion of the shell is covered with plates that are derivatives of skin and offer additional strength and protection.

Protecting service air requires revisiting the covenant on a regular basis. All covenants depend on clear expectations understood and agreed upon by both parties. When a flight attendant goes through the FAA safety drill before talking about the meal or the movie, it reaffirms the promise of a safe flight. When a restaurant posts the letter given by the health department or a physician hangs license and degrees in the waiting area or exam rooms, it is a subtle but important reiteration of their promise to the customer.

Smart organizations perpetually pursue feedback from customers regarding their expectations. They recognize that expectations constantly change and must be updated. When the FedEx delivery person walks with a sense of urgency, customers expect the mail carrier to do likewise. When a top-notch insurance company answers customers' phone calls on the first ring, those customers expect the power company to do the same.

Consider the following half-dozen service experiences and how customer expectations have changed in the last 10 years:

- The entire car-buying experience

- Getting a boarding pass to board a plane

- Waiting (with an appointment) to see a physician

- Product knowledge of a sales clerk when buying a TV

- The quality of care given clothes taken to a dry cleaner

- Withdrawing funds from a bank checking account

Covenants updated by changing customer requirements have been counterbalanced by changes in expectations on the service provider side. There was a time when banks, faced with a customer's overdrawn check, took the time to call the customer, waited for a deposit to match the check, and did not charge an overdraft fee. Fast forward to today. With razor thin margins, most banks bounce and fine most customers who write hot checks.

There was a time when airlines delayed their departure when a gate attendant announced there was a late passenger running through the terminal to make the flight. Today, due to the cost of flight delays and its domino effect on crowded schedules, no pleas from passengers screaming "I'm coming!" will delay the airplane door from being closed for an on-time departure. Smart companies give customers lots of warning and lead time before imposing changes like these to the covenant.

ASSESSING AIR DEFENSE

Air defense operates in the realm of customer perception. The tricky part about air defense is how it is interlocked with service air. When passengers lower a serving tray on an airline and notice coffee stains, their negative reaction might not be about a sloppy cabin maintenance crew. It could trigger an intuitive leap to the condition of the plane's engine and a fearful concern that the plane might crash. Passengers will not likely separate cabin maintenance from engine maintenance, leaving the entire perception of the flight painted with the sloppy brush. Just like the 10-year old did in the opening story.

Assurance is the word that service researcher Leonard Berry of Texas A&M has wrapped around many of the key factors of air defense. Assurance was one of the five factors his team's research found accounted for 85 percent of customers' satisfaction with the service they received.[1] The concept of assurance envelops all those things in the covenant that produce and reduce customer confidence. The warm and friendly nurse about to draw blood might provoke extra uneasiness if the patient spots the nurse's nervous hands. Accuracy in a customer's bank statement might say to customers less about carelessness and more about the potential for identity theft.

Why do we put bent cans of vegetables back on the grocery store shelf? Why do inexperienced flyers take out flight insurance before boarding the plane? Why do we FedEx or UPS a large check when speed of arrival is not a requirement? An important part of understanding air defense is that it involves perceptual features that, if missing, mangled, or in jeopardy, trigger alarm, not anger. The opposite of confidence is fear, not fury. Research shows that experiences characterized as frightful are remembered long after irritating moments are forgotten.[2]

Air defense is not always about our anxiety over service air but rather our anxiety over the impact of the service or product failure. We expect our dry cleaners to properly clean our clothes. And, while we may get angry over an occasional cracked button or poorly creased pants, there is little about those service encounters that would provoke anxiety. However, there are some types of failures that can indeed leave customers nervous. Consider these two vignettes:

> *His son's wedding is on Sunday morning. He goes to the dry cleaning pickup station to get his tuxedo that was promised by Saturday. He learns that the tux is not back from the site that does the actual cleaning, and that site is only open Monday through Friday.*
>
> *She has an important interview and needs her hair done right before the interview. When she goes to her hairdresser for a long-standing appointment she is told that the person who has done her hair for 10 years is unexpectedly out sick. The only consolation they can offer sounds like this: "But our new girl is open and will be glad to style your hair."*

No assurance there. Just two customers who are not only unhappy but distressed and agitated. The point is that there are service failures that cause disappointment and there are other service failures that yield stark terror. The service provider often misses the gravity of a service breakdown for the customer because the missed detail or minor hiccup is read by the customer as a much graver issue than the service provider assumes.

MANAGING AIR DEFENSE

How do service providers interpret customer complaints about minutiae? When is customer fault-finding just plain nitpicking and when is it born of anxiety about whether service air is threatened? If air defense comes largely from factors that customers sense and infer, how can organizations get their customers to teach them about the link between assessment and anxiety? The search begins with an eye and ear for detail.

ANXIETY MONITOR

We were doing a focus group interview with a group of employees of a large Midwestern hospital. All had frontline roles providing service to patients. We were running through our battery of customer intelligence questions when the discussion turned to patient anxiety. There were several comments about the fact that patients are not always candid with their caregiver if they are uneasy about their welfare.

"We were swamped one day," said one nurse, "and it took me longer than normal to respond to a maternity ward patient's call button. Since she had been only two centimeters dilated ten minutes earlier, I was confident her call was not an emergency. By the time I got to her room, she was hysterical. She finally calmed down enough to tell me she could not locate her lunch menu. I thought it odd that something so small would make her so upset. But, as I was leaving her room, she asked me, "How soon will you come if my new baby is in serious trouble?' I got a new appreciation for the symbolism behind the call button."

FEAR SCREEN

One learns early in Psychology 101 that anger is sometimes a mask for fear. Customers bold enough to "give them a piece of my mind" might be reluctant to admit they were actually more scared than livid. Looking through the lens of fear at a customer's angry letter or hostile comments on a survey might reveal insights into the subtle features of air defense.

We were assisting a large construction company with customer forensics on an important customer who had yanked his business from the company in anger and frustration. One of the goals of the customer forensics effort was to equip our construction company client with tools for future customer intelligence efforts. While sifting through correspondence between the departed customer and the construction company, their marketing director suddenly commented, "We have given this poor customer plenty of reasons to keep him up at night."

The comment triggered a renewed look at the data—not as evidence of anger, but as examples of fear. The fresh interpretation triggered a deeper, richer understanding of those factors that signaled to the customer that his construction project was in jeopardy. Without the project, his business was at a high risk of bankruptcy. Without his business, his upwardly mobile wife would likely leave him. With a history of heart problems, his life could be threatened by such a chain reaction. Thus, his outbursts of anger were actually a cover for his fear-laden cries for help—all misinterpreted by the construction company as simply the grumblings of a high-maintenance customer.

CUSTOMER SOUNDING BOARD

Any kid who ever owned a dog or cat no doubt used the pet as a sounding board. Timid or shy at school, one could be courageously outspoken and heroic with Rover or Boots. Customers often have someone who will turn a willing and patient ear to their grievances and concerns. For the organization looking to manage air defense, candid conversations with the customer's confidants can often yield a solid understanding of how the customer truly feels about their service experience.

When John Longstreet (now with Dallas-based ClubCorp) was the general manager of the Harvey Hotel in Plano, Texas, he realized the taxi drivers who transported guests to DFW airport after their stay were an informational goldmine. John reasoned that Harvey guests would more likely volunteer their impressions and be candid with the taxi driver than to answer the smiling desk clerk's "How was your stay?" question. He set up periodic focus group meetings with the drivers. Their conversations not only revealed ways to improve service but pointed out subtle aspects of the guest experience rarely found on a comment card.

Taxi drivers taught Longstreet that missing toiletries in the bathroom caused guests to worry about how accurate room service would be, the smell of slightly scorched towels from overheated dryers could trigger concerns about a potential hotel fire, and a poorly lighted parking lot potentially brought worries about safety in hotel hallways. In the customer's mind, room service hours were linked to hours of security guard coverage; dust balls under the bed could conjure up images of unwelcome bugs in the room. These minors were actually warning signals that spotlighted potential majors in jeopardy.

COMPLAINT FORENSICS

Conventional service wisdom is to examine complaints to spot patterns and trends. Many organizations do complaint-frequency counts to ascertain the most prevalent issues that leave customers disappointed. Some use customer focus groups to help gain a deeper understanding of high-priority customer complaints. Complaint forensics involves looking at complaints with the assumption they are simply a symptom camouflaging the real customer concern. Like the TV character Columbo, key complaints are examined with the healthy skepticism that what is being reported is not the real story and that a more methodical investigation will yield a more complete understanding.

A large event services provider learned that their customers' biggest complaint was a lack of timely arrival in the exhibit booth of shipped exhibit supplies. They did complaint forensics to learn more about the issue. The event services provider was responsible for getting an organization's signs, displays, props, and so forth to the right booth so the exhibitor could get set up before the show or convention. Any delays raised anxiety the exhibitor would be late getting the booth ready and thus poorly represented as conventioneers went through the exhibit hall. A delay also meant there would not be enough time to properly display whatever booth merchandise was to be sold. But the real concern was often more about how an unprepared exhibitor might appear compared to a competitor already set up in a nearby booth. Once the full emotional impact on the exhibitor was understood by the event services provider, the more ammunition they had to effectively attack the problems causing delays.

The customer's propensity to connect rational facts with irrational assumptions is the substance and challenge of service air and air defense. It led bestselling author Tom Peters to conclude that "customers perceive service in their own idiosyncratic, emotional, irrational, end-of-the-day and totally human terms. Perception is all there is."[3] Service wisdom lies in appreciating its complexity, understanding its impact, and shepherding the details that trigger angst in customers.

Smart organizations major in the majors when it comes to ensuring customers reliably get exactly what they expect from the organization. But they also major in the minors—taking the initiative to care for and protect subtle but vital service hygiene.

CHAPTER 11
Scout's Honor

"The customer trust gap is the emotional space between hope and evidence; between expectation and fulfillment."

—John R. Patterson

"I'll be back to get you when school is out," a parent promises as her youngster exits the car with book bag in tow. So begins an all-important trust gap—the space between a promise made in the morning and the promise kept (or broken) in the afternoon. The level of anxiety the child experiences during the day depends on whether past experiences are more "Mom always comes" or "Sorry I'm late again; traffic was terrible."

We all live our lives on promises. From the time a child can grasp the concept of "cross my heart and hope to die," there is a forever realization that anxiety can be reduced only through proof of trust while waiting for a promise to be kept. From "scout's honor" to "I do" to "the whole truth and nothing but the truth," we seek cues that allay our worries. Lifeguards, the bus schedule, and the spotlessness of a hospital room are all obvious artifacts of promises waiting to be kept.

Scout's honor is a take-their-breath-away service strategy crafted around various forms of promises waiting to be kept. We recollect the evident power of a scout's honor strategy when we see brand names that have attached guarantees to their offerings—FedEx, Domino's Pizza, Hampton Inn, Nordstrom, and

L.L. Bean. And we sense its subtle power when the hotel finds our reservation, the newspaper is on the front porch, and the bank statement is completely accurate. Making trust the centerpiece of imaginative service can catapult a service provider, unit, or organization into a position of distinction in the eyes of the customer.

Scout's honor is all about paying attention to the customer trust gap, the emotional space between hope and evidence, between expectation and fulfillment. Scout's honor works because customers are exactly like that child waiting to be picked up at the end of the school day. Service begins with a promise made or implied: "I'll be here when school gets out," "We'll be landing on time," "It will be ready by noon," or "Your order will be right out." Granted, great service recovery can transform an aggrieved customer into a satisfied customer. But the residue of betrayal will leave a disappointed customer perpetually on guard for the time when letdown reoccurs.

Trust is the emotion that propels customers to the other side of the gap between expectation and experience. The manner in which a person, unit, or organization *manages* the trust gap drives every other component of the service encounter. The manner in which a person, unit, or organization *capitalizes* on the trust gap takes a service given to a service gift.

Understanding the Customer Trust Gap

The trust gap cannot be avoided when a promise to a customer is made or intimated; it can only be managed. Insecurity and doubt are not necessarily present in every customer's trust gap. But requiring customers to walk on the high wire of faith is clearly an inescapable component of every service encounter.

Dr. Leonard Berry, famed author and marketing professor at Texas A&M University, has done compelling research on service quality. His work repeatedly affirms this finding: Reliability is the most important factor customers use in gauging the quality of their service experiences.[1] David Aaker, renowned brand researcher and professor of marketing strategy at the University of California at Berkeley, confirms a similar research finding: Brands retain their influence power only as long as customers associate iron-clad trust with the brand.[2]

The Penguin

They mate for life. They live in colonies. Male and female take turns warming eggs. Chicks count on parents for food until they grow up. Females hunt for food while males keep the eggs warm. When females return they have food for the winter in their stomach.

As customers, our journey across the high wire of faith is a trip with or without anguish depending on how strong the net of trust the service provider has put there to support our passage. Customers' perception of that net of trust makes all the difference in how they grade their experiences. No net, no loyalty; shaky net, no loyalty. The critical concept is this: It is the *customer's* perception that tells the tale. No matter how much an organization believes they create and sustain a "you can trust us" approach, it is what customers believe that counts.

Smart organizations—those that retain the best customers the longest time—know that managing the trust gap can never be taken for granted. They know that customer trust must always be treated as a fragile bond, as if it can be shattered with a single malfunction, misunderstanding, or mishap. Examine how service superstar JetBlue Airways went from champ to chump with a single incident of extreme delay on the tarmac. Prudence suggests building up the customer's storehouse of trust through repeated reminders of promises kept.

Smart organizations also know that trust is an animated, always-in-motion dimension of all relationships. Here's why. As humans, our concept of value perpetually changes. Apples are less valuable after you have two dozen in the pantry than when you had none. Loud music is less valuable when you are past 50 than when you were 15. Making a difference gets more valuable with maturity; making the team, less valuable.

If trust is a covenant of value exchange and value is nomadic, it suggests the pursuit of trust building needs to include some mechanism for updating the proposition. Think about expectations. Every service experience we have alters our expectations for future service. Customers today want every service to be FedEx fast, Amazon.com easy, Disney friendly, and Southwest Airlines thrifty. Consequently, the object of any implied covenant, agreement, and pledge must be in perpetual motion.

Take-their-breath-away service providers know that treating trust as a moving target requires an active, ever-changing relationship with customers. If customer expectations are part of what trust is made of, and those expectations are in perpetual motion, service providers must find ways to stay current. They gather up-to-date customer intelligence from the scouts on the front line and turn what they learned into improvements. They use myriad ways to get customer feedback. They perpetually work to look at service through customers' eyes. This does not mean an organization must be completely accurate 100 percent of the time; customers know service providers are not able to read their minds. It does mean that the relationship with customers must have built-in ways for updating.

You may be thinking, "This sounds wonderful for small enterprises, but such customer faith wouldn't work with the financial challenges of our organization." However, L.L. Bean's success is tied to faith in customers, and they're far from small potatoes! And, when a customer has a problem with a computer purchased from Dell Computer, the company with $61 billion in revenue[3] sends the customer a replacement, a program to move files from the old to the new computer, and mailing labels to send back the defective computer. How many organizations would manage the return process the other way around—"Send us the computer and then . . ."? Winning organizations bet on the long-term relationship and demonstrate trust.

TAKING THE ANGST OUT OF CUSTOMER HOPES

If trust is the Big Kahuna of customer service, why do so many customer encounters end with dashed hopes? Why are we, as customers, so frequently let down by some aspect of our service experience? Part of the reason lies at the core of human relationships: To err is human. But the lion's share of fault comes from organizations taking for granted their responsibility to practice persistent trust building.

Recall the example of the child dropped off by the parent who promises to return at the end of the school day. The foundation of this particular encounter is the perception that mom (or dad) always comes. However, there are approved variations on this theme. One could be: "Susie, your mom is held up in traffic, and Ms. Jones, your neighbor next door, is going be there to get you after school." It could also be something like this: "Susie, your mom called the school. She is running about 10 minutes late, but she will be there to get you at the usual place."

Customers, like children, do not expect service providers (or parents) to be perfect. They do expect them to care enough to manage the trust gap so customers retain unwavering trust. Operating without paying attention to trust it is somewhat like asking customers to take a walk on the high wire without a net—or worse, asking customers to take the walk blindfolded and uncertain if there really is a net in place at all.

Examine the companies that make the "best in . . ." lists and you will see poured into their practices an unmistakable understanding of the importance of trust. Learning the anatomy of trust can yield ways to keep customers' anxiety out of their trips across the gap. If you put trust under a microscope or could dissect it in a lab, what would you find? Trust comes from five tactics key to all customer relationships or service encounters: caring actions, competence, core protection, constraint-free execution, and consistency.

CARING ACTIONS

Customers trust people and organizations that repeatedly and sincerely demonstrate they care. When Nordstrom joyfully allows customers to return merchandise that disappoints, it is proof Nordstrom cares more about the worth of the relationship than the economics of the transaction.

The grounds maintenance team at Crow Canyon Country Club in Danville, California, demonstrated over-the-top caring by creating a magic moment for a member's recent celebration. The member had booked the club ballroom for a bar mitzvah and realized two days prior that the colorful annuals planted at the entrance to the club had been removed due to aeration of the grounds. After the member panicked about not having flowers at the entryway, the very next morning the maintenance crew dug out the flowerbeds at the ninth tee and replanted them in front of the clubhouse.

Trust in all relationships begins with risk—the gamble that the experience will not fall short of expectation. Trust is gained through encounters that meet or exceed hopes. These two facts insinuate that the sooner customers get irrefutable evidence they made a good bet, the faster trust occurs. This is why successful automobile salespeople follow up immediately after the customer takes delivery on a new car. Follow-up is more than an antidote to buyer's remorse; it is an assertive reminder that a strong and caring trust net undergirds all future encounters. Placing guarantees in the brand promise plus customer-friendly return practices can accomplish a similar role.

Excuses like "I did my part," "It's still stuck in operations," or "The system is down" may assuage our guilt, but they only serve to remind the customer there is no net they can count on.

Such explanations are most often viewed by customers as excuses that really say, "We do not really care enough about you or your business to keep disappointments from happening." Customers expect backup arrangements to cover for people out and systems down. Customers assume their needs and expectations to be valued over employees blindly following bureaucratic procedures.

COMPETENCE

Competence communicates to customers they are in the hands of a professional. Customers need to know (or perceive) that service providers not only have the commitment to deliver great service, they possess the capacity to do so as well. The roofing contractor who shows up without a ladder does not engender trust. Home Depot's early claim to fame came through putting in their aisles employees from the trades. Instead of dealing with a clerk in the plumbing section, customers enjoyed the advice of a real plumber. Best Buy's Geek Squad and well-trained sales associates dramatically raise customers' evaluation of Best Buy because it signals they are dealing with experts, not order takers.

Walk into the lobby of a five-star hotel and watch a one-click-above-minimum-wage bellstaff associate make you feel like you just stepped into the arena of the hospitality Olympics. Compare the superior product knowledge of any Starbucks barista with the nearby fast-food restaurant employee who has been hired from the exact same labor pool. Scrutinize the service ways and means behind what you see in these settings and you learn those organizations spend many times more per employee on training than their competitors. And training is not relegated to sporadic offerings from a teaching staff at corporate; it is a part of the mentoring role of every leader.

CORE PROTECTION

In the last two chapters, we examined the power and promise of service Air and Air Defense. It cannot be overstated that trust comes when customers sense the unit or organization is taking care of the basics. Think of *air* as core protection, meaning the service provider is ever vigilant to maintain the core offering—what the customer came to the organization for in the first place. Taking care of air means a noticeable effort is expended on looking after the core components of what customers expect.

When the child expects to be picked up on time, showing up late at the end of the school day driving a flashy new car is not likely to erase the anxiety of an unanticipated wait. Southwest Airlines receives great marks for customer service, not because they do glitzy extras but because they do the airline basics very well—landing on time in the right city safely, with luggage in tow. They are the only major U.S. airline without an incident involving fatalities.

CONSTRAINT-FREE EXECUTION

Promise keeping requires an organization working without silos to ensure seamless operation, flawless handoffs, and constraint-free execution. Customers do not like being passed from Patty to Paul to pillar to post. They want to believe the organization is designed and managed around their needs, especially since they are the ones generating the funds needed for the company to survive. USAA Insurance is one of the service super stars because of seamless execution. They achieve extraordinary results by, in the words of one of their senior leaders, "having the customer standing right in the middle of our service team. There are no handoffs, no transfers; it is literally one-stop service."

Let's say you wrote USAA a letter about a claim. A few days later you called to follow up. Mary answers your call. You say, "Mary, I wrote USAA a few days ago about a claim." And, Mary stuns you by saying, "Yes, I am looking at your letter right now. You were inquiring about. . . ." USAA scans every piece of correspondence—thousands every day—to make them available in an instant to every single one of its customer service agents.

Interview USAA customers and the most frequent word you'll hear is "trust." The accolades are born from USAA's making it super easy to get service and by having which server you get be completely irrelevant to the transaction. Compare that claim to your next trip to the grocery store checkout line!

CONSISTENCY

Consistency reminds customers that effectiveness was neither accidental nor unique to a particular person or touch point. Consistency is frequently posited by wise organizations as a vital component of great customer service. However, we too often forget the rationale for consistency and the major role it plays in trust building. Consistency is all about promise-keeping evidence. When the hotel *always* has a friendly greeter at the front door no matter the property, when the fast-food restaurant *always* has a clean bathroom at all locations, and when the flight attendant *always* underscores the importance of safety, we are comforted. Consistency promotes the continuous renewal of trust.

One key tool for ensuring consistency is a service vision. A service vision is a description of the enterprise's unique or signature experience it seeks to create for customers at every touch point. An effective service vision serves as the lens through which every part of the service experience is examined and aligned. The Ritz-Carlton Hotel Company's service vision is "We pledge to provide the finest personal service and facilities for our guests who will always enjoy a warm, relaxed yet refined ambience. The Ritz-Carlton experience enlivens the senses, instills well-being and fulfills even the unexpressed wishes and needs of our guests."

"Warm, relaxed yet refined ambience" suggests attentive service. "Refined ambience" implies employee language that is classy, not folksy. It means a style that is noticeably elegant, yet completely devoid of arrogance. "Fulfills even the unexpressed wishes and needs" evokes images of employees knowing or reading guests well enough to anticipate their aspirations and expectations. It means being superconscientious about details. It means communicating across unit lines so the right hand always knows what the left hand is doing. This vivid picture or vision of service enables frontline employees to do it consistently every time, with every guest, at every hotel property. The byproduct is a trusting (a.k.a. devoted) guest.

PUTTING THE "US" BACK IN TRUST

In the end, trust comes through relationships. What makes service different from product is the presence of feeling, not just form. While we expect all the Model 423B trash compactors from the same manufacturer to be identical; we know the next cashier at the mega-mart will not be a carbon copy of the last (for better or worse). As customers we admire the absence of variability in products; we find that same trait in service to be robotic and mechanical. We like our products uniform, but we want our service unique—crafted just for us.

This reality underscores the power of trust handmade by people. Handmade trust is fashioned through the small acts of communication and caring that make customers feel that every service person is on their team, not on the opposition's squad. When the mechanic takes the time to explain all of your car repair options—from the cheaper quick fix to the more expensive long-term solution, without trying to cross-sell you on a list of other needed repairs they just happened to discover while under the hood—it reminds us of the "us" in trust. When the pilot takes the time to explain why your plane has sat on the tarmac 15 minutes past its scheduled departure and provides a new estimated take-off time—rather than leaving you sitting in the dark, wondering if there's been a terrorist incident—it begins to build a relationship of trust.

Every time a customer deals with a service provider, a *trust walk* is involved. Whether the customer experiences that walk as a high wire over snarling crocodiles or as a safe path surrounded by sensitive caregivers depends on the efforts made to avoid the trust traps and utilize the trust maps. Since trust can be dashed by a single incident of unfaithfulness or cemented by a solitary memorable act, it rests on the leadership of the unit or organization to make the pursuit of trust a never-ending part of the way the organization serves its customers.

CHAPTER 12
Firefighter

"Customers don't expect you to be perfect, but they do expect you to care."

—Ron Zemke

Ask a group of elementary students what they want to be when they grow up and we guarantee you that "fireman" will land in the top 10. We heroize people willing to risk life and limb on our behalf. But what about a unit or organization that has its best moment of glory when there is a problem?

A classic example is a utility. We take them for granted until we smell gas, the lights go out, or the faucet runs dry. Thought about your cable company lately? Let your favorite channel go down and the cable company will come roaring to the forefront of your brain! Otherwise, they are nowhere to be found between your ears.

The firefighter strategy applies to more than organizations like utilities, forgotten until there is a problem. Best Buy's Geek Squad was so successful it became a separate subsidiary. Geek Squad precincts are located in all Best Buy stores, but there are a number of stand-alone locations—the Geek Squad Stores. Employees in these locations are full-time "Winjas" who specialize in PC repair, troubleshooting, data rescue, in-home PC setup, and wireless networking, and they operate 24/7. Apple Computer stores created the Genius Bar, staffed by specialists primarily for hands-on technical support and repairs.

The firefighter strategy is one that deliberately makes a distinction out of turning an oops into an opportunity. In other words, the service provider choosing this strategy is opting for relative invisibility until a hiccup happens. Obviously, the pursuit of "take us for granted until something goes wrong" is a completely different path from the "remember us as extraordinary" pursuit of most service exemplars. Customers don't impress their neighbors by saying, "Guess what? I haven't thought about my power company in years. Isn't that wonderful?"

Achieving this brand of invisibility also has another challenge. Unless properly managed, it can fail to give employees the kind of personal pride and bragging rights that they might have if they worked at Disneyland. Firefighters without a fire can be simply a bunch of folks sitting around watching television. Again, unless managed.

 The Spider

All spiders make silk. Spider silk has been used for cross hairs in telescopes, levels, and surveying equipment. Cobwebs have been used for dressing wounds. There seems to be an anticoagulant in the silk. The web acts like an air filter, trapping insects that cannot see the fine silk. Most webs are rebuilt every day.

Many organizations treat recovery as a forum for damage control—what can we do to soothe the customer's contempt and get out of this negative encounter as quickly as possible? Some focus on the physical side of the breakage, working to fix the problem, not necessarily the customer.

When an organization is siloed, the "fix the problem, not the customer" mentality exacerbates the customer's upset. Customers unsatisfied with the outcome or the experience seek solace only to hear messages from employees that communicate indifference or a soiled view of that part only. These units or organizations fail to recognize that recovery is not over until the customer is returned, at a minimum, to a state of satisfaction. It is for this reason that betrayal management is a more fitting perspective than mere problem resolution.

How Customers View Service Recovery

Understanding the components of a firefighter strategy starts with understanding how customers view service recovery. Service recovery is about keeping customers satisfied after the worst happens. Remarkable recovery means doing it in a way that makes customers even more devoted to the unit or organization after the fact.

Nothing creates a stronger bond between service provider and customer than having a problem fixed with competence, speed, and—most important—empathy. Such a recovery ensures the pieces that have been glued back together after a mishap are even stronger than the original, unshattered whole. That is because, prior to any problems, customers operate purely on hope—a hope that in the event of a breakdown, the unit or organization would respond in good faith. In the aftermath of great recovery, they have proof of that commitment and surging confidence in the service provider.

Service Recovery Principles

Remarkable recovery happens not through steely resolve, but through preparation and practice. There are several principles that prepare service people to create remarkable recovery.[1] Some of these deal with the support that organizations must provide the front line. Others are more about the psychology of betrayal management. Implemented together they can turn aggrieved customers into committed believers who evangelize about the service provider to colleagues, friends, and family.

Principle #1: Remarkable Recovery Begins with Planning

The kind of remarkable service recovery that transforms at-risk customers into walking billboards isn't the result of random acts committed by a handful of good-Samaritan employees. Remarkable recovery is the result of a planned, systematic process. The process includes creation of (1) a clear problem-resolution process, (2) a subsystem that captures and analyzes customer disappointments, and (3) a way to recycle that information back into the system to reduce repeat mishaps. Remarkable recovery is delivered by employees trained in the quick-thinking, problem-solving tact and diplomacy—the performance skills—necessary to convert disdain into delight.

Great firefighter employees exude confidence because of a well-devised plan, specialized competence, and the empowerment to take action when something goes wrong for the customer. They know they can work with their customer to find creative solutions rather than defer to "my boss." At Ritz-Carlton Hotels, for example, all associates from the general manager to the housekeeper have blanket authorization to refund or spend up to $2,000 to solve a guest's problem. That empowerment allows everyone to perform acts of remarkable recovery for guests. The empowerment did not come without training in smart decision making. Empowered ignorance is anarchy!

Principle #2: Customers Have a Clear Image of How You Should Fix Their Problem

All service recovery begins with the expectation of fairness. Customers enter a service experience with a clear idea of how the service provider should react in the event of a problem. Recovery expectations can vary by geography, customer demographics, and even the recovery process customers are familiar with from the gas company or the telephone company. If a large percentage of customers also are customers of great service organizations like FedEx or Amazon.com—or even the stellar mom-and-pop dry cleaner on Main Street—their experiences with those organizations will inform their expectations of all service providers.

All upset customers want personalized treatment—"Here's how we're going to fix your *particular* problem, Mr. Jones." Just the same, those individual visions usually include similar basic expectations. The longtime bank customer with multiple high-balance accounts and the month-old customer with a minimum balance checking account may have similar recovery expectations if there's a significant error on a bank statement: *Fix it fast, and don't let it happen again*. But the customer who has had repeat problems may expect—and indeed require—some personal hand-holding as well, likely a call plus a sincere apology from a bank manager. The customer with a small, first-time hiccup, on the other hand, will probably be satisfied with an e-mailed form letter and evidence in his online account that the problem's been resolved.

Principle #3: First Fix the Customer—Then Fix the Customer's Problem

The first response of most organizations to service breakdown is to do what's necessary—often minimally so—to fix the problem, and then send the customer on his or her merry way. But customers also have a need to be repaired psychologically. Service breakdown threatens the very glue of any business relationship: essential trust in the service provider's ability to deliver what was promised. The first step toward remarkable recovery is letting customers vent about the problem, and for service personnel—like it or not, and regardless of who caused the problem—to apologize and grovel a bit before moving on to the business of fixing the problem. Letting the customer tell her tale, provide her take on the problem, and release the pressure valve a bit helps provide this emotional repair.

How that apology is handled makes all the difference. It's important for service workers to take full responsibility, not blame the problem on a misunderstanding or miscommunication or place the burden on a third party. A direct and simple "I'm sorry this happened, I can appreciate its impact on you, and I'll make sure it's fixed right away" is often all the customer needs to hear.

Customers do make mistakes, and they know those mistakes often cause or contribute to their problems. But they assume their view of what should happen to atone for that mistake—whether they or the organization caused it—is the only right course of action. When an employee challenges that view—when the end game becomes determining who's right—then the customer assumes he is being coerced, patronized, or even lied to. Focusing on who gets to be right puts the long-term health of a relationship in jeopardy. It is far better to focus on collective discovery and problem resolution with the customer, rather than on finger pointing. Bottom line, even if you're ultimately right in your position, you still lose.

Principle #4: Offer a Fair Resolution to the Problem—Then Atone for Any Inconvenience

While apologizing and showing empathy are crucial to fixing customers' emotions, they are only the opening salvos to a remarkable recovery effort. Plenty of organizations think their recovery work is done with an act of contrition, when the damage inflicted actually requires some further atonement or compensation to the customer. Understanding that need separates remarkable recovery efforts from those that leave customers with a lingering sense of being coerced or marginalized. In short, it pays to remember that for many customers, a brusque refund beats a smiling rebuff any time.

Contrary to popular belief, most customers bring a sense of fair play to the table when the situation calls for atonement.

These are the small, reasonable "symbolic gestures that say, "We understand your frustration or disappointment, and want to do something to make up for it." The good news is that research shows, in the majority of cases, what customers expect by way of atonement costs less and is easier to deliver than you might guess.

Involve the customer. Research also shows that customers who participate in the problem-solving effort tend to find the problem resolution more satisfying. This doesn't mean shifting the burden to customers to fix the problem. It *does* mean asking the customer what he or she would like to see happen next to fix the problem, which gives them a sense of regaining control. And that control can be essential to customers who feel they've just been abused by the unit or organization.

Principle #5: No Recovery Act Is Complete without Follow-Up

Nothing enchants a customer like a follow-up call at home or the office following a service problem. When the service provider takes the time to check back to ensure the solution is still satisfactory, it makes a powerful statement. The return on investment from such follow-up phone calls is huge in terms of the goodwill created and the devotion captured.

Following up serves another important purpose. There are some breakdown situations where customers feel if they voice upset or frustration during the transaction or experience it may put them at risk. Research in the health care field, for instance, has found that due to fear of retaliation, many elderly hospital patients keep quiet about service problems, particularly regarding nursing issues, until after their discharge. Following up with a phone call or survey gives an organization a second chance to resolve the customer's problem, and potentially win back their trust and devotion.

Let's look at an example of recovery done well. Cliff and Debbie Dickinson in Villa Rica, Georgia, filled the gas tank of their

Yukon to the tune of more than $100. The relatively new vehicle
had never had engine-health challenges. However, the SUV began
making rude sounds. The Dickinsons took the SUV to the dealership mechanic. The diagnosis was clear: bad gas! No, not what
you're thinking! Bottom line, it cost more than $400 to rid the
Yukon of the problem. Returning to the Petro Sun gasoline station where they had bought the fuel, the Dickinsons were braced
for a fight. Instead, the very friendly attendant listened patiently
to their saga, apologized, and suggested they call the district manager together. Within minutes they were on the phone to the DM,
already briefed by the attendant. She too sincerely apologized and
agreed to pay for all their expenses. The Dickinsons faxed her
their repair receipts. A few days later they received a check for all
their expenses, a handwritten note of apology, and a gift certificate for a tank of gas at the newly repaired Petro Sun gas station.
Needless to say, the Dickinsons are now devoted customers.

TACTICS OF A FIREFIGHTER STRATEGY

The firefighter strategy requires several tactics for effectiveness.
Some relate to the people or culture side of the unit or organization; some relate to administrative processes and practices.

PARTNERING

From the customer's standpoint, there are only three elements in
play in a service recovery situation: the customer, the disappointing incident, and the organization (as a single entity). Any hint
of departments, units, or division of labor implies bureaucratic
delay and the challenges of misinterpretation when communicating across lines. Now, if you asked customers, "Is XYZ company
organized into various units?" they would reply in the affirmative.
However, in the middle of disappointment they want nothing
that suggests there will be any delay or any potential for added
error due to structure. They simply want a complete, end-to-end
seamless response.

This requirement means that extraordinary partnering is necessary to pull off seamless recovery. It also means that the customer gets a single point of contact—end to end. And, if additional human encounters are required, they are done in a fashion that feels to the customer like, "My partner Judy in the call center told me about your situation and asked me to take really good care of you" and "I will call your service person, Judy, and update her on what I did for you here today." The message to the customer is that the entire organization is completely mobilized around a single person to serve this one customer.

Partnering is both structural and cultural. Units that must work well together can be brought in on a quarterly basis for breakfast, updates, and joint problem solving; that addresses the structural part. But the human side of partnering involves the habit of approaching customer problems with the perspective of collaboration. For example, if the call center operator is told by an irate customer that "I'll turn my Doberman loose on you people," they immediately think of ways to give the field service representative a heads up to watch out for a mean dog.

The cultural side of partnering comes from the array of actions that reinforce and support partnerships between units and teamwork within units. That reinforcement includes units that must work together being trained together. It means they spend enough time in each other's areas to completely understand and appreciate their partner's work role and environment. It includes all the elements that make any partnership great: opportunities for joint problem solving, common vision, collective goals, worked-out-in-advance protocols, mutual trust, constructive feedback, closed-loop communication, partnership incentives, and norms that reinforce collaboration and discourage working at cross purposes.

CONNECTIVITY

The firefighter strategy requires a special focus on connectivity. This tactic is a blend of systems and cultural elements. The systems side would let any service person know at any given point in time where a customer's problem is in the path from report to resolution. But it also means the customer would be able to do likewise.

Connectivity also has a cultural component in that it requires a tradition of openness. Issues that are hidden, conflicts that are avoided, and candor that is shunned, all work to inhibit, even sometimes alienate, interpersonal connections needed for people in the system to be kept informed so the customer can be informed. When customers hear a field service representative saying, "Those people in the call center don't have a clue about what we are dealing with out here," it communicates a problem with cultural connectivity. When the customer hears a service person say, "I'm still waiting to hear from so and so," it really means, "My partner is not telling me what I need to know to respond to you right now." To the customer it communicates, "*Their* administrative chores are more important than *my* problem."

Connectivity also includes follow-up with customers, both for customer closure, as well as learning increased competence that can be fed back into the culture. Connectivity entails end-to-end thinking and accountability. As a cultural factor it requires trust and collective responsibility for the customer's whole experience. It shifts the internal focus from simply "completing my part of the task" to "healing a broken customer relationship." Connectivity is not just about the right hand knowing what the left hand is doing. Connectivity is also about the right hand *caring* about what the left hand is doing.

PROBLEM-SOLVING PROWESS

Remarkable firefighter units are world class at problem solving. That prowess is an attitude and aptitude that is woven into what is valued and rewarded in the organization. It is a virtue that causes one department to engage another department in joint problem solving rather than simply passing their completed task off to the next unit. Customer disappointment is viewed synergistically and creatively, not linearly. Root cause analysis trumps task completion; problem prevention leads problem resolution. And all the while the prevailing perspective is one of "how is the customer viewing this?"

With problem-solving prowess, blame is viewed as an obstacle to learning and healing. This tactic values reality and authenticity over image and form and honest dialogue over rehearsed posturing. Problem-solving prowess means the organization seeks the best talent for finding the solution rather than some political criteria for assembling problem solvers. It is also a perspective that insists anyone who assembles a problem-solving forum also provide a skilled resource to facilitate that forum.

RECOVERY LEGENDS

The remarkable recovery organization makes heroes of people who effectively turn disdain into delight. It is an environment that captures stories of recovery greatness and feeds them back into the organization as tools for learning, affirmation, and role modeling.

The challenge every unit or organization faces in pursuing a firefighter strategy is how to keep the shiny from wearing off. The early elation of the "The Year of the Customer" big deal kickoff can quickly turn to exertion when the umpteenth irate customer makes some unreasonable demand on an already exhausted frontline person. How do remarkable recovery organizations ensure excitement wins out over despair? A part of the answer is to celebrate heroics.

Effective service celebrations begin with "see." The telling of heroic recovery stories provides a graphic picture of what remarkable recovery looks like. But, too often, those witnessing a service celebration—"And this year's 'CSR of the Year' award goes to . . .,"—learn *who*, but not *why*. They depart such an event with very little to emulate. And, at a deeper level, they never discover the real message.

Great recovery organizations make certain the story is told in intricate detail, along with the philosophy or attitude demonstrated by the story. People are thus reminded of the importance of daily remarkable recovery, not the fact that the way to get the big award next year is to send customers home in an unbudgeted limousine because "we screwed up their bill."

Paul "Red" Adair's Houston-based company (The Red Adair Company) had a long and famous history of putting out oil fires around the world. (John Wayne portrayed Red in the 1968 movie *Hellfighters*.) The work is a world of high-pressure danger where split-second timing can mean the difference between a gigantic explosion and a successful cap that saves millions of dollars. When an employee was asked, "Why do you put up with the long nights, remote sites, intense pressure, and life-threatening danger?" he did not mention the premium pay his role commanded. He simply, but poignantly, answered: "Because I feel valued." Red's words to an interviewer went like this: "It scares you—all the noise, the rattling, the shaking. But the look on everybody's face when you're finished and packing, it's the best smile in the world; and there's nobody hurt, and the well's under control."

Affirmation is a key component in an employee's sense of self-esteem. Why is self-esteem important to a recovery culture? Because, it is a high self-esteem that enables an employee to withstand the customer's expression of wrath when things go wrong and not take that attack personally. It is a high self-esteem that prevents employees from burning out as a response to repeated barrages of negative confrontations. At the time when a customer is most insecure is the time when customer-facing employees need to be most confident. Confidence is born of self-esteem; self-esteem comes from affirmation—affirmation as an individual contributor; affirmation as a valued member of a team.

RECOVERY TRAINING

Confidence also comes from competence. Just like solid preparation is the antidote to nervousness by the public speaker, training
is the component that equips the service provider with the assurance to deal with a scenario of discord and quarrel. Competence
also quells the customer's anxiety when things go wrong. It says
to the customer: you can rest easy during this crisis with the
knowledge that you are in the capable hands of an expert.

Training is an important part of any take-their-breath-away
service culture. But, in the realm of firefighting, it is the kind
of training that imitates a military unit planning an invasion or a
firefighting team preparing for a forest fire or apartment building
ablaze. Such training is as much group or team as it is individual.
Like war games to a soldier, recovery training relies on simulation,
planned accidents, and dry runs.

Training also encompasses approaches that enable service
people to view recovery from all perspectives, not just "my part."
This view from all sides might include job rotation that helps
units understand each other. It might entail briefings that facilitate
cross-unit understanding.

Great recovery looks like a well-oiled machine in action. That
disciplined and seamless execution comes from a careful plan
and is the byproduct of countless what ifs that make handling an
accident almost look as if it had been done on purpose.

RESPONSIBLE FREEDOM

Empowerment! The word is spoken with apprehension by most
managers. What too often races through their heads are scary
images of employees giving away the store and bosses giving up
control. Some employees want more of it; some want to be told
what to do and not worry after five o'clock.

Empowerment is ensuring employees closest to a problem or
need have the authority to make judgments on how the problem

is solved or the need met. Empowerment does not mean unlimited license: "Just do whatever you need to do." It means responsible freedom. It means employees who balance the freedom to go the extra mile for the customer with the responsibility of taking care of the unit or organization. It is a blend of service with stewardship. Fundamentally, it means thinking and acting more like an owner, and not like a brainless slave who simply does what he or she is told.

METRICS AND MAPPING

Recovery metrics are like maintenance dials on the dashboard. One of the most important for the firefighter strategy is what we call *hang time*. A positive term in football (it is the time the kicker makes the football hang in the air to allow the kicking team to run downfield), it is a negative metric in the world of service recovery. It measures the time that has elapsed from the problem alert by the customer to the time the problem is satisfactorily resolved in the eyes of the customer. Another useful dashboard reading comes from tracking the frequency of a given type of problem, hopefully triggering root cause analysis. Ideally the process includes complaint analysis to ascertain patterns so that problems can be resolved instead of symptoms merely bandaged.

Think of process maps as working like the dye a cardiologist puts into your blood stream to find blockages. With process maps you delineate the steps involved in a specific process to determine its weak points, those accidents waiting to happen that might result in the kind of service breakdown that throws customers into disappointment and the service provider into recovery.

As a particular process (perhaps one that yields frequent customer upsets) is closely examined, components of that process might be streamlined, redesigned, repaired, overhauled, or eliminated to yield a more resilient or more robust process—one that is less accident-prone. Process maps can also surface areas where redundant systems are needed to allow service failure without customer disappointment. Another use for process maps is to identify processes that are labor intensive and thus more vulnerable to error or breakdown; automating those processes might not only reduce their susceptibility to failure, but also lower costs and free up service providers to engage in other take-their-breath-away service strategies.

The firefighter strategy takes more than a singular focus on great service recovery. It requires the pursuit of zero defects at the same time. The components of a zero-defects focus are well known. They are pursued in most organizations that get dinged by their marketplace when things go wrong. We walk into a McDonald's restaurant not expecting a gourmet meal or terrific service. But we do expect the Big Mac we order to be exactly like the last one we consumed, and we count on it to be served in a hurry with limited inconvenience. We need to know little of the mechanization of burger preparation or the assurance that sufficient buns will be inventoried. We simply want the outcome: a predictably okay hamburger served quickly and without a hassle.

Most organizations achieve greatness through a single focus—Nike or Johnson & Johnson for great products, Ritz-Carlton or USAA Insurance for great service, and McDonald's or Wal-Mart for operational excellence. The firefighter strategy can work only through a dual distinction: the pursuit of zero defects and the pursuit of remarkable recovery. Coupling zero-defects outcomes with remarkable recovery has advantages. If extraordinary recovery is what is valued and rewarded, employees may be inadvertently enticed into creating problems they can resolve in an amazing fashion. With both focal points, each is moderated by the other.

The manner in which service disappointments are handled can have a dramatic impact on the customer's overall perception of the service provider. Smart organizations look for ways to get customer feedback on service breakdowns. They keep track of the most common customer complaints. They devote time in meetings to talk about service recovery and plan ways to deal with recurring service failures until they can be permanently fixed. Remember, the difference between a good service operation and great service operation is not how they perform in normal times; it's how they perform when the customer is disappointed.

PART TWO

❋ ❋ ❋

The Take-Their-Breath-Away Execution Plan

Even if you could genetically engineer a six sigma goat,
if your market is a rodeo, your customers will probably
prefer a four sigma horse.

Selecting a new way to think about a service process is fun and
energizing. However, no matter how creative, the ultimate test
is whether your plan will work and, more importantly, work
with *your* customers. In the end, it must be filtered through
several reality checks. The old adage is true about idea generation: "It is easier to tone down than think up." So, we started
with "think up"—examining 12 take-their-breath-away service
strategies in Part One. Now, we must consider the "tone down"
side—deciding what will work, what can be sustained, and how
to make it work.

Jack Daniel's whiskey has been Chip's adult beverage of
choice for many years. The making of Jack Daniel's provides a
helpful metaphor for the process of selecting the right service
strategy. All whiskey is made by fermenting grains (wheat, corn,
etc.), yeast, and water. The result is then distilled to produce a

clear spirit. Moonshiners put this brew directly in glass jars, often without diluting it; fancy brewers put the spirits in charred oak barrels, giving the concoction its brown color. After aging, the spirit is then diluted with water and bottled.

The secret to Jack Daniel's quality and taste is, first, the pure, iron-free water taken from a spring that flows from a cave near the distillery in Lynchburg, Tennessee. However, what happens after the distillation process is unique. Local sugar maple trees are cut, cross-stacked, and burned. The ashes are placed in a large vat. The fermented mixture (called *sour mash*) is then poured into the vat. It takes 10 days for the liquid to reach the bottom of vat. It is then stored in handcrafted barrels made from new lightly charred white oak trees.

Think of the Jack Daniel's whiskey-making process as having three major steps: pick the right ingredients, ferment the mixture (a rather creative process in itself), and use the right filters to make it work. The process used to chose the right take-their-breath-away service strategy is very similar (Figure II.1). Hopefully, the outcome will be equally intoxicating for your customer.

First, select a particular service offering or process. Enterprise Rent-A-Car has essentially the same cars that all other rental car

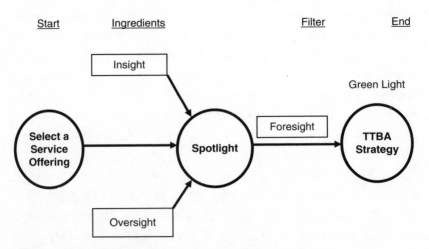

Figure II.1   Strategy Implementation Framework

companies have. So they needed to reinvent the service process that customers go through to get a car. Cabela's has essentially the same merchandise as other outdoor recreation supply companies. They needed to transform the shopping and buying experience that surrounded the objects customers purchased.

The ingredients step of your take-their-breath-away strategy process includes two parts. First and foremost is identifying and understanding your target customer. Trying to be all things to all customers is foolhardy. While you may serve an array of customers, knowing your primary customer is essential. Courtyard by Marriott, for example, serves couples on their honeymoon, vacationers who travel one week a year, and guests seeking a home-away-from-home for a month while awaiting a new house to be completed or a loved one to get discharged from the hospital. However, Courtyard's primary customer is the frequent business traveler. And they make certain the requirements of that target customer take priority.

We have labeled the process of understanding your customer insight. It involves getting many perspectives on your target customer. In *Product Development Performance,* authors Kim Clark and Takahiro Fujimoto relate how Mazda went about creating a new high-performance car for Japanese yuppies.[1] Its first step was to put together a team of people who would design it, manufacture it, deliver it, and sell it; every step of the drawing-board-to-showroom process was represented. But team members didn't sit back in the office and sift through reams of market research printouts or computer-generated engineering designs. Instead, Mazda sent them out for six months to live with the people who the company hoped would be buying the car. They went skiing with their targeted owners. They went out to eat and to the nightclubs with them. In some cases, they literally moved in and lived with them.

They came back with such an intimate understanding of what their customers wanted this new car to be and do that they created a metaphor instead of a set of expectations: The perfect car, to its customers at least, would come across as "a rugby player in a tuxedo"—rugged but feline, socially recognized, polite, sports-manlike, strong and secure, orderly, likable, bright, and, above all, elegant. It is important you have an up-to-date view of your cus-tomer's wants, needs, hopes, issues, and aspirations. That may involve using a data-gathering tool or process for continuously renewing that picture.

Another key ingredient is a clear-eyed view of your unit's or organization's strengths, weaknesses, opportunities, and threats (SWOT). What assets do you bring that may enhance your capac-ity to be distinctive? What liabilities do you have that, if not properly managed, could undermine your efforts to influence your customer? What are the unique opportunities that could be capitalized on—timing, location, resources, contacts, and so forth—to increase your success? What are the threats—changing economy, turnover, competitor plans, and the like—to watch out for, circumvent, manage, or compensate for to be effective? We call this step *oversight*. Think of it as gathering an essential and realistic understanding of the platform from which you will launch your take-their-breath-away strategy.

The next step is the selection of a take-their-breath-away strat-egy. This step involves examining the strategy benefits against what you learned in insight and foresight. We call the selection step *spotlight* since it is aimed at zeroing in on the take-their-breath-away strategy that is right for you. But the process does not stop here. Planning is great, but it's execution that makes the difference.

The chosen strategy must now be poured through another filter we call *foresight*. It is important you use this filter to ensure your strategy has the pragmatism for success. Too often, organiza-tions get so enamored with their exciting new offering that they forget it must have a return on investment. That test is relevant for profit-making organizations as well as not-for-profit or expense-only units. Your customers may not write checks payable to your unit but there is an investment of their time and energy. Will the new service offering or reinvented process yield an experience that increases customer devotion? Will it enhance or improve your unit's reputation?

The foresight filter is crucial because it is aimed at assessing exactly what will be required to make your chosen take-their-breath-away strategy work. Think of it as clearing out the implementation obstacles and adding the resources and practices required for success. It is also the step that determines if the chosen strategy can be sustained by your culture. In other words, to paraphrase the famous *Field of Dreams* movie line, "If you build it, are you confident that customers will come?"

Armed with an execution plan, you are now ready for launch. In the chapter called "Green Light" we have provided ideas on how to implement your take-their-breath-away strategy as well as identified few potential potholes that have derailed some of the best-crafted plans. Since launches are generally collective efforts, we have crafted the chapter around the role of the leader. However, we included tips for individual contributors as well.

In executing a new take-their-breath-away service strategy, remember that a strategy launch is the beginning, not the ending. It is important to continually support, reinforce, and fan the flames of change. The excitement associated with newness can soon give way to the hard work required to sustain a strategy. New people joining the unit or organization, and who therefore were not a part of its creation, may not embrace the strategy with the same passion as its authors. Customers change; their needs, expectations, hopes, and aspirations must be continually assessed and updated. That intelligence is vital to knowing whether you are still heading in the desired direction and help provide alerts when you might be going off course and a take-their-breath-away strategy review and relaunch is called for.

CHAPTER 13
Insight
Understanding Your Customer

A map confiscated from an enemy courier revealed the location of shallow caves each containing a cache of weapons used to resupply enemy troops. However, when a wise Army lieutenant sent the captured map to a friend he knew could provide a deeper assessment of the terrain covered by the map, he learned that the caves shared striking similarities—same type of soil, same topography, same elevation. Checking other areas with the characteristics of the cave sites produced another major discovery: There were many more caves not marked on the map that contained even larger collections of weapons.

Customer intelligence is like that captured map, a means of unearthing valuable information about your customers. The security guard's assessment of the demeanor of a departing key customer can sometimes be more instructive than 40 focus groups and 60 surveys; talking with a customer you lost last year might be more helpful than talking with the one you acquired last week.

Acquiring customer intelligence is an intentional effort to understand the customer. This search is typically combined with known socioeconomic, demographic, and psychographic data. With contemporary market research tools, investigators can know the specific buying preferences of a particular zip code.

Their fact-finding techniques can tell you what magazines customers read, the TV shows they watch, and what they name their pets. However, such data points are more like searching the caves marked on the map rather then discovering unmarked ones. Understanding customers requires the pursuit of wisdom and insight, not just the quest for knowledge and understanding.

Customer intelligence is different from market intelligence. Market intelligence teaches us about a segment or group and discerns how they are similar. Customer intelligence informs us about the individuals who make those buying decisions in that market. As one peruses car counts, per capita statistics, and economic projections, it is helpful to remember the wisdom attributed to Neiman Marcus founder Stanley Marcus: A market never bought a thing in my store, but a lot of customers came in and made me a rich man!

Knowing what customers are really like starts with the recognition that looking at the results from customer interviews, surveys, and focus groups is at best like looking in a rearview mirror. Today's customers change too rapidly to rely solely on what they reported. Instead it is important to anticipate where they are going. In the words of one infantry captain, "Any military unit can figure out where their enemy is. Victory comes with figuring out where their enemy will be."

Customers have many dimensions. They are more than a bundle of needs and expectations. They are also issues and concerns, hopes and aspirations. Figure 13.1 depicts myriad customer dimensions. Imagine this figure is like an iceberg. Market research can tell us the public information and some of the needs and expectations above the customer's waterline. The objective of customer intelligence is to learn as much as possible about what lies below the surface of the water but above the forbidden area marked "private."

Smart customer intelligence teaches us that customers often behave differently from the way they predict they will. The implication for insight is that we must examine more than what

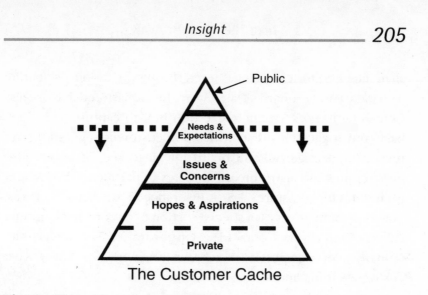

The Customer Cache

Figure 13.1   The Customer Cache

customers report in an interview or survey. For example, Professor Jerald W. Young at the University of Florida compared the key reasons patients gave for switching physicians with the reasons these same patients said would influence their decision. There was a major difference. "Quality of medical practice" was the factor patients consistently said would send them in search of a new physician. However, "bedside manner" was the factor that actually triggered a change of physicians.[1]

Continuum, a Massachusetts-based consulting firm, was hired by Moen, Inc. to conduct customer research for use in the development of a new line of showerheads.[2] Continuum felt the best way to really understand what customers wanted in a new showerhead wasn't to ask them via surveys but rather to watch them in action. According to *The New York Times*, the company got permission to film customers taking showers in their own homes and used the findings in the new design. Among the insights gleaned were that people spent half their time in the shower with their eyes closed and 30 percent of their time avoiding water altogether. The insights contributed to the new Moen "Revolution" showerhead becoming a best seller.

Customer expectations are a perpetually moving target. It means smart customer intelligence must value real-time feedback as much as historical data gathered through traditional scientific methods. Stew Leonard's Dairy Store, headquartered in Norwalk, Connecticut, uses a giant suggestion box to capture daily feedback and suggestions. Every morning customer suggestions are posted on a huge bulletin board for all to see. Managers also make copies and distribute them to key departments throughout each of their eight stores. USAA Insurance in San Antonio, Texas, posts customer ideas on a special section of its corporate intranet called ECHO (Every Contact Has Opportunity). The key is to let as many people as possible—as quickly as possible—know what customers think and feel.

CAPTURING INTELLIGENCE IN THE FIELD

Who is in charge of customer intelligence gathering in your unit or organization? If you were in command of a fort you probably would value the observations of your scout over the guesses of your cook or paymaster. Yet, examine the structure of many organizations and you will find the researcher down the hall has more credibility than the boots in the field.

Customer intelligence, like military intelligence, can be guided and resourced from the command post, but it must come from those who interact with customers. Surveys and focus groups can be very helpful. However, by the time such customer research data is captured, analyzed, synthesized, sanitized, and exported to a PowerPoint slide, it is more about history than the future.

How to Get a High Response Rate on a Customer Survey

- ♦ Provide advance notice of the survey.

- ♦ Telephone precontact works better than a letter.

- ◆ Promise of a contribution to a charity does not produce a significantly higher return rate. A cash incentive does produce a higher return rate.

- ◆ Create a survey that is attractive, easy to complete, and easy to return.

For E-Surveys

- ◆ Let respondents know upfront how long the e-survey will take or the number of questions involved.

- ◆ Allow respondents a way to save a partially completed e-survey to finish it later.

- ◆ Provide ample space for open-ended questions.

For Mailed Surveys

- ◆ Stamped envelopes yield a higher return rate.

- ◆ Use a personalized cover letter with a real signature.

- ◆ If the respondent recognizes the name and thinks positively of the person it significantly increases the return.

Customer-centric organizations look for countless ways to facilitate and nurture field reconnaissance. They make the gathering of customer intelligence, even in its rawest form, an act of value and importance. Victoria's Secret Catalog required the company's top 50 officers to spend time in their call center listening to customer calls and interviewing call center reps on what they believed were customers' most frequent requests, most common complaints, and most unfulfilled expectations. The quarterly exercise led to powerful lessons and innovative insights. Most valuable were early warnings on emerging customer issues that had not yet made their way into customer surveys.

Below are some of the most effective means take-their-breath-away service providers have discovered for acquiring timely, relevant customer intelligence.

SCOUT REPORTS

Position all field personnel as customer scouts. Scouts see a lot, hear a lot, and know a lot. Yet they are probably the most under-utilized source of brilliance about what customers really value. Teach them to ask the customers with whom they have contact: "What is one thing we can do to improve our service to you?" and report what they hear. Provide them the time, tools, processes, and incentives to share their insights. Start every field meeting with "what are our customers telling us?" Encourage frontline people to share stories about "the good, the bad, and the ugly." Have leaders listen to them on the phone and ride with them in the field with the intent of learning, not of critiquing. Create a way for the collective learnings to get upstream to senior leaders as well as into the hands of those who can provide a timely response.

ESTABLISHING BOARDS OF CUSTOMERS

Some customers are more influence-shapers than others. Mayors know who among their constituents they can count on to tell it like it is. They also know the informal leaders whose views shape the opinions of others. Duke Energy borrowed from the play book of small-town mayors to create a Boards of Customers program in the regions they serve. These experienced customers volunteered their time each quarter to act as sounding boards for new products and services. They also became a key neigh-borhood conduit for feedback and ideas on improvement. Before implementing what could be an unpopular policy or controversial decision, these Boards of Customers could often help soften the impact or offer suggestions on timing and tone. Not only did the admiration of the chosen members of the boards climb with experience, they had unique opportunities to become advocates for the Charlotte, North Carolina–based utility.

TOWN HALLS SQUARED

The town hall meeting concept is used by many units and organizations as a way to get up close and personal with customers. Many leaders report these gatherings are at best marginally useful. The reason is the fact that these sporadic events typically have all the openness and authenticity of the town hall format used for presidential candidates to secure TV footage. The exchange is reduced to rants and raves from the scripted, the disenchanted, and the fevered fans. However, if the town-hall concept is done locally and frequently, it can shift from being a predictable set piece to being a true conversation. And the town-hall format can work equally well with employees.

Maureen Foster, head of financial services for Kaiser Permanente, holds quarterly town-hall meetings with employees. The focus is not only on employee issues and concerns but getting input on what employees hear from customers. That's well and good, but the secret for making these sessions so effective is the way they catalogue the changes, improvements, and plans based on what was reported in the last town-hall gathering. Customers and employees are less likely to keep giving feedback if they do not believe it fuels change.

Questions to Ask an Acme Customer Focus Group

When you think about getting service from Acme, what are the features or attributes that are most important to you?

If (your favorite customer service organization) were to be in charge of Acme's service experience, what is one thing they would likely do?

(continued)

(*continued*)

What are the features you would expect of a terrific customer experience from Acme? Now, what would each of these features look like if we super sized them or put them on steroids?

If Acme wanted to increase their fees/prices by 50 percent and still have you view the value that you received as a good one, describe the service experience they would have to provide.

If Acme offered a 100 percent money-back guarantee if you were not happy with your service experience, what part of your experience with Acme would likely get you your money back? What would Acme have to do to never pay you that service guarantee?

Recall a time when you were disappointed with your experience with Acme? What did Acme do to make you feel better about your disappointing experience? What should they have done?

What is one thing Acme could do that no one else in the industry or function is doing that would make you feel valued and special?

DEAR COMPANY

Log onto CVS/pharmacy's new Web site www.foralltheways youcare.com and you will get a spectacular example of the power of customer input. The company created the Web site for customers to communicate examples of ordinary miracles performed by CVS/pharmacy employees. According to CVS/pharmacy President Larry Merlo the site not only has become an important array of best practices for all employees, but it also serves as a valuable source of timely information about what is important to customers. Reading the incidents that triggered customer accolades taught the company that positive emotional connections with customers were a key to repeat business. They could also erase customer memories of excessive wait time and out-of-stock situations.

Some corporate communication departments warn that opening up the floodgates for customer letters can create an administrative nightmare, like the fabled full moon that brings out all the crazies. But consider this: Would you rather have an irate customer vent their grumble to the CEO or to their neighbor? Customers who take the time to pen a passionate letter or e-mail probably have a few worthwhile lessons to teach.

CUSTOMER INPUT CONTEST

Most employees are subtly trained to keep bad news to themselves. Their fear is that the customer pot shots they report will ricochet around the organization, potentially turning the messenger into a casualty. Changing the frame from *blame* to *aim* requires finding ways to incent employees to get beyond their reserve and share their stories. When St. Luke's Medical Center in Milwaukee changed the labeling of patient concerns from "patient complaints" to "patient suggestions," more employees shared what they heard in the cafeteria, hallways, and waiting rooms.

EDiS Corporation, a large construction company headquartered in Wilmington, Delaware, made "customer reporter" a part of the expectations they have of employees and put their money where their mouth is by providing incentives for employee candor about customer concerns. "How can we fix what we do not know about?" asked CEO Andy DiSabatino at an officer meeting. "And, who better to tell us about customer hiccups than our frontline employees who know about them? We have to find a way to make them want to share what they know." If frontline people are punished for bringing forth customer complaints or feedback, they will find ways to keep future feedback to themselves.

BIG DEAL MEETINGS WITH A CUSTOMER AGENDA

Boards of directors are becoming more forceful in their direction to organizational leaders. Long viewed as rubber-stamping friends of the firm, boards now more quickly fire CEOs, more scrupulously examine organizations' foibles, and more aggressively constrict undisciplined expansion. In take-their-breath-away organizations, the customer is on the agenda of all big deal meetings just like this quarter's goals or earnings. Some boards even invite key customers to periodically join their board meeting just to ensure that the organization keeps a proper focus on their raison d'etre. If the board has a finance committee, a strategy committee, and an audit committee, why not have a customer committee charged with keeping an ear to the voice of the customer?

CUSTOMER ADVISORY TEAMS

Customer advisory teams are not new. But their relevance is more important than ever. Today's customers are much more vocal than they have ever been. And customers are a lot smarter consumers than they have ever been. Take-their-breath-away organizations tap into this assertive wisdom and turn that insight into improvements. Take eBay, which every 60 days invites 12 eBay users to journey to San Jose, California, to participate in the company's Voice of the Customer program. These select people visit almost every department to talk about ways to improve service. This focus group methodology goes one step further. Every month thereafter for six months these same users are reassembled to explore emerging issues. As users evolve from being interviewees to feeling like members of the organization, they get bolder in their input. The byproduct of these customer conversations has been important service enhancements for eBay.

Emerald Peoples Utility District, a small public power co-op based in Eugene, Oregon, gets customers involved in various committees and study groups. Arizona Public Service (APS), a much larger regional utility based in Phoenix, has recruited some of the public interest advocates who once dogged its every step to bring their interest and energy inside the walls, where they can be applied in useful ways.

How to Have a Great Customer Focus Group

Hold it on neutral turf in a comfortable, quiet setting

Limit attendance to 8 to 10 customers

Make it convenient for customers—location, time, and length

Only include customers' recent experience on the topic

Use a focus group leader who can lead a good discussion

Listen to learn, not to teach, preach, or defend

Start with general questions and then go to more specific

Keep comments completely nonjudgmental

Ask probing questions aimed at clarifying information

Ask about expectations, importance, and experience

Ask about service failures and service opportunities

CUSTOMER WEATHERPERSON

The TV weatherperson provides us with early warnings about environmental changes. A customer weatherman is a person or unit charged with keeping up with any piece of intelligence important to the direction of the organization as it relates to customers. Communication departments routinely Google the company's name to find out how the company is being perceived in news reports, articles, and customer blogs. However, this is just the beginning. Think about what would be learned from googling your competition or a best–in-class company in the same industry.

The purview of the customer weatherman could range from industry best practices, to regulatory changes, to the election of a legislator known to be a foe of the company. The customer weatherman can go to Chamber of Commerce or Rotary Club or local government budget meetings to learn about issues and concerns relevant to the organization. Who in your unit or organization is tracking industry inventions, breakthroughs, and R&D that might ultimately shape the customer's experience? Who in your organization has an ear tuned to the academic circles conducting research and discussions about the future of the industry?

MULTICHANNEL RESPONSE SYSTEMS

Make it easy to listen to customers by making it easy for customers to contact the organization through 800 numbers, e-mail, Web-based text chat, and more. Many service-focused companies today have Web-enabled call centers that route, queue, and prioritize incoming e-mail from customers, enabling customer service reps to handle e-mail and real-time Web requests just as efficiently as calls to their 800 numbers. Don't make trying to find an 800 number on your Web site like a game of Where's Waldo? Many customers have a good reason for wanting to contact the organization via phone versus sending an e-mail or visiting the Web site's frequently asked questions (FAQ) page—for example, they often can't find answers to their particular questions using those resources or they need more detail and nuance than those avenues provide. List your 800 number boldly on every Web page.

Understanding your customer requires making certain you don't listen to one source of information at the expense of others. Marketing professor Leonard Berry of Texas A&M University tells the story of a new manager at the Chicago Marriott a number of years ago.[3] One day, while going over year-end budget requests, he came across a $20,000 line item to upgrade the small black-and-white television sets to color in the bathrooms of the rooms on the concierge level. At first glance, it seemed like a nice enough service improvement. But something teased at the edge of his service vision.

So the manager started asking questions of his people, based in part on the implicit assumption that they had been listening to customers and hence would have a good handle on guest preferences and requests. First, he asked the concierge level staff and the people in engineering how many requests they had received for color sets in the bathrooms on that level. "Actually, none," came the reply, "but we thought it was a neat idea." He checked with guest relations to determine if the guest comment cards had ever had a request for color sets or a complaint the TVs were black and white. There were none.

Then he asked the entire housekeeping staff to tell him what was the most requested item that was not readily available to guests. Their reply: irons and ironing boards. While these are common amenities today in most hotels, at that time they were delivered to the room only after a call to housekeeping. Guess what he authorized for purchase under that line item? And as an unexpected reward for listening for understanding, it turned out that the cost of putting in irons and ironing boards in all the hotel rooms was less than the cost of upgrading black-and-white television sets to color on the fancy floor. Diverse customer information results in rich customer intelligence, the basis of customer understanding. And understanding is an essential part of the platform from which a take-their-breath-away strategy is selected and launched.

CHAPTER 14
Oversight
Assessing Your Launch Pad

Warning. This is the toughest chapter in the book! Before selecting a take-their-breath-away strategy it is important to take a clear-eyed, sober assessment of your capacity to launch and sustain the chosen strategy.

Take it from Mary Jones and her husband, Tom. For several years, Mary and Tom had enjoyed having friends over for dinner. While doing a year's graduate study in Italy, Mary had learned to make superb pizza. Tom prided himself on having an enormous knowledge of wines. After Mary's high school teaching position was cut during a budget squeeze, she and Tom decided to put their savings into a classy wine and pizza shop. Mary could supervise the cooking; Tom could buy the wine and handle the business management while continuing on a moderately demanding job as an electrical engineer.

They leased space in a new inner-city shopping mall and began their new career as restaurateurs. Within six months, they were out of business! Mary had learned she lacked the patience and desire to supervise people. Tom had been unable to keep up with the continuous paperwork. Even worse, the mall mainly generated lunch traffic; less than 25 percent of the business came from dinner customers. The waiting time for their specialty, made-to-order pizza precluded the rapid customer turnover required to capitalize on the lunch business. They went into bankruptcy, bitterly resigned, exhausted.

You may be saying to yourself, "I would never make that kind of mistake." Perhaps not. But there are other potholes we can easily trip on if we do not systematically assess our take-their-breath-away strategy launch pad. In the world of strategic planning, the process is called SWOT—strengths, weaknesses, opportunities, and threats. And even the most creative, forward-thinking organizations have stepped in a hole because they failed to do a thorough SWOT.

In the 1980s, FedEx (then Federal Express) came up with a very creative strategy to shorten the time required for the delivery of documents to less than two hours. If customers took their documents to a Federal Express location the documents could be faxed to the Federal Express location nearest the destination and a courier would then deliver the faxed documents. Zap Mail was a disaster, costing the company more than $400 million. FedEx missed the fact that the Japanese were launching fax machines so cheaply that every business quickly had their own.

STRENGTHS

What are strengths? They are first and foremost assets that set you apart from others. A car dealership would not list "have cars" as a strength unless the other dealerships had run out of cars. Strengths come in many forms. Strengths can be features of your reputation or resources important to customers (or important for you to be able to deliver those resources). They could be advocates (friends of the firm) other than the customer. They could be a convenient location, resources to weather a change in approach, being in a recession-resistant niche, or talented people. Keep in mind, you are cataloging those strengths that will help you select or implement a service strategy.

A strengths assessment is not an invitation to boast. It is a chance to carefully determine what assets you bring that might lead you to select a particular take-their-breath-away strategy and/or shape how you might launch that strategy. Use the questions below to start your thinking. Then, invite others to build on the list. Your colleagues, employees and customers are three great sources for your strengths-list review. They can give you a reality check on what you consider your strengths. Be prepared to remove some of the items you initially thought were strengths.

When your customers compliment your service, what is the subject of their accolades?

If you could divide the service you provide into parts, and you could put a price on each part to sell it in your marketplace, what parts would bring the greatest return?

If you went out of business tomorrow, who would be the first to notice? What would they likely miss the most?

What aspects of your service do you and others enjoy the most? What do your customers experience?

When you think about others in a similar business or function, what part of your operation are you most proud of? What are you most grateful for? What would your customers say?

What is your secret sauce, a strength you have that, if supported, amplified, reinforced, or nurtured, could really set you apart?

WEAKNESSES

What is a weakness? It is a limitation that you can or cannot control. It is a shortcoming or restriction. This part of your oversight analysis is not about listing your imperfections as much as it is getting an up close and personal view of the drawbacks that might make your strategy selection flawed. For example, if you are considering launching an animation strategy but you have a unit with limited or rare customer contact, the infrequency of contact would be a weakness of that particular strategy.

The first reaction most people have to cataloging weaknesses is to assume weaknesses are completely different from strengths. They sometimes are. But often the most useful approach is to look at the dark side of your strengths. Your greatest strength can be your biggest blind spot. Answer the questions below and then review them with your SWOT jury (colleagues, employees, and customers).

> When your customers complain about your service, what is the subject of their complaints?

> If you could divide the service you provide into parts, and you could put a price on each part to sell it in your marketplace, what parts would bring the least return?

> What are the aspects of service employees fuss most about? What is the customer seeing?

> What do you wish most for when considering improvement?

> What do others in a similar business or function have that you wish you had? What can they do that you cannot do?

> When you were asked in the strengths section above about your secret sauce, did you have a challenge thinking of one? What could that teach you?

OPPORTUNITIES

Opportunities are openings for success. Opportunities come in many forms. They could range from the sudden departure of a competitor to the availability of unique resources. They could be as small as a break in the weather or as large as a merger. Opportunities could be created by other events that leave you with an edge. They could be a change in a regulation that formerly was restrictive or the introduction of a new technology or product that gives you a unique break. Answer the questions below and then get feedback from others.

What is an emerging theme or trend in your business or function on which you could capitalize?

What is an asset or talent you have that is unique or rare?

What part of your business or function is underdeveloped that, if developed, could provide you with a distinction or advantage?

What is a key value in your unit or organization that might serve as a springboard or foundation for your take-their-breath-away strategy?

What are resources currently not available but obtainable in the future if your take-their-breath-away strategy is a major success?

Where has your competition failed and why? Where is your competition most vulnerable to failure?

THREATS

A threat is anything that could hamper or trip up your implementation of a take-their-breath-away strategy. It could be a pending regulatory change or shift in what your customers want or value. Competitor actions often constitute threats. Threats can be changes in the geography in which you serve or the introduction of a new competitor into the area. It could be oversaturation in the marketplace by similar enterprises. Threats can be the aftermath of negative publicity. As important as going green has been, there are service providers that no doubt have taken a hit by being branded as "greenwashers." Getting thin, lowering cholesterol, or being fuel-efficient have all created winners and losers. Some of the concepts in the chapter called "Foresight" may provide you added potential potholes to consider.

What is the likelihood a competitor could scoop your take-their-breath-away strategy and preempt your launch, leaving you having to abandon your strategy or risk looking like "me too"?

What is a key constraint in your marketplace (shareholder dissatisfaction, budget cuts, social concerns, etc.) that a new take-their-breath-away strategy could aggravate?

What are anticipated changes within your unit or organization that could adversely affect the timing of your take-their-breath-away strategy?

How will your take-their-breath-away strategy be impacted by reduction factors (turnover, economic downturn, loss of a key license, loss of a key advocate, reorganization, loss of a key customer, etc.)?

What if, after launching the take-their-breath-away strategy, you discover that the lead time required for your strategy to be sustainable is much longer than you expected?

Where has your competition succeeded and why?

FORGOTTEN VOICES

There is one more perspective to add to the SWOT analysis. Much can be learned from listening to people often overlooked in our capacity-assessment process. The security guard or receptionist can sometimes tell you more about current reality than the familiar voices in market research or the sales department. Consider listening to some of these oft-forgotten voices:

What can lost customers tell you about your SWOT? Even the ones you lost for legitimate reasons often can provide valuable insight.

What perspective can you learn from prospective customers, those considering you as a service provider?

What can you learn from all the consumer-generated media (blogs, Web sites set up for complaints, Better Business Bureau, etc.)?

What do the most common complaints teach you about your customer?

What can frontline employees—those who frequently talk with customers—tell you about your SWOT?

What could you learn from stakeholders (owners, inspectors, vendors, regulators, legislators, etc.)?

AIR FILTER

Chapter 9 focused on the *air* strategy—making the core offering done extraordinarily well by the take-their-breath-away strategy to gain customer devotion. Air as a strategy works particularly well when customer expectations are generally low for your industry, sector, or offering and/or no one else is doing the basics very well. However, faltering on service air can derail all the take-their-breath-away strategies. The super friendly, convenient, inexpensive dry cleaner that cracks buttons on your shirts or improperly presses your skirt gets no accolades from its patrons. Taking their breath away assumes the core offering—the basic value proposition you make to your customers—is being met.

One important step in selecting and implementing a take-their-breath-away strategy is to ensure it will mix well with service air. Consider the following questions about how your customers are served at the most basic and foundational level. With the answer to each question, consider how that service encounter will be impacted. Enterprise Rental reinvented one component of the service offering—bringing the car to you—but it also altered how rental customers interacted with the agent. Answering a few rental agent questions over the counter is different for the customer than the chitchat with the agent expected in the field.

NetFlix added easy and efficient to renting videos but eliminated contact with Susie down at the video store.

How do your customers currently communicate their needs and expectations? Phone, face-to-face, mail, e-mail? Will the nature of that communications change with your take-their-breath-away strategy?

What role does customer wait time play in the current service encounter? Will that time (or the perception of that time) change with your take-their-breath-away strategy?

How would you describe or characterize the relationship between the customer and the customer contact people in your unit or organization? Will that relationship be altered in any way with your take-their-breath-away strategy? If so, will that alteration be viewed as negative, neutral, or positive by customers?

Which of your policies, procedures, or business practices (e.g., packaging, response time, delivery, returns, guarantees, etc.) are customers currently accustomed to? Will these be impacted in a way that customers care about?

How do your customers relate or interact with other customers of yours? Will that change through your strategy selection?

Is there another take-their-breath-away strategy that is already in operation? Will it be eliminated, changed, or enhanced through the new strategy? Will it conflict or clash with the new take-their-breath-away strategy?

Is there a side benefit to your current service offering important to a segment of your customers (for example, Starbucks sells coffee, tea, and food; they also sell CDs and coffee cups)? Will the side benefit be impacted in a fashion customers will find negative?

Will implementation of a new take-their-breath-away strategy require structural changes impacting customers (new building, different machinery, etc.)? Will they have to learn anything new to get service?

Will implementation of a new take-their-breath-away strategy require those who deliver service to learn anything new, thus changing the service experience for at least some period of time?

How will follow-up with customers be altered by a new take-their-breath-away strategy?

We take automatic teller machines for granted today. Most customers would rather hit the ATM than stand in even a short line to see a bank teller. But, when the first true bank ATMs were introduced in 1971, they were met with widespread customer resistance. Not only were customers not ready to give up the social interaction, they worried about the safety of a deposit put into a machine. It took years for ATM usage to spread beyond the 15 percent of customers who were early adopters.

Introducing a new take-their-breath-away strategy can have an impact on the implied service contract service providers have with the customer. It is vital you take a studied view of your service air, paying particular attention to how that contract will be impacted. It is easy to get caught up on the newness of the strategy and lose sight of the heart of service—meeting a customer need.

IMPORTANT VOICES

The selection and implementation of the take-their-breath-away strategy does not happen in a vacuum. It happens under the influence of leaders and through the enthusiasm of employees. The most cleverly crafted strategy can be quickly overturned by the indifference of those who must make it important to the organization and/or through the resistance of those who must make it work. It was this imperative that made Bank of America executive Dick Nettel comment, "Culture will eat strategy for lunch, every time!"

The word *organization* could be defined as the "workings of interdependent organs." Your body is an organization of sorts. If the heart is not functioning properly, all the other organs are adversely impacted. If you are an employee and a service provider, you operate as an organ of an enterprise body. If you supervise a group of employees, you run a collection of organs, much like the digestive system or the respiratory system of the body.

The biology of change tells us that effective interdependence is vital to the health of an organization. An organization's culture includes all the norms, agreements, values, and beliefs that enable the parts of an organization to work well (or sometimes not so well) together. Think of culture as a lot like the blood and nerve cells in a human body. The hand needs blood from the heart and signals from the brain to pick up this book. The operations department relies on patterns of communications and agreed-upon practices to function properly with the sales department. Even if an organization has a great strategic plan for outwitting a competitor, without the organs of the corporate body working well together, the best plan will falter. Again, culture eats the strategy for lunch.

So, you are ready to change your game and ratchet up the experience your customers or colleagues receive from you, your unit, or organization. Congratulations. Success comes from more than having the perfect strategy. It must be congruent with the corporate body. It needs to play well with the other organs so to speak. Shouldn't we be mavericks or wild ducks leading the organization toward excellence? Of course we should. But, as long as you are a part of a corporate body, going way too far from what that body considers normal will lead to severance.

The human body reads the introduction of a foreign body (think disease) as an invasion. It sends its warriors (white corpuscles) to wage war until the intruder is either eradicated or contained like the pearl that began as a grain of sand in an oyster.

It is what makes transplants or organ replacements particularly tricky. The corporate body reacts similarly. Mavericks can be tolerated; rebels, on the hand, are ousted, penalized, or completely marginalized. There can be patience for eccentrics, but a defiance of insurgents. If you are compelled to exceed your organization's outer barriers, start your own company or get the organization to set your unit up as separate subsidiary or as a project team allowed to play by different rules.

Beyond Setting Target Dates

The ability to influence only comes with *capacity* to influence. And, unless the corporate body at least tolerates your platform, the most zealous plan is just that: simply a plan. How can you ensure you become an illustrious model of take-their-breath-away excellence instead of a forgotten kamikaze pilot? How can you or your unit become an exemplary model for change without finding yourself on the outside looking back in? There are two important keys to being a maverick with a domicile: intention and enlistment.

Intention requires a close examination of your real ambition. Look yourself in the mirror and be completely honest. How much of your intended service metamorphosis is for your customer and how much it is all about you? True noble purposes are rarely viewed by the corporate body with mistrust. However, if there is even the hint of a self-serving ambition, your efforts to embark on a new strategy are at risk of being rejected or sabotaged. Should your success elevate you or the reputation of your unit? Hopefully, that will happen. We all laud those who get rewarded for delivering excellence. But the payoff should be a byproduct, not the target. Management guru Peter Drucker sagely reminded us, "There is only one valid definition of a business purpose: *to create a customer*."[1] Financial success is one measure of accomplishment at that purpose.

Enlistment entails identifying key advocates. Advocates could be leaders more senior in the organization or leaders in other units that are likely to be impacted by you or your unit. Advocates can serve you in many ways. They can offer advice, they can provide early warning, and they can downfield block to help neutralize key resistors. They can also be a part of your cheerleading squad that starts a positive buzz about your efforts. Get them involved early. Use them as sounding boards. Help them become your advisory team or informal board of directors.

Enlistment also includes identifying key resistors. Resistors can be people likely to impair your plans by their silence (when affirmation is expected), by their objection, and by their taking steps to incapacitate your implementation. Get them involved early as well. People will care if they share. Their participation enables you to more accurately gauge, and thus prepare for, their opposition. And, by getting their participation in some form early you may sway they position and neutralize their impact when you are prepared to launch your take-their-breath-away strategy.

And what if you own the place? You may be the owner of your business and thus not answerable to a boss or board. The concepts of intention and enlistment still apply. Just as the corporate body can sense a self-serving mission by one of its organs, your marketplace has the same sonar. We live in a time when the customer's greedometer is especially fine-tuned. Customers are ready to consider, even embrace, enterprises eager to serve them; customers reject those organizations eager to only serve themselves.

Inclusion is also a powerful marketing concept. Who are the important voices in your marketplace? Like Duke Energy, creating your own board of customers could be a boon to selecting and launching a new strategy. Before finalizing your decision on a new take-their-breath-away strategy, why not run it up the flagpole of a few advisor-customers? Passing their early snicker test could save you great expense now and embarrassment down the road.

The *New Yorker* magazine ran a clever cartoon in the early 1980s that portrayed an obviously well-to-do businessman in a three-piece suit reading the newspaper while sitting on a park bench. Beside him sat a dingy street bum. The businessman's reading is interrupted by the bum, who says this in the caption under the cartoon: "You know where I think I went wrong? I never set target dates!"[2]

The cartoon captures the core of the challenge. Strategy selection and planning are important to achievement. However, success in the execution of a take-their-breath-away strategy requires a lot more than setting target dates.

CHAPTER 15
Spotlight
Choosing a Take-Their-Breath-Away Strategy

Customer service excellence is not about what units or organizations say they are; it is about how customers consistently experience the organization. When Bain and Associates asked the senior leaders of several hundred large companies if they believed they delivered a superior proposition to their customers, 80 percent indicated that they did. However, only 8 percent of their customers agreed with them in the same study.[1]

The units and organizations that get solid marks from their customers are not necessarily those that pursue the absolute pinnacle of service greatness. Marriott Hotel service is very good, but it's not at the level of their high-end chain, Ritz-Carlton Hotels. But, then, it is not supposed to be. That's why we advocate the process we call "spotlight" to choose your take-their-breath-away strategy.

Preparation for spotlight requires the two previous chapters. First, you must have insight into what is important to your customer. Second, you must give oversight to your capacity to deliver the take-their-breath-away strategy. Launching into spotlight without insight and oversight is like an actor stepping onto the stage on opening night without learning his lines.

Spotlighting the right take-their-breath-away strategy comes through three steps, which are examined in this chapter. First, it is important to select the level of service that best fits your customer and matches your sweet spot. Second, it is vital you pick the take-their-breath-away strategy with the features most suited to you and your goal.

But there is an important third step. You must craft the form you will use to spotlight that take-their-breath-away strategy. Spotlighting a strategy involves forming a clear picture of what the take-their-breath-away strategy will look like in action (a service vision). Bottom line, it is all about knowing who you want to be and then consistently executing against that vision.

CHOOSING A SERVICE LEVEL

Just as customer loyalty is a much higher level of affinity than mere customer satisfaction (think Nordstrom versus Sears) and customer devotion is even a higher level above customer loyalty (think Lexus versus Jaguar), we consider customer centric the pinnacle of a unit or organization's dedication to the customer. The less the customer's experience dominates how a unit or organization is led and managed, the lower the grade the customer will bestow (Figure 15.1).

Customer indifference is a dangerous characterization by customers. Indifference is not viewed as uncaring; it is seen as arrogant—one of the traits most loathed by customers. Organizations hostile to customers do not remain in business. Customers avoid such organizations if possible and typically speak ill of them to others.

A	B	C	D	F
Customer Centric	Customer Focused	Customer Friendly	Customer Aware	Customer Indifferent

Figure 15.1   Customer Report Card

Customer aware cultures are those that are cognizant of the customer since they are reminded of their presence via frequent complaints. However, their overall attitude is one of accommodation rather than support. These organizations typically survive if they lack competition or if they have a product, price, or convenience that customers desire and will simply put up with the poor service in order to get it. Their customers are often disappointed with their experience.

Customer friendly is a label reserved for organizations that give enough lip service to customer service that it shows up in pockets of service delivery but not consistently. A typical bank might be one example—a friendly branch in one location and another simply going through the motions. Their efforts yield customers who are generally satisfied. Satisfied customers only remain as long as a better (or sometimes simply different) option is unavailable. They essentially take the organization for granted! Customer friendly organizations can survive if they can keep the price-service-product (or outcome) in proper balance.

Customer focused cultures are found in organizations that get consistently good marks from their customers. They not only do the basics exceedingly well, but also they periodically take actions that yield a great story customers enjoy repeating. They place extensive effort on ensuring offerings are based on up-to-date customer intelligence and feedback. They ensure employees are resourced, supported, and motivated. They ensure service is comfortable and convenient. Their efforts produce customers who are loyal.

Customer centric cultures are very rare. A positive customer experience is almost guaranteed. Employees seem to have unlimited authority to take care of customers and exercise obvious initiative to ensure customers get a consistently great experience. Enormous effort is put into training and continuous improvement. These organizations hire the best, expect the best performance, treat their employees as the best, and hold leaders accountable for achieving the best. Their over-the-top service creates a strong, almost cult-like following among customers. Their customers enthusiastically speak of them in terms that reflect love.

We live in a culture that values an "A" performance. And, clearly customers enjoy the "A" service performance that typically comes from a customer centric organization. However, as any responsible CFO can tell you, there are more components to marketplace success than the customer's grade on the quality of the service they receive. L.L. Bean and Starbucks depend on a good product to go with the service experience. Best Buy and Lexus count on having stores in the right location to reach their target market. USAA Insurance and Amazon.com depend on great information systems to support their superfriendly customer contact people. Great service can only go so far in covering mediocrity in other aspects of the value proposition.

There is also the issue of the economics of operation. If a budget hotel decided to start delivering luxury hotel service, it not only might irresponsibly exceed their customers' requirements, it might bankrupt the hotel. We expect to get great service when we are paying extremely high prices. There is also the issue of the role that customer service plays in gaining competitive advantage. When Bass Pro Shops goes head to head with Cabela's, or Lexus tries to one-up Infiniti, it is more likely their customer service that tips the scale for consumers. How much difference is there between a Marriott hotel and a Hyatt in the same geography, between Hertz and Avis at the same airport, Sears and JCPenney, or United and Delta Airlines, except for the service experience delivered by their front line?

Characteristics of Top-Grade Service Providers

The Customer Centric Service Provider

Customer issues are the primary concern of all leaders.

Customer-designed processes.

Customer input/feedback is constant, pervasive, and viewed as crucial.

Customer metrics drive the enterprise.

Customer service shapes all recognition.

Internal service is a matched set with external service.

Customer-handling manners rule selection for everyone.

The Customer-focused Service Provider

Customer issues an important concern of leaders.

Customer comfort is a key criterion for processes.

Customer input is frequently pursued and used to improve and correct.

Some customer metrics used for monitoring and improvement.

Customer heroes frequently affirmed in a pronounced way.

Good internal service is the rule and frequently discussed.

Service manners criteria are used for selecting people in obvious service roles.

The Customer-friendly Service Provider

Customer issues a concern only due to an event/report.

Customer comfort is a consideration for processes.

Customer input is sometimes pursued and used primarily to correct.

Very few customer metrics are used, primarily for monitoring.

Customer heroes annually affirmed in a limited fashion.

Good internal service is the exception and rarely discussed.

(continued)

(continued)

Service manners criteria are used for selecting people in external customer contact roles only.

While making the customer service dean's list may not be required, being below average in the eyes of customers can carry a heavy toll. Customers who give organizations a "D" or "F" are far less trusting of that enterprise. Absent trust, when inevitable hiccups occur, their customers are much less patient, far sharper in their criticism to other customers, and more hostile in the treatment of the frontline employees they encounter.

JetBlue Airways made the evening news for leaving passengers stranded on the runway for many hours during a winter storm. Some thought it would topple the airline. However, JetBlue's long-term reputation for superior customer service had built up such a large reservoir of trust that the company was quickly back on its feet.

Organizations labeled only "customer aware" (D) and "customer indifferent" (F) are often the butt of "ain't it awful" dinnertime stories. Such an unfavorable reputation erodes employee pride. Harassed and embarrassed by neighbors, employees find themselves hiding their company nametags while standing in the checkout line at the grocery store. It makes it challenging for such an organization to attract and retain the best employees. With low morale fueled in part by customer anger, employees exhibit ever-declining efficiency and productivity.

Choosing the right customer grade to aim for has a wild card in the deck. When it comes to reliability, customers compare their power company to the cable, water, or other utility. When it comes to a restaurant, customers judge the quality of the food against the offerings of other food service providers. But when it comes to the service experience they receive, customers compare an organization to all organizations they encounter delivering great service. When the FedEx delivery person walks with a sense of urgency, customers expect the mail carrier to do the same. When the call center operator of an insurance company answers customers' phone calls on the first ring, their customers expect the cable company to do the same. People judge Delta and United through their Southwest Airlines eyes. And Amazon.com has raised the make-it-easy bar for every e-tailer on the planet. This means the overall standard for customer satisfaction has been raised.

As you consider a level of service relevant for your unit or organization, consider these questions:

What level of service do your customers expect?

What level of service would your customers value and pay for?

What level of service can your employees deliver?

What level of service will leaders support?

What level of service can your culture sustain?

COMPETITIVE ANALYSIS OF THE TAKE-THEIR-BREATH-AWAY STRATEGIES

Once you have chosen a service level to pursue, the next step is to select the right take-their-breath-away strategy. While some take-their-breath-away strategies have obvious ethereal or emotional appeal, in the end they must work for you and for your customers, and they must fit the service level you plan to pursue. Choosing a strategy also depends on the state of the marketplace around you, even if that marketplace is within your organization.

Strategies are like rooms in a house, they serve different functions. The kitchen has a different role than the den or garage. A way to zero in on your best strategy is to first consider the room they represent. Figure 15.2 shows how the various take-their-breath-away strategies serve a particular function.

Animation, reinvention, decoration, and camouflage serve a *revitalization* purpose. They are particularly valuable when service needs a jumpstart or reinvigoration. *Revitalize* literally means "to give new life." Such strategies help overcome service deemed rather plain vanilla, dull, functional, just adequate, or in the doldrums. In an industry such as retail or hospitality, they can be a catalyst for turning good service into something imaginative and positively memorable.

Concierge, partnership, cult-like, and luxury all serve to enhance, improve, or enrich the *relationship* with the customer. Each of the strategies is helpful when the personal relationship with customers needs new, deeper meaning. They help transform industries that focus on transactions to ones that value the on-going relationship with the customer.

Air, air defense, Scout's honor, and firefighter all impact *reliability*. They come into play when customer mistrust has been created through too many service hiccups. They can be great strategies for helping employees refocus on the basics of the service offering.

Animation holds a special role. While it is clearly a take-their-breath-away strategy that helps liven up the customer's experience, animation has a big star next to it in Figure 15.2 because animation should really characterize all service offerings. That's why we started the book with animation. As you review the "Energize" and "Celebrate" sections of the last chapter, you will discover we also end with it.

What benefits does each strategy bring? Figure 15.3 outlines some of the competitive advantage of each take-their-breath-away strategy.

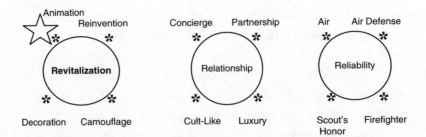

Figure 15.2 Functions Performed by TTBA Strategies.

Figure 15.3 Competitive Advantages of the Take-Their-Breath-Away Strategies

TTBA Strategy	Intent	Competitive Guidance for When to Use This Strategy
Animation	Energy	Industry viewed as dull or boring Service with a lot of people contact Industry where high spirits can fit Examples: Financial services; low-end retail
Reinvention	Transformation	Industry ready for change Market with plenty of early adopters Competitors all seem alike Examples: Car rental; airlines
Decoration	Attraction	Customers are open to novelty Industry viewed as rather functional Employees willing to experiment Examples: Retail; food service; hospitality
Camouflage	Magic	Service in the industry is boring Service delivery contains processes customers dislike Service with frequent repair (e.g., returns) Examples: Retail; financial services
Concierge	All About You	Service with high touch Some service tailoring is necessary Competitors are largely all alike Example: Personal services (e.g., barber)
Partnership	All About Us	Customers have frequent or intense contact Long-term relationship is possible Service requires high touch Example: Professional/personal services

(continued)

Figure 15.3   (*continued*)

TTBA Strategy	Intent	Competitive Guidance for When to Use This Strategy
Cult-Like	Identity	Service with high touch Service with high value potential Service with easy word-of-mouth Examples: Retail; professional services
Luxury	Refinement	Industry without a luxury offering Customers willing to raise service standards Service with discretionary spending Examples: Hospitality; retail
Air	Focus on Core	Service has a routine nature Service with lots of regulation Industry with poor service reputation Examples: Airlines; banks; utilities
Air Defense	Core Protection	Service with health/safety aspect Service where air is often threatened Service with very frequent or infrequent contact Examples: Utilities; food service
Scout's Honor	Trust	Industry where good service relies on trust Industry with low consumer trust Industry frightened by negative PR Examples: Airlines; financial services
Firefighter	Repair	Industry with frequent breakdowns Industry with major breakdowns Customers willing to forgive hiccups Example: Utilities; government

FROM SERVICE STRATEGY TO SERVICE VISION

How do you get everyone in the organization rowing together as one to deliver consistently imaginative service—the kind of reliable, trustworthy, yet inventive performance that keeps customers coming back again and again? It starts with a compelling and actionable service vision. Consistent service excellence demands a game plan that makes it easy for every employee to make decisions that align with the company's overarching mission. Creating a service vision provides a critical alignment anchor.

Virtually every business book, keynote speech, or consulting proposal on culture change starts with "Get a vision." Yet a quick check with the truth tellers on the front lines and back offices who actually survive the brass band, banter, and ballyhoo announcement of "our new vision" will reveal that most visions end up as a framed fixture, not as a valued compass. If a clear vision is needed for successful change, yet most vision efforts fail to pass the snicker test with the typical employee, where does it falter? Is the error from poor preparation or inadequate wordsmithing? Or perhaps a flawed vision development process?

The truth is that too many service visions die because they are not integrated as a valued part of the unit or organization's DNA. The service vision should be the lens through which you look at your entire operation to ensure everything is lined up with the picture. But, if you never wear the lens, you'll stay blind to the actions that are out of sync.

What exactly is a service vision? It is a simple, yet compelling word picture of the signature experience that consistently expresses the take-their-breath-away strategy at the level of service chosen. When Hotel Monaco Chicago speaks of "indulging in the sights, sounds, textures, and tastes of its environment" or "truly imaginative accommodations," the spirit of enchantment is ever present. Such images instruct and guide employees in the type of experience they create, one uniquely different from the

Hyatt-Hilton-Sheraton down the street. A service vision is not only aspirational, it is inspirational and illustrative. It is not just used to point out a destination; it is used as service experience audit tool.

Manheim is the largest wholesale auto auction company in the world. Dealers come to one of 140-plus auction locations to buy and sell cars, over 10 million a year representing a value of over $59 billion. The company has a 60-plus year history as an auto marketplace that values honesty, fairness, and integrity. Dealers told Manheim they wanted an auction experience that "felt like home" and employees who worked as a knowledge-able, proactive team. Manheim chose a concierge strategy. Their service vision became "We are a team of success-makers—for customers, partners, and each other. Our integrity and passion fuel us; our values and legacy guide us; and our commitment to proactive and personalized service unites us." To this they added the slogan: "Fueled by employees; driven for customers."

Starbucks also chose a concierge strategy to re-create the feel and ambiance of the old-fashioned coffeehouse. Every employee carries the *Green Apron Book*, a guide to the unique experience Starbucks seeks to create. At the end of this book are the words: "Creating the experience that keeps people coming back relies on the magical combination of three things: our products, our places, and our people. They come for coffee, stay for the inviting warmth, and return for the very human connection." And then there is a special charge to associates: "Now go ahead, welcome your next new regular."[2]

An effective service vision should reflect a blend of insight—what matters the most to your customer—and oversight—a clear-eyed review of the unit or organization's strengths, weaknesses, opportunities, and threats. It should enable the chosen level of service to be possible and to be an expression of the take-their-breath-away service strategy. An effective service vision becomes the tool for aligning plans, practices, and performances to ensure they are consistent with what is expected by customers.

Often added to the service vision are organization-wide standards and norms. When the Ritz-Carlton Hotel Company coaches its associates that "any employee who receives a guest complaint 'owns' the complaint," it is communicating a necessary standard for being "ladies and gentlemen serving ladies and gentlemen." When Walt Disney World establishes a standard that "no guest is allowed to see a cast member out of character," it is honoring the "code of the Mouse" to keep the Magic Kingdom truly magical. Norms describe behavioral and performance examples of the standard in action so there is absolute clarity resulting in unmistakable consistency.

PULLING IT ALL TOGETHER: A CASE EXAMPLE

High Point University is a private liberal arts college located in High Point, North Carolina. Obviously named for the town, it could have easily been named for the attitude it seeks to create in its students—a high point! When Dr. Nido Qubein assumed the presidency in January 2005, he realized the enormous potential of this academy of higher learning. Using the input of parents, faculty, and the board, a strategy was crafted to transform the college into an extraordinary center for holistic education committed to helping its graduates move on to advance with both success and significance.

The HPU focus on their customer—the student—was captured in their service vision (they call it a branding statement): "At HPU, every student receives an extraordinary education in a fun environment with caring people." Each of these three components is expressed in a fashion that reflects a relentless emphasis on excellence, life values and maximizing potential. *U.S. News & World Report* picked HPU in 2008 as #1 among "up and coming schools" and #5 among all comprehensive colleges in the South. The 2008 freshman enrollment is up 238 percent from 2005. Retention has skyrocketed and SAT scores have jumped 55 points on average.

"Extraordinary education" includes a professor-student ratio of 1 to 14. Over 85 percent of the HPU faculty teaching 68 majors has earned doctorates or terminal degrees in their field. There is an Early Alert program which signals professors to intervene when there are signs a student is not fully tracking toward success. Free tutoring is provided to students who need a little extra help. Even the commencement speakers reflect an emphasis on excellence—Former New York Mayor Rudy Giuliani, Queen Noor of Jordan, Supreme Court Justice Clarence Thomas, and legendary comedian Dr. Bill Cosby. In the 2008-2009 year students heard baseball legend Cal Ripken, former President Bill Clinton, best-selling author Tom Friedman, astronaut Buzz Aldrin, and a dozen major CEOs. HPU student athletes had a cumulative GPA of over 3.0 (B). One of the unique features of a student's education is a focus on community service. HPU students annually donate 27,000 hours and tens of thousands of dollars to causes like cancer research and the United Way.

Extraordinary also extends to character building. When John's son, Chad, visited the campus, President Qubein spoke of the importance of a positive attitude, daring to be extraordinary, and being a leader. "We have a no-whine philosophy here," he explained to the prospects. "Every student gets a tin cricket clicker. Anytime a student hears someone whining they click it. It is a way for everyone to be a leader."

"We are more than student-centered," says President Qubein. "We exist to bring out the very best in our students. We tell our students that this is a partnership. We provide phenomenal housing, delicious food, and a wonderful student life. Their side of the partnership is to excel in the classroom."

The "fun environment" component is easy to spot. The wireless campus sports an immaculate setting with a promenade displaying the flags of the 50-plus countries their diverse student body represents. Speakers play classical music as students change classes. However, everything about the student's experience is done to model a value. Kiosks have free snacks, fruit, and drinks that students can grab as they walk to class (modeling generosity). There is a concierge in their dorms (modeling service), valet parking at night (modeling security), a free car wash on Saturday, and an ice cream truck that meanders the campus on hot days (modeling joy). There is live music in cafeteria to attract students to stay and chat instead of eat and run (modeling fellowship). HPU's Director of Wow! Roger Clodfelter focuses on creating wow experiences for students all year long. He also works to eliminate all that is un-wow, ranging from cracks in the sidewalk to chipped paint. Every detail is managed to ensure the campus is decorated in the color of extraordinary. Log on www.highpoint.edu for a picture of a concierge strategy extraordinarily implemented.

Caring is never taken for granted. Students get a birthday card with a free Starbucks card inside. A large suggestion box encourages student feedback on anything they feel needs improvement. President Qubein knows nearly every student by name, eats lunch with them in the café, and encourages them to stop by and talk anytime. Every freshman takes the president's seminar on life skills. "We are interested in the product. We are *more* interested in the product of the product," Dr. Qubein told us. "We do not measure our effectiveness by the size of our enrollment. We measure it by the vertical impact our graduates make on our world and how our current students feel in their hearts." The success of this glorious experiment is overwhelmingly obvious. A visit to the campus will take your breath away. "Our students are our best promoters," concludes Qubein. "And our parents are our best advocates."

Creating strategy can be exciting. However, great planning will not create devoted customers, only great execution. As Tom Peters warned years ago, the error of "Ready, Fire, Aim" is topped only by "Ready, Aim; Ready, Aim." Planning takes contemplation; execution, however, takes courage. Preparation entails discipline; but implementation evokes daring. In the end, it is important to launch. That means starting the countdown and pushing the button. In the two chapters to follow, we will provide guidance on managing the path on the other side of the plan.

CHAPTER 16

Foresight

Unearthing Potential Customer Stressors

Archeologists excavating the pyramids discovered an unexpected treasure—wheat seeds that dated back to around 2,500 BC. As in the tradition of antiquity, the seeds were there for the dead Pharaoh to have something to eat if he got hungry. The find was important because it would enable scientists to determine what variety of wheat was in use in the ancient world and could be invaluable for engineering and launching new strains of the grain. Out of curiosity, the scientists planted the 4,500-year-old wheat seeds in fertile soil and an amazing thing happened. They grew!

Foresight is about taking an advance look at the factors likely to derail the launch of an effective take-their-breath-away strategy execution. While employees are among the early causalities of wrecked execution, customers suffer the greatest blow as their expectations are raised only to be dashed by unkept promises.

Our look into the process of foresight will be a lot like a treasure hunt. We will examine seven areas where hiccups-in-the-making are likely to be hidden. We call these potential customer stressors *treasure faults*. You may be able to eliminate (or at least minimize) some of these stress creators in advance of your take-their-breath-away strategy rollout. Even if you can neither eliminate nor minimize them, being aware of their influence can shape ways to more effectively roll out your strategy.

"Planning is bringing the future into the present so that you can do something about it now," wrote time management guru Alan Lakein.[1] Have you ever planned a party only to discover at the last minute that the date or time conflicted with a holiday or major athletic event likely to be attended by your invitees? Have you ever planned a meal for guests only to discover as they were ringing your doorbell that you were out of salt or wine or an essential ingredient to finish your recipe?

Effectively launching your take-their-breath-away strategy requires future perfect thinking. That means examining as many of the what ifs as you can with full recognition that there will always be twists and turns as well as highs and lows on your journey to success. In the words of the Indian proverb: "No one was ever lost on a straight road." And there are no straight paths on a journey that involves altering the habits, patterns, and practices of people.

Two Strategy Launch Helpers

There are two helpers important to develop and nurture before your take-their-breath-away strategy launch. One is to have a cadre of scouts. Before customers feel stress, employees are likely to get their version of the stress or at least see the potential to the customer. It is central that employees serve as your early-warning system for these customer stress creators. It requires ensuring employees have a fast, easy, and effective means to send their early warnings. However, their scouting and reporting will only happen if they are incentivized by how much you show you value their warnings. Their candor will come too if they witness your unmistaken dedication to making the new take-their-breath-away strategy work. Be both zealous in your focus and grateful for their help. Remember, if you aren't getting warnings from your scouts, it is a likely indication the new take-their-breath-away strategy is running into problems.

The other helpers to manage prior to take-their-breath-away strategy launch are the skeptics you want to convert. "All hat, no cattle" is the Texas phrase for all form and no substance. It is also the sentiment sometimes expressed by employees when big deal flavors of the month are hurled and heralded from on high. There are skeptics to convert, and there are skeptics to ignore. Convertible skeptics are those who probably have good reason to be skeptics. They have seen their share of programs du jour come and go and are likely to view yours with the same jaundiced eye and this-too-will-pass attitude. The skeptics to ignore are those poor souls who seem to relish staying pessimistic and downbeat no matter the topic.

Converting skeptics can come in several ways. People don't resist change! People resist what they perceive or predict will result in pain over which they have no control. Many skeptics can be neutralized with a "we" approach. It is difficult to feel like a victim when one has a hand in crafting the outcome. Through your early inclusion they share control. Ask for their feedback and ideas. Also, help them see the what's-in-it-for-you side of the effort. Overcommunicate to minimize early rumors instigated by hearsay and half-truths. As people get the information they need, their resistance is quelled since they develop new perceptions of the future that are less painful than they originally imagined. Communication is effective if it is constant, consistent, takes many forms, and, above all, is clear and honest. Convert the skeptics so you aren't dragged down after launch with their nay-saying attitudes.

Treasure Fault #1: Competing Priorities

One of the major potholes you might encounter in your take-their-breath-away strategy launch is the impact of competing priorities. What else is happening within your unit or organization that could conflict with your launch schedule? Could you be conflicting with a major software rollout? Might the timing clash with employees away on vacation or with a community event, industry conference, or required training attended by key people?

Whenever possible, make certain the take-their-breath-away strategy launch is not scheduled for the month the unit or organization is deep into budget preparation. Many budget processes run for a surprisingly long period of time. Often there is one month when the true resource allocation decisions are debated and finalized. Stay clear of that month if you expect to have the focus of your organization. Know your organization's calendar and avoid selecting launch times when key players are absent or distracted.

Conflicting priorities can sometimes grow out of the take-their-breath-away strategy's reliance on processes that cross departmental lines of responsibility. If the departments who are the caretakers of their parts of the processes have conflicting objectives, there will be little hope of a successful launch, let alone sustaining the new initiative. If launching a reinvention strategy, for example, depends on a program change in how a shared operating system communicates information, all parts sharing the output of the system need to have a chance to weigh in on how the program change will impact their requirements. It is vital that take-their-breath-away strategy champions and implementers initiate conversations in which the respective conflict in priorities can be surfaced, discussed, and either resolved or effectively managed. Collaboration is always important to a successful take-their-breath-away strategy launch, particularly when multiple units are impacted.

Treasure Fault #2: Processes That Don't Play Well ... Together

Most often, a new take-their-breath-away strategy impacts certain service processes. It is important there be a thorough examination of all processes even remotely impacted by the strategy. When the front-desk employees of a major hotel found ways to speed up guest check-in they failed to consider that the goal of the guest was not to get checked in quickly, but to get into their hotel room quickly. Failing to integrate speedy check-in with how fast housekeeping could get rooms cleaned resulted in even more stress for the guest. Fast check-in raised guest expectations that were then shattered upon hearing "your room is not quite ready. Give us your cell phone number and we will call you as soon as housekeeping releases the room."

Most units and organizations depend on cross-functional processes and practices supported and/or enhanced by specific technology. When considering the implementation of a new take-their-breath-away strategy, review the organization's key processes and practices to determine if they are aligned with the new take-their-breath-away strategy. Such a process review can be tedious and detailed work, dissimilar from the creative and innovative process of developing and designing the strategy. Yet it is at least as important as any other element in the process. Great take-their-breath-away strategies too often fail in execution when derailed by an unaligned process or practice.

Freeman, a company headquartered in Dallas, Texas, provides services for exhibitions, conventions, and corporate events. Attend any large trade show around the country and odds are Freeman has supplied much of the furnishings and merchandise you see around you. Freeman has always provided an exhibitor service desk at each show for exhibitors who need additional display items and/or encounter problems with their order.

Freeman was dissatisfied with the service quality at the service desk, particularly at peak times when lines could be long or staff too swamped to deliver rush items. During a spirited discussion on how the service desk could be reinvented, then-SVP of Operations Keith Kennedy, a 35-year Freeman veteran, suggested, "Why don't we eliminate the service desk all together?" Attendees were stunned; most assumed Keith would be protective of his turf. Keith continued, "Why are we making our customers come to us when we could have our folks out on the exhibit hall floor taking immediate action to solve exhibitors' issues?"

Freeman turned to their customers for input. Customers let them know they wanted a service desk—a place they were confident could typically solve their problems and handle their requests. However, they also let Freeman know they needed faster response times on the floor. The result? Today, Freeman's customers get the best of both worlds. Freeman scaled down the exhibitor service desk but added roving concierges on the show floor to provide on-the-spot service via electronic hand-held devices. This has allowed exhibitors to stay in their booths and avoid waiting in line at the service desk when requests need to be handled promptly.

Treasure Fault #3: No Sustainability Plan

Sustainability is the ongoing nourishment a new take-their-breath-away strategy will require to maintain momentum, overcome the inevitable bumps of all new changes, and conquer the boredom that sets in as soon as the shiny and excitement of new wears off. It is imperative to plan for ongoing nourishment. Without planned sustainability there is great risk that less-than-enthused employees will turn their attention to other priorities before the new take-their-breath-away strategy gets an opportunity to take and become a part of the organization's DNA. The length of a sustainability plan is tied to the complexity of the take-their-breath-away strategy, the length of time needed for implementation, and the amount of change it triggers. Most plans run a minimum of six to nine months; there is no maximum period.

Waning interest in any change effort is predictable. Like New Year's resolutions and diet programs, the planned change is susceptible to all manner of influences and diversions until it is fully integrated into habit and pattern. Sometimes new people with different priorities can sidetrack a change effort. Sometimes a shift in business direction, distractions from other change efforts, or a downturn in the economy can doom efforts. However, the greatest influence is the insidious pull to forsake awkward new practices for more comfortable old routines. Building in stopgaps can help bridge the distraction.

A large business-to-business company was a year into a new service strategy. Early warning that excitement was waning came with a simple staff meeting. There was nothing on the weekly leadership agenda even remotely related to customer service. The company president called the consultant assisting with the change effort to voice her concern. The two began planning a major service audit. Patterned after the service components of the Malcolm Baldrige National Quality Award, they assembled a team of key customers to serve as examiners. Units within the company revved up their "needs improvement" engines to compete for various service awards. The renewal effort was so successful in preserving a focus on the service strategy it became a valued annual event. Like the unexpected treasure from the pyramids, the seeds of permanence were planted.

An effective way to help your take-their-breath-away strategy weather the challenges of sustainability is organized learning. Change requires growth, a state that can often put people in a position of public awkwardness. Leaders especially prefer to appear competent rather than in the potentially embarrassing position of being viewed as a greenhorn. Many a change effort has faltered and failed simply because leaders were unwilling to be exposed. However, if everyone is in the same circumstances, then resistance to putting themselves in a vulnerable position can be significantly less.

Harley-Davidson almost went bankrupt holding onto old methods. Under the leadership of then CEO Rich Teerlink, the company embarked on a massive long-term change effort that ultimately saved the company. A part of that effort was the implementation of Harley-Davidson University, an annual three-day event that included every company officer and every Harley dealer. Opening the event in Ft. Lauderdale, CEO Teerlink included in his presentation the words, "Here's something I screwed up on this week . . . and, what I learned from it." His words signaled that change required learning; learning involved making mistakes.

Treasure Fault #4: "We've Always Done It That Way"

Most of us are creatures of comfort and habit. Stability is comforting since it is predictable. Implementing a new take-their-breath-away strategy is likely to represent novelty. With their pattern-making minds, employees may first question the strategy as being deviant or abnormal when it may simply be at odds with the status quo. But the larger issue will be trying to mentally process a new approach through the filter of old and familiar mind patterns. Like the superlogical, analytical engineer trying to get his head around an emotional, irrational concept, the initial mental awkwardness may lead an early trial to getting an early rejection.

It is for this reason that new take-their-breath-away strategies need champions and advocates who can encourage resistors to fake it until they get it. New take-their-breath-away strategy launches often benefit from a pilot period and a test plan to get new users comfortable before going live. New take-their-breath-away strategies also need to be concretely grounded in the proof that "our customers will want this."

Treasure Fault #5: Uncommitted People, Especially Leaders

People are the number one variable in the quality of the service experience. Ultimately, much of the customer's experience is delivered and determined by the people involved. And people are the main make-or-break feature of all culture change efforts. The people most essential to success are leaders.

Leaders daily walk under a floodlight. They stay in the unblinking watchful eye of their employees. Leader actions proclaim priority; leader priorities telegraph values. When roles and responsibility for implementation are left ambiguous, it communicates that activity takes precedent over results. When direction is not coupled with interim check-ups and feedback, it says to employees that leaders are more interested in checking a box than accomplishing an outcome. Employees pay less attention to whether the leader delivers an eloquent charge to go forward and more to whether there are leader-directed consequences that follow performance or nonperformance.

Commitment is vital to fuel the energy needed to stay on course. Anne Morriss contributed the following quote to "The Way I See It" on the side of a Starbucks coffee cup: "The irony of commitment is that it's deeply liberating—in work, in play, in love. The act frees you from the tyranny of your internal critical, from the fear that likes to dress itself up and parade around as rational hesitation. To commit is to remove your head as the barrier to your life."[2] Since leaders often have more than their share of rational and head-driven logic, Morriss' counsel is valuable to leading change.

Change always contains an element of the fear of the unknown. One way to minimize the fear is for employees to get lots of clear, timely information about the new take-their-breath-away strategy and feedback about their performance contribution. Fear is also reduced when leaders are very visible and approachable, especially as the new take-their-breath-away strategy is being launched. "A body can pretend to care, but they can't pretend to be there," wrote Texas Bix Bender in his book *Don't Squat With Yer Spurs On!*[3] Visibility can be a key indication of buy-in.

Treasure Fault #6: Out-of-Sync Performance Management

Most organizations have a performance management process designed to help managers and employees determine and agree on the employee's work goals and plans. These performance plans are typically related to employee compensation and development. One by-product of performance planning is the clarification of roles, expectations, responsibilities, and consequences. Performance management, done effectively, ensures a meeting of the minds that helps promote focus and discipline to work performance and understanding and agreement to the leader-subordinate relationship. It can be the foundation of fairness, morale, and support that all contribute to worker productivity and unit accomplishment.

Effective implementation of a take-their-breath-away strategy will not only require a quest for excellence, but also it will take collaboration and coordination with others when collective effort is involved. Clarity and discipline are imperative. Without an effective performance management process there will be no method for synchronizing effort and harmonizing contribution. The by-product will likely be disjointed performance that is viewed by the customer as a lack of congruence and consistency. Haphazard and disorganized all spell a lack of trust to customers, ramping up their stress and lowering their devotion.

Treasure Fault #7: Inadequate Competence

Studies have shown that customers, given a forced choice, would rather have a surly expert than an incompetent Pollyanna. As much as customers like passionate, pleasant servers, throw "competent" into the mix and it races to the top of the list.[4] All take-their-breath-away strategies assume the people who bring the strategy to the customer have the knowledge, skill, and expertise to pull off the strategy. Employee competence is a precursor to customer confidence. And, confidence is one of those *air* factors that must be present for devotion to exist. No customer ever proclaimed, "I really love them, but I can't trust them!"

One type of this treasure fault could be the failure to accurately determine if there is a gap between the skills and knowledge needed to successfully execute the take-their-breath-away strategy with the competence present. Another fault might be a lack of understanding regarding the most effective way to close the gap—whether through training existing employees or hiring new people who already have the needed competence. Too often, organizations—in their pursuit of cost effectiveness—stretch employees into a new arena when hiring a new person might be the smartest approach. While there is always wisdom in maximizing employee potential, taking employees way beyond their capacity can set them up to be a casualty.

Why wheat in the pyramids? Wheat is one of the most nutritious plants in the world. It can be used to produce many different types of food. A plant cultivated for more than 10,000 years, every part of the wheat plant—from stalk to grain—has some valuable purpose. Because wheat is generally a self-pollinating plant, each plant tends to produce clones of itself. Take-their-breath-away service has many of the same features.

The features of wheat serve as a powerful metaphor for what fertilizes and sustains the implementation of a new take-their-breath-away strategy. Change lasts if it helps nourish the unit or organization in a manner that is healthy and productive. Change takes if it empowers people to be fully functioning, wholesome, and emotionally strong. Bottom line, change moves from experiment to permanence when it enables the organization to be self-pollinating.

CHAPTER 17
Green Light
Launch Lessons for Leaders

If you checked the list of most-admired to the least-admired occupations, car sales would not be in the top 20! In fact, we sometimes use used-car salesman as the epitome of distrust. The typical car dealership has too many cars, salespeople who are too aggressive, service that is too slow—like they are quick to sell you and slow to serve you—and receptionists with the personality of a concrete block. But there is a bright shining exception: Dallas-based Sewell Automotive!

Take a visit to Sewell Lexus in Dallas, Texas. The first thing you notice as you approach the bone-colored building is the oversized glass door with a large brass door opener proudly displaying the Lexus logo. Both door and opener are polished to perfection. A huge overhead light shaped like an upside down diamond bathes the bone-colored tile of the showroom in a soft glow. Offices are done in rich cherry paneling. Large plants are everywhere, as are colorful fresh flowers. The sitting area has overstuffed couches centered on a rich oriental rug. If this were a home it would be in *Architectural Digest*!

You realize you are in a classy place when you are warmly greeted by everyone like you are a guest in their home, not like easy prey for salespeople in search of a kill. Instead of the proverbial sleaze talk—"Have I got a special for you," or "Let me help you drive away in the car of your dreams," or even, "Anything in particular you looking for today?"—you get "Please let us know if we can be of assistance." The walls are adorned with numerous J.D. Power Awards, telegraphing an unmistakable allegiance to quality.

There is no pressure and no hassle. The focus is on you, not on the vehicle. Sales professionals build relationships grounded in trust, not hype; they are clearly on a quest for a thrilled customer, not just a higher notch on the "number of cars sold" chart. Conversations about the vehicle tell you in an instant you are dealing with expertise. Not an arrogant, smarty-pants "Let me show you how brilliant I am" attitude, but a quiet, understated style that leaves you feeling very confident. Salespeople show the kind of bubbly pride and solid confidence in what they sell that convinces you they have fallen in love with the brand.

The buying process is without the mysterious sales manager you never see in the back that is approving the counteroffer of the powerless salesperson. Salespeople at Sewell can take the sale to the end without checking with someone. And, the first move they make after closing a sale is to take the new customer to meet the service manager. They make these handoffs with the finesse and grace of an Olympic relay team.

Now, walk into Sewell Cadillac Saab, Sewell Infiniti, Sewell Hummer, Sewell Buick-Pontiac-GMC, or any of the 16 Sewell auto franchises and you get the exact same quality experience. Talk with the U.S. headquarters of all of these brands and Sewell will be at the very top of their "best of the best" dealerships. Many dealerships around the country dream of being #2 behind Sewell. It is a brand that puts customers first, and customers have rewarded Sewell with their long-term devotion. Sewell dealerships enjoy one of the highest repeat business rates in the industry. But where did all this customer devotion begin? And, how has it been sustained since 1972, when Carl Sewell Jr. took the reins of a business his father started in 1911?

In 1980, Sewell built a state-of-the-art Cadillac dealership on Lemmon Avenue in Dallas. Three giant brass chandeliers adorned the showroom over a floor so shiny it mirrored the array of new cars. Restrooms looked as if they were imported from a five-star hotel. Service technicians (not mechanics) kept the service bay with the spic and span of a hospital operating room. Upscale pastries, designer coffee, antiques, and leather couches helped decorate the waiting area. But the centerpiece of this talk-of-the-industry dealership was its unrelenting focus on creating devoted customers.

Customer service Sewell-style was heralded in Carl's best-selling book, *Customers for Life*. It is chock full of stories and sermons. Like the customer who broke his key off in the door trying to leave the airport and called Sewell for help. Help came instantly at no charge. Like inviting customers to call if they need help 24/7. Or like a guaranteed estimate of charges for repairs, or complimentary chocolates when you pay your bill, or a fleet of over 150 loaners. Sewell Village Cadillac quickly became the standard of excellence for all Cadillac dealerships. Launching this bold strategy required imaginative leadership that reflected five features: trumpet, exhibit, energize, harmonize, and sponsor.

TRUMPET

Since Carl Sewell selected a decoration take-their-breath-away strategy, it was important the launch match the service strategy. When Sewell Village Cadillac introduced new model cars, Carl took a page from the Neiman Marcus Christmas catalog—some extravagant items are always included to help set the tone for the catalog. Carl held an annual coming-out party for the new cars, complete with champagne, roast beef, and fancy desserts. He hired a band, dressed his salespeople in tuxedos, and made a big deal to show off the new cars. He even invited devoted customer and celebrity Larry Hagman of the TV show *Dallas* to help with the festivities. Over 5,000 people attended. At first Sewell only invited customers. Then, he opened it up to anyone driving a Cadillac!

Trumpet includes all the actions that signal a change is in the offing. When Bass Pro Shops opened their new store in Spanish Fort, Alabama, they featured an Evening for Conservation event with fishing legend Bill Dance, NASCAR driver Martin Truex, Jr., and Major League Baseball veteran Ryan Klesko. When luxury hotelier Rosewood Resorts opened their Acqualina property in Dubai, the launch included 40 VIPs, 400 guests, a fashion show, formal beachside buffet, and silent auction. Contrast that with Southwest Airlines, master of the air strategy, who opened at BWI airport with balloons, soft drinks, popcorn, and recorded music. Both launches were successful for their targeted customer.

When Banco Continental de Panama rolled out their new customer-focused take-their-breath-away initiative, the CEO demonstrated the organization's strong sense of commitment by holding what they labeled "The Big Event." Every employee and officer attended one of three one-day events held at an extraordinary rainforest resort an hour from their headquarters. The buses that transported employees were decorated. Tour guides on board taught them a special song written for the event as they were en route. The event started and ended with huge celebrations. Between the celebrations the CEO, key leaders, and over 50 employees acted as facilitators for one of several mini-shows that participants rotated through. When participants came to work Monday morning following "The Big Event" all the computer screen savers had been changed to reflect the new focus. Signs, mementos, tools, and a host of supportive procedural changes all helped communicate to employees the service strategy was real, relevant, and ready to become permanent. Monthly thereafter, leaders held special sessions to reaffirm and reinforce as the take-their-breath-away initiative moved from a fun high to a valued habit.

So You Are a Solo Act

Even if you are not in charge of a unit or organization, you still need to carefully launch your take-their-breath-away service strategy. Here are a few tips for making it take.

Always underpromise and overdeliver.

Be patient with impact; the change may take longer than you had planned.

It is normal for some customers to be skeptical of any change you make.

Know that your service might decline before it gets better as you and your customers learn new ways.

Some of your customers and co-workers will not like "the new you." Just deal with it.

Let your customers and coworkers see your passion for the new take-their-breath-away strategy.

Make sure your strategy is not at odds with your organization's mission and values. Reread "Important Voices" in Chapter 14.

Create an advisory team of a few important customers to give you continual feedback.

Create an advisory team of colleagues to give you emotional support.

Take-their-breathe-away service is a journey, not a destination. Once you have started, the focus must be continually nurtured.

Give it your very best. If you want something to really grow, pour champagne on it!

EXHIBIT

The day Sewell Lexus opened, Carl was out of town for the morning. The new dealership was filled on opening day with prospects and well-wishers. The paint was barely dry, and carpenters were still working on the building on opening day. When Carl arrived that afternoon, he found cups and empty boxes lying around outside. He began picking up the debris only to be silently joined by several of his salespeople. A couple of guys noted, "The contractor was supposed to do this." Carl's response: "But they didn't and this is our house, so we have to take care of it."

"If you're the boss, you can't fake it," wrote Sewell in *Customers for Life*.[1] "You either believe in the goals you've set or you don't, and if you don't you're going to get found out. Employees watch their leaders too closely for them to be able to fake anything. Once people catch you not caring about a goal you've set—you said we always have to treat customers *honestly*, and they watch while you deliberately short-change someone—it's all over. They'll stop caring because they see you don't. Once that happens, all the banners and pep rallies in the world aren't going to change things. With everything we do, we're sending a message to both our customers and our employees about what kind of place we're running and what we think is important."

Exhibit is our word for model. Too often *model* conveys an up-on-a-pedestal quality, on display and removed, not elbow to elbow in the trenches. Carl lives his values every minute, not just at big-deal events when the spotlight is shining. Model also does not mean a replica of perfection; leaders should be real, not ideal. Exhibit implies what is quietly demonstrated and subtly revealed. It means leaders using their actions as evidence of what is important. This is particularly important with a new strategy.

"If you want your employees to be polite to your customers," says Carl Sewell, "you have to be polite to your employees." How employees treat customers and colleagues is often a function of how leaders treat them. When leaders show curiosity and interest, the message to employees is that they are valued. Valued

employees have high self-esteem and are better able to demonstrate confidence when serving others.

One thing that take-their-breath-away strategy leaders exhibit
is high standards. Carl would never ask an employee to do something he was not himself doing. He knows employees do not
watch a leader's mouth, they watch the leader's moves. Lexus Corporation has a CSI (Customer Service Index) program centered
on a national score. "It is our job internally to meet or exceed the
national Lexus CSI average," says Dawn Betrus, a top salesperson
for Sewell Lexus in Dallas. "For instance, when an inquiry from
the Lexus Web site comes in, the Lexus standard is that it must be
answered within 60 minutes. But, Sewell's expectations are that
it be answered in 10 minutes."

Take-their-breath-away strategy leaders make themselves visible. Leaders can't exhibit by staying in the office. To lead by
example requires being there working shoulder to shoulder during a busy time or when there is a need. When leaders don
the same uniform as employees and view work through their
employees' eyes it speaks volumes about priority.

ENERGIZE

It only takes a few seconds with Carl Sewell to read his passion
for customers. His eyes light up and his smile broadens when
hearing a positive comment or a helpful suggestion from a customer. Framed customer letters adorn his office, not awards (and
he has won a gazillion of them). Books about customer service
are in his bookcase, not policy manuals. He lives, breathes, eats,
and sleeps "the customer." And, his regular meetings are domi-
nated by customer-talk. "Mr. Sewell energizes his employees to
be passionate about the customer by priding himself and our company on his name and what that means to our clients," say Dawn
Betrus. "The Dallas area knows the Sewell name is synonymous
with great customer service." It is our job as employees to carry
on this important legacy and make sure our clients are always
very pleased with their Sewell experience."

"Repeating our values and beliefs over and over again is a lot like why they hold church every Sunday," wrote Sewell in his book. "Even when you know what you're supposed to do you sometimes can forget. And, that's why we keep repeating what we believe in—and celebrate each time we meet one of our goals: to remind ourselves."[2]

A fundamental component of energize is the collective creation of purpose. It entails creating contexts in which everyone enters the dialogue about direction. "Just like when you go to any five-star establishment, you have expectations of what your experience will be and should be," Dawn Betrus told us. "And I believe that's what Mr. Sewell has created with our dealerships. You can trust that walking into our showroom isn't like walking into your average car dealership." Collective creation of purpose involves getting every person impacted by the new take-their-breath-away strategy to have an honest, non-pressured say in how it impacts them and what they will need to do to make the new strategy effective.

Carl Sewell has been for many years an energizer leader. Allison Cohen, top salesperson for Dallas-based Sewell Infiniti, puts it this way: "Mr. Sewell excites us by giving us the tools we need to be successful so we are able to treat our customers the exact same way he treats employees. He always keeps us up to date on what is happening with Sewell and things that are coming down the pipeline from Infiniti. Mr. Sewell is always asking for feedback and inquiring about what he can do to make us more successful."

HARMONIZE

Customer trust comes through consistency. And consistency is built on aligned efforts. When the customer's experience exactly matches the organization's covenant implied by ads, marketing, prior customer experience, and word of mouth, the customer comes to rely on the experience as trustworthy. To achieve such an end, it is crucial leaders act noticeably in sync with the promise. More than role modeling, it is the deliberate effort to think and act congruently with the promise implied by the covenant.

When Simon Cooper, president of The Ritz-Carlton Hotel Company, treats the doorman at a Ritz property with the same respect he might give a frequent guest, it is harmonizing in action. When Zappos.com CEO Tony Hsieh attends training sessions and departmental happy hours it communicates the egalitarian, open culture needed for their concierge take-their-breath-away strategy to foster customer devotion. When Larry Kurzweil, president of Universal Studios Hollywood, requested that the theme park turn up the volume on the street music and to make it peppy, walking-somewhere music, it was harmonizing the ambiance with the decoration take-their-breath-away strategy.

The leader's role as a harmonizing influencer is to search for areas where the new take-their-breath-away strategy's implementation may create dissonance. The clash may come from processes out of sync with the new strategy. If the take-their-breath-away strategy calls for creating customer partnerships yet the returns policies communicate mistrust, there is dissonance. If an air strategy is selected and yet employees are allowed to be lax on safety procedures, the mixed message spells mistrust to customers.

As Carl Sewell states, "Being nice to people is just 20 percent of providing good customer service. The important part is designing systems that allow you to do the job right the first time. . . .[3] Systematic approaches are 80 percent of customer service. They're what's *really* important, not the smiles and thank yous. The key is to devise systems that allow you to give the customer what he wants every time."[4]

SPONSOR

The word *sponsor* means to champion, inspire, or advocate. Leaders who sponsor invite inventiveness among employees. A major study done on the most productive research and development organizations in the world—those with the most patents and the most profound breakthroughs—found their employees labeled R&D leaders as inspiring.[5] They did not mean charisma or charm. Rather, they pointed to the leader's willingness to be bold in their decisions, courageous in the support, and ethical in their nature.

Leaders who sponsor are *spirit-full leaders*—they let go of *proving* who they are in exchange for *being* who they are. They are givers whose curious interest in others drives them to be completely absorbed in whoever is on the other end of their conversation. They are patient listeners eager to learn, not anxious to make a point. Leaders who sponsor cultivate pioneers—employees who think imaginatively in their quest to leave customers with a sparkly experience and a story to tell.

Leaders who sponsor know and practice the power of expectations. One of the single most powerful phenomena in human behavior is the self-fulfilling prophecy (also called the *Pygmalion effect*). The leader's belief, demonstrated in behavior and attitude, has a significant impact on the individual or team's performance. If the leader believes the team or a team member is going to be successful and treats them that way, they generally are successful. If the leader believes the team or a team member is likely to fail, and treats them that way, they generally fail. It suggests it is critically important how leaders communicate high, positive expectations to the team. Even tone of voice and emphasis on key words can impact what is interpreted as leader belief.

Leaders who sponsor know that celebrations are spirit refreshments! Celebration is a way of nourishing group spirit. This is especially important when knee deep in the challenging tasks of implementing a new take-their-breath-away strategy. A well-executed celebration represents a moment in time when a glimpse of a transformed organization—a product of the efforts of people from many levels—can be seen, felt, and enjoyed. In highly human terms, celebration reaffirms to people that they are an important part of something that really matters.

"Internally we celebrate with recognizing those employees that go the extra mile for our clients as well as our employees," Dawn Betrus of Sewell Lexus told us. "Each week we receive numerous letters from our clients detailing the special service and great experience they had at Sewell. Our managers read them and present them to the employee during our weekly sales meetings."

Carl Sewell has refined the art of celebration. Allison Cohen of Sewell Infiniti describes Carl's approach in this fashion: "We do have some great celebrations. We always have our end of year awards ceremony dinner. We also have a 20 group dinner. For every salesperson that sells 20 cars at least one time in a month, we have a dinner and are given our checks. If you sell 20 cars more than 3 times then you are invited to Carl's house for drinks, eat dinner at the five-star Rosewood Mansion on Turtle Creek and then stay overnight. When we wake up, we all have breakfast. This is always one night I look forward to because I know for sure that my husband and I will have a night out without the kids!"

Leaders who celebrate are quick to affirm and slow to critique. And, they seek the means, moments, and methods to convey gratitude and encouragement for service greatness. Leaders who celebrate know that the most powerful affirmations are those that matter to the one on whom they are bestowed. They also know that servers who feel affirmed are more likely to pass that same feeling on to the customers they serve.

RAINBOWS EVERY DAY

The summer rain stopped and the golden sun melted away all the dark clouds. Left in the sky was a brilliant rainbow, a perfect half circle prism that caused every observer to think of pots of gold. "Wouldn't it be wonderful," muses the observer, "if you could have a rainbow every day?" Take-their-breath-away service is a service wonder that makes customers remember that enchantment is not only possible, it is something they deserve. But, what prevents it from being something you give or receive every day?

All organizations are challenged by the economics of extras. Take-their-breath-away service is the perfect substitute for value-added when adds cannot be funded. Avis Bell and Liz Patterson are children of the Great Depression. They also happen to be our mothers. Their stories of living through the worst economic times of the last century are peppered with joyful memories of special Christmases when there was no money to buy gifts. Handmade original surprises had to replace store-bought ones. The restriction forced the giver to think about the uniqueness of the recipient; it enabled the receiver to appreciate the labor of love over the expediency of purchase.

We were in midtown Manhattan and hailed a taxi. "Thank you for stopping," we said to the pilot of the cab. "We're running late and need to quickly get to 51st and Madison." The taxi driver asked if we wanted to hear music; we agreed. He continued: "Would you like to hear music like you have never heard before?" We suddenly felt we were on a musical adventure. "I am from India, and this is a mix I created myself." He began to narrate the music we were hearing as the taxi weaved through early morning New York City traffic. He was as passionate about his driving as he was his musical creation. When we arrived at our destination and were paying the fare, he handed us a copy of the CD and proudly announced, "This is my gift to you; I hope I'll see you again." Thank you, Paul, for taking our breath away.

Take-their-breath-away service is a handmade original surprise. Its power to attract and retain customers lies in its capacity to make the customer feel they have been bestowed a value-unique expression that honors the very nobility of service. Its originality and imagination telegraph an innate commitment to excellence. Its handmade distinction signals an unmistakable spotlight on the customer. And, like a perfect rainbow, it leaves us astonished, affirmed, and served.

Notes

INTRODUCTION

1. The American Customer Satisfaction Index reports scores on a 0–100 scale at the national level and produces indexes for 10 economic sectors, 43 industries (including e-commerce and e-business), and more than 200 companies and federal or local government agencies. The ACSI is managed by the University of Michigan Ross School of Business.
2. Seth Godin, "In Praise of the Purple Cow," *Fast Company* 17 (January 2003): 76.

PART ONE A CALL FOR IMAGINATIVE SERVICE

1. Kendall Anderson, "Alzheimer's Patients Find Homes in Past," *Dallas Morning News*, April 15, 2002.
2. Thomas L. Friedman, "The Hot Zones," *The New York Times*, February 12, 1997.

CHAPTER 1 ANIMATION

1. Photo of White's Restaurant courtesy of White's Restaurant, Salem, OR.
2. Pete Blackshaw, *Satisfied Customers Tell Three Friends, Angry Customers Tell 3000: Running a Business in Today's Consumer-Driven World* (New York: Doubleday Business, 2008), p. 11.
3. Rollo May, *Love and Will* (New York: Dell Publishing, 1969), p. 312.
4. Viktor E. Frankl, *Man's Search for Meaning* (New York: Washington Square Press, Simon and Schuster, 1963), p. 104.

5. Stanley Herman, *Authentic Management* (Reading, MA: Addison-Wesley, 1977), p. 25.

Chapter 2 Reinvention

1. Aldous Huxley, *The Doors of Perception* (New York: Harper & Row, 1954), p. 18
2. Photo of the Dung Mug courtesy of its manufacturer, Mocha in Essex, U.K. (www.mocha.uk.com) and was designed by Dominic Skinner in London
3. Jena McGregor, "High Tech Achieve: Netflix," *Fast Company*, (October, 2005).

Chapter 3 Decoration

1. Photo courtesy of Stew Leonard's Dairy Store in Norwalk, CT.
2. Sharon Hori, "Zany Servers at Ed Devebic's Dish Out Attitude to Diners," *UCLA Daily Bruins*, December 1, 1999.
3. Donald A. Norman, *Turn Signals Are the Facial Expressions of Automobiles* (Reading, MA: Addison-Wesley, 1992). Quoted in *The Experience Economy*, by Joseph Pine and James Gilmore.
4. Russell C. Brumfield, *Whiff! The Revolution of Scent Communication in the Information Age* (New York: Quimby Press, 2008), p. 39.
5. Photo of Frank and Sammy's business card courtesy of Nicholson-Hardie, Dallas.
6. Photo of the gumball machine courtesy of Miller Brothers, Atlanta.

Chapter 4 Camouflage

1. Bill Price and David Jaffe, *The Best Service Is No Service* (San Francisco: Jossey-Bass, 2008), p. 38.
2. David Kirkpatrick, "Dell in the Penalty Box," *Fortune* (September 18, 2006): 26.

CHAPTER 5 CONCIERGE

1. John Goodman, Stephen Newman and Cynthia Grimm, "The ROI of Delight," *Customer Relationship Management* 8 (2003): 12.

CHAPTER 6 PARTNERSHIP

1. Robert E. Pierre, "A Lot on Worried Restaurant Owner's Plate," *Washington Post*, December 9, 2007, C3.
2. Photo of the "Got Mayor" poster courtesy of the City of Santa Clarita, CA.

CHAPTER 7 CULT-LIKE

1. Karl Albrecht and Ron Zemke, *Service America in the New Economy* (New York: McGraw-Hill, 2002), p. 13.
2. Tennessee Squire Association story used with permission from the Jack Daniel Distillery in Lynchburg, TN.
3. Peter Drucker, *Adventures of a Bystander* (New York: Harper & Row, 1979), p. 255.
4. Leonard L. Berry, *Discovering the Soul of Service* (New York: The Free Press, 1999), p. 233.
5. Photo of the broom straw against the door courtesy of Reynolds Plantation on Lake Oconee, GA.

CHAPTER 9 AIR

1. Henry Martin, *The New Yorker* cartoon, August, 1978. Used with permission from the Tribune Company Syndicate, Inc.
2. Frederick Herzberg, *One More Time: How Do You Motivate Employees?* Harvard Business Review Classics (Boston: Harvard Business Press, 2008). Originally published in *Harvard Business Review* 46 (1968): 53–62.
3. Photo of the bathroom courtesy of Columbia Tower Club, Seattle.

4. Tom Peters and Robert Waterman, *In Search of Excellence* (New York: Warner Books, 1982), p. 123.

CHAPTER 10 AIR DEFENSE

1. Valarie A. Zeithaml, A. Parasuraman, and Leonard L. Berry, *Delivering Quality Service*, p. 25.
2. Louise Faber, "How Are Emotions Processed and Stored in Our Brains?" *Australian Science* (October 2005): 21.
3. Tom Peters and Nancy Austin, *A Passion for Excellence: The Leadership Difference* (New York: Random House, 1985), p. 71.

CHAPTER 11 SCOUT'S HONOR

1. Valarie A. Zeithaml, A. Parasuraman, and Leonard L. Berry, *Delivering Quality Service*, p. 25.
2. David A. Aaker, *Managing Brand Equity* (New York: The Free Press, 1991), p. 46.
3. Dell revenue figures, http://www.dell.com/content/topics/global.aspx/about_dell/investors/financials/index?c=us&l=en&s=corp (accessed September 13, 2008).

CHAPTER 12 FIREFIGHTER

1. Ron Zemke and Chip R. Bell, *Knock Your Socks Off Service Recovery* (New York: AMACOM Books, 2000).

PART TWO THE TAKE-THEIR-BREATH-AWAY EXECUTION PLAN

1. Kim Clark and Takahiro Fujimoto, *Product Development Performance* (Boston: Harvard Business School Press, 1991), p. 62.

CHAPTER 13 INSIGHT

1. Jerald W. Young, "The Effects of Perceived Physician Competence on Patient's Symptom Disclosure," *Journal of Behavioral Medicine* 3 (September 1980), p. 86.

2. William C. Taylor, "Get Out of That Rut and Into the Shower," *The New York Times*, August 13, 2006.

3. Chip R. Bell and Ron Zemke, *Managing Knock Your Socks Off Service* (1st ed.) (New York: AMACOM Books, 1992), p. 38.

CHAPTER 14 OVERSIGHT

1. Peter Drucker, *The Practice of Management* (New York: Harper & Row, 1954), p. 39.

2. Henry Martin, *The New Yorker* cartoon, August, 1980. Used with permission from the Tribune Company Syndicate, Inc.

CHAPTER 15 SPOTLIGHT

1. James Allen, Frederick Reichheld and Barney Hamilton, "The Three D's of Customer Experience," *Harvard Business School Working Knowledge* (November 7, 2005), p. 12.

2. Quote from the *Starbucks Green Apron Book* used with written permission from Starbucks Corporation.

CHAPTER 16 FORESIGHT

1. Alan Lakein, *How to Get Control of Your Time and Your Life* (New York: New American Library, 1973), p. 92.

2. Quote found on a Starbucks cup on February 25, 2009 as a part of their "The Way I See It" program.

3. "Texas" Bix Bender, *Don't Squat With Yer Spurs On! A Cowboy's Guide to Life* (Layton, UT: Gibbs Smith, 1992), p. 46.

4. Lesley White and Mark Galbraith, "Customer Determinants of Perceived Service Quality in a Business to Business Context" (white paper presented at ANZMAC 2000, Australia and New Zealand Marketing Academy Conference, Griffith University, Gold Coast, Australia, November 28–December 1, 2000).

CHAPTER 17 GREEN LIGHT

1. Carl Sewell and Paul B. Brown, *Customers for Life: How to Turn That One-time Buyer into a Lifetime Customer* (New York: Doubleday, 1990), p. 107.
2. Carl Sewell and Paul B. Brown, *Customers for Life: How to Turn That One-time Buyer into a Lifetime Customer* (New York: Doubleday, 1990), p. 108.
3. Carl Sewell and Paul B. Brown, *Customers for Life: How to Turn That One-time Buyer into a Lifetime Customer* (New York: Doubleday, 1990), p. 24.
4. Carl Sewell and Paul B. Brown, *Customers for Life: How to Turn That One-time Buyer into a Lifetime Customer* (New York: Doubleday, 1990), p. 26.
5. Tom Burns and George Stalker, *The Management of Innovation* (London: Tavistock Publications, 1961), p. 232.

About the Authors

Chip Bell is a senior partner with The Chip Bell Group and manages their office near Dallas, Texas. Prior to starting CBG in 1980, he was director of management and organization development for NCNB (now Bank of America). Dr. Bell holds graduate degrees from Vanderbilt University and the George Washington University. He was a highly decorated infantry unit commander in Viet Nam with the elite 82nd Airborne. Chip is the author or co-author of several best-selling books, including *Customer Loyalty Guaranteed, Magnetic Service, Service Magic, Customers as Partners*, and *Managing Knock Your Socks Off Service*. His work has been featured on CNBC, CNN, Fox Business Network, Bloomberg TV, and in the *Wall Street Journal, Fortune, USA Today, Fast Company*, and *Business Week*. Chip has served as consultant or trainer to such organizations as GE, Microsoft, CVS/pharmacy, Marriott, Universal Orlando, Ritz-Carlton Hotels, Hertz Corporation, Harley-Davidson, Pfizer, Lockheed-Martin, Allstate, and Victoria's Secret.

John Patterson is president of the CBG affiliate Progressive Insights, Inc., headquartered in Atlanta, Georgia, and has more than 20 years of executive leadership experience in the hospitality, business services, and real estate industries. John holds a graduate degree in business from the Darden School at the University of Virginia. His consulting practice specializes in helping organizations around the world effectively manage complex culture change built around customer and employee loyalty. Prior to founding Progressive Insights, his work experience included positions with NationsBank (now Bank of America), Homestead Village, Inc., Guest Quarters Hotels, Post Inn Hotels, and Trammell Crow Residential. His clients include

McDonald's Corporation, Freeman, Northeast Utilities, Texas Instruments, Kaiser Permanente, AllState, Southern California Edison, TravelClick, Banco General, Pegasus Solutions, Banco Popular, General Growth Properties, Cousins Properties, EDiS Corporation, Manheim, and The College Board. He is the co-author of *Customer Loyalty Guaranteed* and numerous articles in professional journals.

The Chip Bell Group is a confederation of highly experienced consultants who passionately pursue one core vision: to help clients become famous for the kind of service experiences that result in devoted customers. All the members of this long-term alliance are independent consultants with their own consulting practices. They periodically work together as a high-performance team on selected consulting projects. All members of CBG share key values: making cutting edge contributions both to the profession and to their clients; practicing the world-class service they encourage their clients to emulate; and working to leave their clients with the capacity and competence to be more successful.

CBG also produces training and delivers programs for all levels of the organization from front-line employees to executive leadership. Their blended learning solutions have been rated by *Leadership Excellence Magazine* as among the very best in the nation. Chip and John are both renowned keynote speakers and address thousands every year. Visit their Web site at *www.taketheirbreathaway.com* for additional information about keynotes, consulting, and training.

Chip R. Bell
chip@chipbell.com
214-522-5777

John R. Patterson
john@johnrpatterson.com
770-329-1459

Thanks!

To Tony D'Amelio and Harry Rhoads of the Washington Speakers Bureau; Sherri Shafer of Southern California Edison; Katy Wild and Jeri Yarbrough of Freeman Company; Lynn Dinkins of Buckhead Boutique; John Longstreet and Peter Phillips of ClubCorp; Dr. Nido Quiben of High Point University; Christine Kim of John Wiley & Sons; Debbie and Cliff Dickinson of ELA Consulting; Cindy Collins Smith of SOCAP; Carl Sewell, Neva Bell, Allison Cohen, and Dawn Betrus of Sewell Automotive; Linda Dirksmeyer of Aurora Health; B.J. Dyer of Bouquets; Tina Haddad and Gail Ortiz of the City of Santa Clarita, California.; Ted Dwyer, Andy DiSabitino, and Brian DiSabitino of EDiS Corporation; Greg Miller and Robby Miller of Miller Brothers; Jim McGinty of CIG Companies; Catherine Davis of Davis Financial and Insurance Group; January and Ren Hodgson of Savor Specialty Foods and Tabletop; Nabil Moubayed of Hotel Monaco Chicago; Nick Cabellero of Façonnable New York; Steve Win of Win Signature Service; Archie Bostick and Osman Shaw of Hertz Rental Car-Atlanta Airport; Tom Connellan of The Connellan Group; Don Uselman and Kathleen (Katie) McGee of White's Restaurant; Meghan Flynn of Stew Leonard's Dairy Store; Dave Lockin of Hennessey Automotive Companies; Mama Cole of Cole's Café; Ellen Amirkhan of Oriental Rug Cleaning; Linda Zieller and Lillian Koster of Rocky Hill, Connecticut, Marriott; Richard Schaefer of Awards & More; Ted Townsend of Townsend Engineering; Truett Cathy of Chick-fil-A; James Brown of Brownstone Hotels & Resorts; Michael Tompkins of Canyon Ranch Health Resort; Rick Jelinski and Joy Todd of Cruisers Yachts; Steve Tunnel of Steinway Hall Dallas; Jean Schlemmer and Doug Johnson of General Growth Properties; Howard Behar and Diana Fullerton of Starbucks Corporation; Larry Merlo and Carolyn Castel of CVS/pharmacy; Kimberly Beach of Kindred Health Care; Vickie Henry of Feedback Plus; Joseph Michelli and Lynn Stenftenagel of Lessons for Success; Keith Harrell of Keith Harrell, Inc.; Brian Denn of Wayzata Dental; Bob Dorf of 1to1 Marketing; Corbin Riemer of MedStar; Dean Eisner, Diane Barton, and Donna Goettling of Manheim; Lee Olivier and Johnny Magwood of Northeast Utilities; Jill Applegate of Performance Research Associates; and Susan Oldham, Sandra Tacuri, Fran Sims, Lisa Gaspar, Lindsay Willis, Catherine Glawson, Mike Horn, Andy Crook, and Mari Pat Varga of The Chip Bell Group.

A SPECIAL THANKS

This book has had a special cast of helpers. Leslie Stephen, our world-class editor and long-term friend, was there, as always, with her special brand of vernacular wisdom. She amazed us with her capacity to quickly and skillfully make our chatter sound clever. Shannon Vargo of John Wiley & Sons supportively managed the entire book production process from contract to bookstore. She was always there when we needed her. Lauren Freestone of Wiley, our production editor, did a terrific job setting up the manuscript for printing. Matthew Holt of Wiley has been our advocate. When we first approached him with our book idea he was very excited. We are happy to report he was equally passionate at the end of the process. Megan Beatie of Goldberg, McDuffie Communications is our world-class publicist. She and Lynn Goldberg got what the book wanted to be just from reading one rough chapter. They have been champions for us from the beginning. Finally, we give a special thanks to our life partners, Nancy Rainey Bell and Katie Bunch Patterson, for their unconditional love, unrelenting patience, unending support, and enthusiastic devotion. They are the very essence of what this book is all about. To all of you, our heartfelt thanks.

Bibliography

Aaker, David A. *Managing Brand Equity*. New York: The Free Press, 1991.

Albrecht, Karl and Ron Zemke. *Service America in the New Economy*. New York: McGraw-Hill, 2002.

Bell, Chip R. and John R. Patterson. *Customer Loyalty Guaranteed: Create, Lead, and Sustain Remarkable Customer Service*. Avon, MA: Adams Business, 2007.

Bell, Chip R. and Bilijack R. Bell. *Magnetic Service: Secrets for Creating Passionately Devoted Customers*. San Francisco: Berrett-Koehler, 2004.

Bell, Chip R. *Customer Love: Attracting and Keeping Customers For Life*. Provo, UT: Executive Excellence Press, 2000.

Bell, Chip R. *Customers As Partners: Building Relationships That Last*. San Francisco: Berrett-Koehler, 1994.

Bell, Chip R. and John R. Patterson. "Don't Skip Dessert." *Customer Relationship Management* (June 2004), pp. 20–23.

Bell, Chip R., John R. Patterson and Lindsay Willis. "Focusing on a Customer Experience Survey." *SBusiness* (Spring 2008), pp. 46–51.

Bell, Chip R. and John R. Patterson, "Customer Intelligence: Connecting the Dots for Service Insight." *Customer Relationship Management* (Summer 2008), pp. 27–32.

Bell, Chip R. and John R. Patterson. "Competing with Service Air." *Customer Relationship Management* (September 2007), pp. 27–32.

Bell, Chip R. and John R. Patterson. "What Loyal Customers Really Want." *Recognition Review* (September 2007), pp. 10–15.

Bell, Chip R. and John R. Patterson. "Bridging the Customer Trust Gap." *MWorld* (Winter 2007), pp. 3–5.

Bell, Chip R. and John R. Patterson. "Service Metrics: Using the Dashboard to Drive Customer Intelligence." *Customer Relationship Management* (December 2004), pp. 6–9.

Bell, Chip R. and John R. Patterson. "Customer Intelligence through New Eyes." *Customer Relationship Management* (March 2004), pp. 12–14.

Bell, Chip R. and John R. Patterson. "New Rules for Mining Customer Intelligence." *Customer Relationship Management* (October 2003), pp. 18–21.

Bell, Chip R. and John R. Patterson. "Command Presence: Animate and Engage People." *Leadership Excellence* (December 2005), p. 7.

Bell, Chip and Oren Harari. *Beep Beep! Competing in the Age of the Road Runner*. New York: Warner Books, 2000.

Bell, Chip R. and Heather Shea. *Dance Lessons: Six Steps to Great Partnerships in Business and Life*. San Francisco: Berrett-Koehler, 1998.

Bell, Chip R. and Ron Zemke. *Managing Knock Your Socks Off Service* (2nd ed.). New York: AMACOM Books, 2007.

Bender, "Texas" Bix. *Don't Squat With Yer Spurs On! A Cowboy's Guide to Life*. Layton, UT: Gibbs Smith, 1992.

Berry, Leonard L. *Discovering the Soul of Service*. New York: The Free Press, 1999.

Blackshaw, Pete. *Satisfied Customers Tell Three Friends, Angry Customers Tell 3,000: Running a Business in Today's Consumer-Driven World*. New York: Doubleday Business, 2008.

Blanchard, Kenneth and Sheldon Bowles. *Raving Fans*. New York: William Morrow, 1993.

Brumfield, C. Russell. *Whiff! The Revolution of Scent Communication;1; in the Information Age*. New York: Quimby Press, 2008.

Clark, Kim and Takahiro Fujimoto. *Product Development and Performance*. Boston: Harvard Business School Press, 1991.

Connellan, Tom. *Bringing Out the Best in Others*. Austin: Bard Press, 2003.

Drucker, Peter. *The Practice of Management*. New York: Harper & Row, 1954.

Ellis, John. "Strategy." *Fast Company* (October 2002): 74.

Gitomer, Jeffrey. *Customer Satisfaction is Worthless; Customer Loyalty is Priceless*. Austin: Bard Press, 1998.

Godin, Seth. *Purple Cow: Transform Your Business by Becoming Remarkable*. New York: Penguin Books, 2003.

Godin, Seth. *The Big Moo: Stop Trying to Be Perfect and Start Being Remarkable*. New York: Penguin Books, 2005.

Godin, Seth. *Free Prize Inside! The Next BIG Marketing Idea*. New York: Penguin Books, 2004.

Griffin, Jill. *Customer Loyalty: How to Earn it, How to Keep It*. New York: The Free Press, 1995.

Griffin, Jill and Michael Lowenstein. *Customer Winback*. San Francisco: Jossey-Bass, 2001.

Gross, T. Scott. *Positively Outrageous Service*. New York: Warner Books, 1994.

Heil, Gary, Tom Parker and Deborah C. Stephens. *One Size Fits One*. New York: Wiley, 1997.

Herman, Stanley. *Authentic Management*. Reading, MA: Addison-Wesley, 1977.

Hill, Sam and Glenn Rifkin. *Radical Marketing*. New York: HarperBusiness, 1999.

Keiningham, Timothy and Terry Vavra. *The Customer Delight Principle*. New York: McGraw-Hill, 2001.

Lakein, Alan. *How to Get Control of Your Time and Your Life*. New York: New American Library, 1973.

Levinson, Jay Conrad and Seth Godin. *The Guerilla Marketing Handbook*. Boston: Houghton-Mifflin, 1994.

McEwen, William J. *Married to the Brand*. New York: Gallup Press, 2005.

McNally, David and Karl D. Speak. *Be Your Own Brand*. San Francisco: Berrett-Koehler, 2002.

Michelli, Joseph A. *The New Gold Standard*. New York: McGraw-Hill, 2008.

Michelli, Joseph A. *The Starbucks Experience*. New York: McGraw-Hill, 2007.

Naylor, Mary and Susan Greco. *Customer Chemistry*. New York: McGraw-Hill, 2002.

Osborn, Alex. *Applied Imagination: Principles and Procedures of Creative Problem Solving* (paper). New York: Scribners, 1963. Rev. ed. Originally published 1958.

Peppers, Don and Martha Rogers. *Return on Customer*. New York: Doubleday, 2005.

Peters, Tom. *The Pursuit of Wow!* New York: Random House, 1994.

Peters, Tom and Robert Waterman. *In Search of Excellence*. New York: Warner Books, 1982.

Peters, Tom and Nancy Austin. *A Passion for Excellence: The Leadership Difference*. New York: Random House, 1985.

Pine, B. Joseph II and James Gilmore. *The Experience Economy: Work Is Theatre and Every Business a Stage*. Boston: Harvard Business School Press, 1999.

Pine, B. Joseph II and James Gilmore. *Authenticity: What Consumers Really Want*. Boston: Harvard Business School Press, 2007.

Price, Bill and David Jaffe. *The Best Service Is No Service*. San Francisco: Jossey-Bass, 2008.

Ragas, Matthew and Bolivar Bueno. *The Power of Cult Branding*. Roseville, CA: Prima Venture, 2002.

Reichheld, Frederick. *The Loyalty Effect*. Boston: Harvard Business School Press, 1996.

Reichheld, Frederick. *Loyalty Rules*. Boston: Harvard Business School Press, 2001.

Rosen, Emanuel. *The Anatomy of Buzz*. New York: Doubleday, 2000.

Sanders, Betsy. *Fabled Service*. San Francisco Jossey-Bass, 1995.

Sewell, Carl and Paul B. Brown. *Customers for Life: How to Turn That One-time Buyer into a Lifetime Customer*. New York: Doubleday, 1990.

Spoelstra, Jon. *Marketing Outrageously*. Austin: Bard Press, 2001.

Travis, Daryl. *Emotional Branding*. Roseville, CA: Prima Venture, 2000.

Vance, Mike and Diane, Deacon. *Think Out of the Box*. Franklin Lakes, New Jersey: Career Press, 1995.

Wiersema, Fred. *Customer Intimacy: Pick Your Partners, Shape Your Culture, Win Together*. Santa Monica, CA: Knowledge Exchange, 1996.

Wiersema, Fred. *Customer Service: Extraordinary Results At Southwest Airlines, Charles Schwab, Lands' End, American Express, Staples and USAA*. New York: Harper Business, 1998.

Zeithaml, Valarie, A. Parasuraman and Leonard Berry. *Delivering Quality Service*. New York: The Free Press 1990.

Zemke, Ron and Chip R. Bell. *Service Magic: How to Amaze Your Customers*. Chicago: Dearborn Trade Publishing, 2003.

Zemke, Ron and Chip R. Bell. *Knock Your Socks Off Service Recovery*. New York: AMACOM Books, 2000.

Zemke, Ron and Chip R. Bell. *Service Wisdom: Creating and Maintaining the Customer Service Edge*. Minneapolis: Lakewood Books, 1989.

Index